THE OFFICIAL
BOOK OF
FIGURE
SKATING

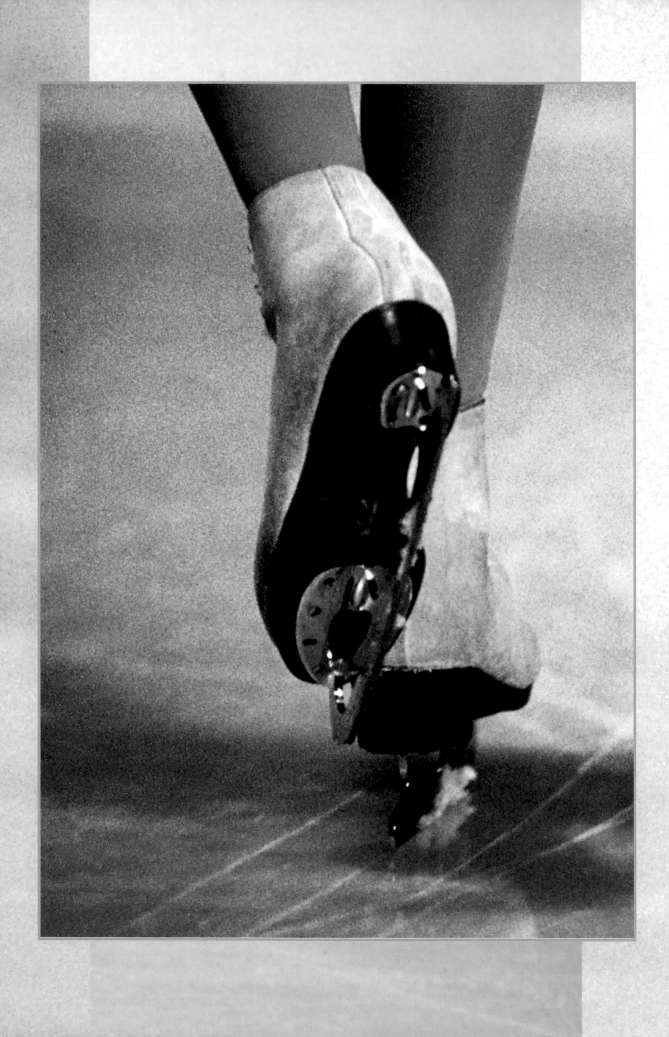

THE U.S. FIGURE SKATING ASSOCIATION

THE OFFICIAL BOOK OF

FIGURE SKATING

INTRODUCTION BY
PEGGY FLEMING

SIMON & SCHUSTER EDITIONS

Simon & Schuster Editions
Rockefeller Center
1230 Avenue of the Americas
New York, NY 10020

BOOK PRODUCED BY
BALLIETT & FITZGERALD, INC.

DESIGNED BY Mary Tiegreen
ILLUSTRATIONS BY Andrew Skuja

Manufactured in the
United States of America

10 9 8 7 6 5 4 3 2 1

Library of Congress Cataloging-in-
Publication Data
The official book of figure skating:
history, competition, technique
/U.S. Figure Skating Association: intro-
duction by Peggy Fleming.
p. cm.
Includes index.
I. Skating. I. United States Figure
Skating Association.
GV850.4.O33   1998
796.91'2—dc2I   98-27343
                                CIP

ISBN 0-684-84673-X

CONTENTS

INTRODUCTION
by Peggy Fleming

What I love best about figure skating is the silence. Even when I was younger, practicing in the early morning to the soft purr of my skates across the ice, a session on an empty rink could put me up in the clouds, fast and free and light as wind, away from the noise. I started skating as a nine-year-old tomboy, a kid who enjoyed sports and music, dancing and playing the violin, but tying on my skates gave me a feeling I hadn't found anywhere else. Skating was easy for me, and my parents encouraged my interest. My confidence grew, and in a few years this shy girl who was once afraid to raise her hand in class became Olympic champion. Standing alone at the center of the ice, in front of thousands and sometimes even millions, I found a quiet place for myself.

But that's my story. Tara Lipinski and Elvis Stojko love getting up in the air, jumping as high and as often as they can. Kurt Browning and Katarina Witt did their best playing characters. Dick Button and Scott Hamilton approached skating as a sport; John Curry and Jayne Torvill and Christopher Dean made it an art form. Every skater, and every skating fan, has his or her own good reason to love figure skating, and while so many people try to find the right

PEGGY FLEMING WITH COACH CARLO FASSI AT THE 1967 WORLD CHAMPIONSHIPS (ABOVE). ON THE COVER OF *SKATING*, WITH ABC ANNOUNCER JIM MCKAY (RIGHT).

pigeonhole for it, they miss one of the sport's most important attractions—the impossibility of pinning it down. There is no proper way to love ice skating, no one way to view what has become one of the world's most popular pastimes and spectator sports. At once it's a strenuous athletic activity and a form of dance; a matter of speed and power combined with dramatic interpretation.

This book, *The United States Figure Skating Association's Official Book of Figure Skating*, was created with the many attractions of figure skating in mind, and the many different kinds of people drawn to figure skating, as well. The whole world of figure skating is here: the costumes and routines; the hard work of fitness and how the moves are performed; the rich history of the sport and the men and women who have made that history; records and skating clubs; a look at each discipline; and an in-depth explanation of scoring. Whether you're someone who enjoys skating or one of the millions who watch the champions on television, you'll find new things to look at and to learn.

As the extremes of athleticism and art have become more visible, the debate over skating's future has grown louder. Some worry that figure skating will become a jumping contest. Jumps are easy for an audience to count, but they're hard to understand; the edges, the postures, the delicacy and explosive strength are often discernible to only the sharpest, most experienced eyes. Still, I believe the beauty and art of the sport are too great to ever let skating slip into simple athletics and that there is a

PEGGY FLEMING SKATING AT AN EXHIBITION IN 1994.

debate is part of the fun. Life is a balancing act, so why shouldn't skating be one too? The achievements of Tara Lipinski and Elvis Stojko are balanced by the smooth artistry of Michelle Kwan and Ilia Kulik. But even that's nothing new; Dick Button's jumps and Ronnie Robertson's spins in the 1940s and 1950s gave way to the elegance and drama of such skaters as the Protopopovs and John Curry in the 1960s and 1970s. If we're lucky, the fans of jumping and the fans of more expressive skating will be arguing for

decades to come because it would certainly mean that the sport is healthy.

And I do believe that skating will not just stay healthy but continue to grow and improve. Another favorite debate is whether or not skaters today are better than those of years past, and as one of the latter I wholly agree that the elite skaters right now are the best ever. Figure skaters will always be pushing the envelope, making the sport more entertaining, more artistic, and more difficult as time goes on. Just witness the number of triple jumps women skaters must perform now to compete. Skaters will always do what is needed to win; the sport breeds tough competitors and if triples were being done back in 1968, I would have done them too if that's what it took to win.

But you don't have to land triple jumps to enjoy figure skating. A gentle skate around a pond, a seat in front of the television for the U.S. Championships; whatever you love about skating, it's in this rich and beautiful book.

—*Peggy Fleming*

SKATERS ON LAKE SILS IN ENGADINE, SWITZERLAND, 1898

CHAPTER ONE

THE HISTORY OF
FIGURE
SKATING

The very first depiction of an ice skater is a 1498 woodcut of Saint Ludwina, a beautiful young woman who became the sport's patron saint after she was knocked down by one of her female skating companions, breaking a rib in the process. Ludwina had fully recovered by the time she was immortalized in the woodcut, proving what every skater learns again and again: Falling down and getting back up again are just part of the sport.

People have been skating—and falling down—for four thousand years, by most accounts. The first skates were merely flat pieces of animal bone tied around the skaters' feet. By the time Ludwina took her historic spill, the wooden blades most skaters wore were a bit more refined than primitive bone skates, but the true leap that began the history of figure skating as a popular sport—and art—wasn't made until the mid-sixteenth century, when Dutch blacksmiths started to produce thin iron blades that allowed skaters to move quickly and with more control—without poles. The simple Dutch Roll—pushing backward on the inside edge of one skate while gliding forward on the outside edge of the other—was invented, and ice skating starting gliding into the world of pleasure. Racing and other, more leisurely, forms of the sport also entered Dutch culture, making skating a vital aspect of winter life.

During his exile in Holland in the mid-seventeenth century, England's rakish King Charles II added skating to his many athletic pursuits, bringing it back to England, along with tennis and yachting, when he took the throne in 1660. The Restoration, then, began

SAINT LUDWINA'S ACCIDENT IN 1396, AS DEPICTED IN A WOOD ENGRAVING FROM 1498. THIS IS THE EARLIEST KNOWN SKATING PRINT. (WORLD FIGURE SKATING MUSEUM AND HALL OF FAME)

PIETER QUAST (DUTCH 1605/06-1647)
"PEASANT WITH A BASKET ON HIS BACK."
COPPER ENGRAVING ON LAID PAPER.
(WORLD FIGURE SKATING MUSEUM
AND HALL OF FAME)

skating's life in England. Weather irregularities limited its immediate acceptance, but the hard winter of 1662 saw skaters on frozen canals in London, as described by both Samuel Pepys and John Evelyn. Although skating had always existed in the marshy fens of eastern England (a low terrain similar to Holland's), two decades passed before a run of cold winters let skating find a place in urban, English culture. In later centuries, the sport became a national mania.

Worldwide, skaters began to develop the basic skills of figure skating in the late eighteenth and early nineteenth centuries, combining athleticism with elements of artistry. By the late eighteenth century, certain moves had already been described in at least three languages—English, French, and German—and the first skating club had been founded in Edinburgh, Scotland. In order to join the Edinburgh Skating Club, skaters not only had to own the requisite formal wear, they also had to pass a test that included skating a complete circle on each foot, then jumping over first one hat, then two, then three, stacked atop each other. As skating evolved, the required circles became much more elaborate expressions of geometry on ice, especially in England and the United States.

An Englishman, Second Lieutenant Robert Jones, wrote the first book on ice skating—*A Treatise on Skating*—in 1772. But from the French came new, revolutionary maneuvers such as spins, pirouettes, and toe steps, which clashed with the more systematic and exacting approach popular among English skaters. Though both styles were in the early stages of their development, this difference in philosophy between precise figures and free artistic expression would have great ramifications throughout the sport's history.

⁑　⁂　⁑

During the nineteenth century, skating's popularity exploded as part of the general formation of sporting culture. As the Industrial Revolution in the United

States and England drew more people into cities—workers whose daily schedules were regulated by factories and offices—the concept of leisure time arose. Sports, both organized and personal, emerged as codified, circumscribed forms of leisure for the working and middle classes. At the same time that baseball in the United States and cricket in England were building competitive structures of rules, standards, and leagues, ice skating swept through the urban centers of the world.

Technological advances—from grooved blades that lent greater speed and agility to steel skates that allowed skaters to clip rather than strap skates onto their shoes— also helped speed the sport's wider acceptance. Mass production made skates more affordable; in 1860 a pair could be bought for less than a dollar.

The biggest skating boom during the nineteenth century took place in the United States. What had been regarded as a boy's sport in the colonial years—a teacher in Salem, Massachusetts, was nearly dismissed in 1801 for rumors that she had taught her female charges how to skate—became an acceptable pastime for both sexes during the 1850s. The first official organization in the United States was formed in 1850. Members of the Philadelphia Skating Club skated not only for pleasure, but also to rescue others who fell through the ice of the Schuylkill River— hence their name change to the Philadelphia Skating Club and Humane Society. There are also reports of skating's growing popularity in Boston at the same time, supposedly championed by Colonel Thomas Wentworth Higginson, who was better known for leading the 23rd Colored Regiment in the Civil War.

In the winter of 1858, New York's Central Park skating pond opened, further propelling the craze. Although skating may have been more popular in Philadelphia, New York's strength as a commercial and cultural center spread the fashion to the rest of the country. The number of figure skaters in New York surged to the tens of thousands, with an estimated crowd of 100,000 at Central Park on Christmas Day, 1860. The first national skating competition—the Championship of

TOP. GEORGE MONTARD WOODWARD (ENGLISH 1760-1809) AFTER "SIX IMPORTANT SKATING POSTURES" BY ISAAC CRUIKSHANK. CIRCA 1809. COPPER ENGRAVING ON WOVE. (WORLD FIGURE SKATING MUSEUM AND HALL OF FAME)

ABOVE. ABRAHAM BLOEMAERT (DUTCH 1564-1651) "YOUTH TRYING ON HIS SKATES." CIRCA 1630. COPPER ENGRAVING ON WOVE. (WORLD FIGURE SKATING MUSEUM AND HALL OF FAME)

America—was held in Troy, New York, in 1863. The winner was Jackson Haines, who would soon change the entire direction of the sport. By the 1870s, rinks existed in cities such as Buffalo, Indianapolis, Cleveland, Pittsburgh, Cincinnati, St. Louis, and Chicago. By then, attempts were being made to organize a national association.

Though it seems an odd connection, the figure skating boom during the Civil War was instrumental in the birth of Major League Baseball as well. Rinks such as the Union Pond in Brooklyn were built to fill the demand for skating venues, but the seasonality of ice skating left the owners in a difficult financial position. William Cammeyer, owner of the Union Pond, decided to use his field in the spring and summer as a ballfield. In 1862 he was the first to charge admission to a baseball game, making him "the father of the enclosed ballpark." The ability to create multiuse, profitable structures intended for leisure added to the momentum of sports in general, and skating in particular. The officials of New York's first skating club also had ties to several baseball clubs, furthering the connection between the two.

Skating's growth in the United States also heralded another important development in sports—the active participation of women. Although in the past, men and women had skated separately (if women skated at all), by the 1860s they were skating together on the same ponds. The presence of women was generally welcomed by the press, who hailed the salutary effects of physical exertion for both sexes. Henry Chadwick, the leading sportswriter of the day, was especially supportive of women ice skating. Thus, figure skating was the first sport in which women participated for the pure joy of it, and with wide public acceptance.

In nineteenth-century England, class, climate, and culture guided the direction of the sport. The figure skating clubs that formed were, as in the United States, primarily social clubs for the emerging middle class and the upper class to which they aspired. Prince Albert became the patron of the London Skating Club in 1850, bestowing great cachet upon the club and the sport, and the Royal Toxophilite Society's grounds in Regent's Park became the place to skate, at least for those gentlemen lucky enough to gain membership in the exclusive club. London's Glaciarium—the first rink with man-made ice—opened in 1876, conquering the often erratic English weather and further anchoring the sport among the urban middle class. The Glaciarium was small, only 40 feet long by 24 feet wide, and the ice was of dubious quality, but within three years there were indoor rinks in Manchester and Southport.

SPECIAL FIGURES

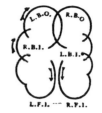

In the early days of figure skating, the marks a skater left on the ice were the real point of competition; how they performed them was secondary, which explains why the sport is called "figure skating." In the late nineteenth century, competition hinged primarily on two elements: creating the compulsory—or school—figures, which were a group of forty-one figures derived from the figure 8; and presenting a new movement or design of the skater's invention. The involved, often fanciful designs some chose to offer were known as "special figures." While skating compulsory figures remained a part of competition until 1990, the creation of special figures was by the early twentieth century already less important than the athleticism and speed of the sport. Special figures are now rarely seen—the special figures on this page were created in competitions during the 1890s.

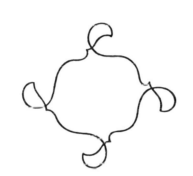

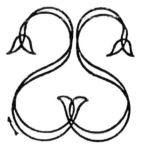

AMERICAN JACKSON HAINES CREATED THE INTERNATIONAL STYLE OF SKATING IN THE MID-NINETEENTH CENTURY. THE COSTUME HE WEARS HERE IS RELATIVELY SEDATE; IN SOME SHOWS HE DRESSED AS A WOMAN, OR EVEN AS A BEAR. HE DIED OF PNEUMONIA IN FINLAND ON JUNE 23, 1875.

Back in the fens, speed skating became popular among the lower classes, now as a betting sport. This sort of rough behavior, especially a sometimes violent rivalry between two Fenland clans, was not well thought of by the sport's more refined advocates. As in all Anglo-American sports that developed during this time, middle- and upper-class Victorian ideals of figure skating emphasized form, sportsmanship, and the moral benefits derived from participation. The essence of the English style was control: The body was to be always upright, the leg in use held straight with the other held behind, arms close to the sides—all to create intricate figures within a small portion of the ice. In short, speed skating was for the masses; figure skating for the elite—an equation that held true for most of the world until the arrival of Sonja Henie, at the earliest. In order to safeguard and promote English skating—and by extension English class ideals—the first skating federation, the National Skating Association, was created in 1879, to oversee first speed skating and then, in 1881, English figure skating.

The need to uphold British skating standards came largely from the immense popularity in Europe of what was called the International style of skating, and that popularity was the product of one man: Jackson Haines. Haines exemplified the International style, and if there is one person who gave form to figure skating as we know it today, it is he. Born in 1840 in New York, Haines grew up amid the arts and embraced music and dance, interests he then applied to skating, much as French skaters had fifty years earlier. The use of dance movements and techniques in skating—musical accompaniment, using the entire ice surface, bent knees, outstretched arms—had not yet been seen in the United States, and Haines's work was not well received. Although he joined numerous skating clubs around the United States and regularly outclassed their best skaters—winning national championships in 1863 and 1864—his fluid, active style offended the stiff Victorian sensibilities of the American and English skating elite. In 1864, at the age of twenty-four, Haines left his wife, Alma, and their three children and emigrated to Europe, never to return. Beginning his new life in Stockholm, Haines found more than acceptance; a tour of the Continent in 1868 turned him into a respected, adored, even revered figure. Haines was more than just a great skater; he was the superstar of his day, with even a perfume named after him. As he traveled Europe from Sweden to Vienna, where he eventually made his home, he pushed the International style of skating figures past the English style in the world's eye and turned skating itself from a pastime into a new form of entertainment. Haines's impact on skating lasted well beyond his early death in 1875 at the age of thirty-five. The city that glorified Haines the most—Vienna—hosted in 1882 what is regarded by some as the first international skating championship. The competition included a mind-boggling twenty-three compulsory figures, an additional figure of the skater's invention ("special figures"), and a program lasting four minutes. One of Haines's pupils, Leopold Frey, won the title.

The formation of the International Skating Union (ISU) in 1892 closed the schism between the International (or Viennese) style and the English style. The first World Championship under ISU auspices was held in 1896, and skaters competed in both free skating and "figuring," creating the two aspects of performance to be judged until figures were eliminated in 1990. New skaters came forward to advance the sport. Norwegian Axel Paulsen, equally adept at figure and speed skating, introduced a new kind of jump at the 1882 Vienna competition in which the skater jumped while going forward and rotated one and a half revolutions.

It became known as the Axel jump and remains (with revolutions added over the years) one of skating's most challenging maneuvers. Ulrich Salchow of Sweden, who invented in 1910 the jump that bears his name, captured a record ten World Championships as well as the first Olympic Men's skating gold medal in 1908. Another Swede, Gillis Grafstrom, succeeded Salchow as the power in men's skating.

Until 1908, Americans had little to do with the International style. Competitive events did take place on U.S. ice: The National Amateur Skating Association was founded in 1886 and held the Championship of America through 1905, a competition then hosted by the New York Skating Club until 1909. But events such as these were more akin to contests of athletic endurance than the increasingly artistic programs and compulsory figures of the ISU. One of the American champions from that period, Irving Brokaw, described the program that won him the 1906 national title as including thirty minutes of spins and thirty minutes of three-turns, "But it utterly lacked grace, beauty of carriage, rhythm, and the long flowing curves inseparably connected with the sweeping strokes of ice."

The International style finally came back to the United States in 1908, when Brokaw gave the first exhibition of what had become the globally accepted approach

ULRICH SALCHOW OF SWEDEN. AS WELL AS INVENTING THE JUMP NAMED AFTER HIM, SALCHOW WAS THE KING OF SKATING IN THE EARLY PART OF THE TWENTIETH CENTURY, WINNING TEN WORLD CHAMPIONSHIPS BETWEEN 1901 AND 1911, HIS LAST AT THE AGE OF 41.

at an event sponsored by George Browne in Cambridge, Massachusetts. Together, Brokaw and Browne were in large part responsible for acceptance of the International style in the United States. Brokaw represented the United States at the 1908 Olympics in London, placing sixth, while Browne played an important role years later in helping establish the United States Figure Skating Association in the 1920s, and wrote two seminal books on skating.

A Canadian and former pupil of Jackson Haines, Louis Rubenstein, who had helped organize a governing body for skaters in that country in the 1880s, was the third vital figure in structuring American skating. He brought his organizing efforts to the United States and by 1914 the International Skating Union of America had been formed, encompassing both the United States and Canada. The first American Championship in the International style was held in New Haven, Connecticut. The whole world was now united in one style of skating.

Brokaw's other major contribution to American "fancy" skating was even more far-reaching than his 1908 exhibition. He suggested to Charles Dillingham, owner of New York's Hippodrome, that he bring Charlotte Oelschlagel, a top German skater, to the United States to perform professionally. Dillingham agreed and Charlotte came. The show was called *Hip Hip Hooray,* and from 1915 to 1918 it

played twice daily in New York's Hippodrome to crowds of up to six thousand. Oelschlagel, a seventeen-year-old with long, blonde hair down to her waist, was very popular, not only because she was the star of a number called "Flirting in St. Moritz," but because she shared her performing tips with many American skaters as well. She also made the first skating-related film, a silent six-part serial called *The Frozen Warning* in 1917 in Chicago. Oelschlagel's pioneering success in the United States as a skating entertainer and her subsequent tours paved the way for another star fifteen years later who would take the sport to a new level of popularity.

To the more traditional, genteel sportsmen, though, this merging of athletics and commercialism was a troubling development. The potential conflict between economic realities— particularly the need to be paid for skating as a livelihood—and amateur

ABOVE. TWO VIEWS OF FIGURE SKATING IN THE UNITED STATES AT THE TURN OF THE CENTURY.

RIGHT. THE PRINCE'S SKATING CLUB IN LONDON WAS THE SITE OF THE FIRST OLYMPIC FIGURE SKATING COMPETITION, HELD IN THE 1908 SUMMER GAMES. THE STRONG BRITISH INTEREST IN SKATING HELPED PUT THE SPORT ONTO THE ROSTER OF THOSE COMPETED AT THE OLYMPICS.

ideals would become an important issue throughout twentieth-century figure skating. Nowhere was this conflict seen more clearly than in the Olympic movement. Created under the leadership of Pierre de Coubertin, the first modern Olympics were held in Athens in 1896 and featured no winter sports, despite the fact that figure skating had been accepted as an Olympic sport by the 1896 International Olympic Committee (IOC) Congress. Because a competition could be held in an indoor rink, figure skating was included on the program for the 1908 (summer) Olympics in London, but it was twelve years before the sport appeared again, this time in Antwerp for the 1920 (summer) Olympics.

Part of the problem was logistical—not every city at this time had ice skating

facilities—but two other issues were more pressing. First, winter sports were still seen as a specialized interest, practiced and followed by only a small segment of the world which was already well served by the competing Nordic Games. Second, winter sports were viewed by some as already professionalized and thus in conflict with Olympic amateur ideals. For both of those reasons, figure skating's presence in 1908 and 1920 was controversial in Olympic circles—hard-line opponents found it downright unseemly. Coubertin's retirement allowed a fresher vision, and separate winter games were held at Chamonix, France, in 1924 that were recognized as Olympics later, in 1926. From then on, the Olympics and figure skating created a mutually beneficial relationship: The Olympics turned a regular, global spotlight on figure skating, and figure skating, by far the most popular winter sport, drew interest to the Winter Olympics in general.

Another significant change in figure skating during this period took place at the 1902 World Championships. England's Madge Syers entered the competition even though it was assumed to be restricted to men, because nothing in the rules specifically prohibited her from competing. Syers's groundbreaking move was more than symbolic; she skated better than all of the men—except Ulrich Salchow, who was already a legend in the sport—and won the silver medal. Her boldness and her undeniable mastery of figure skating made it obvious that women should be included within the competitive structure of the sport. It took four years, but a women's division was finally created in 1906 and—to the surprise of no one—Syers won the first World Championship in 1906 as well as the first Ladies' Olympic gold medal in 1908. The presence of women also allowed for the creation of pairs skating, which made its first appearance at a world championship level in 1908, at both the Worlds and the Olympics. Other competitions, such as Fours, in which two couples skate the Waltz, a precursor to today's ice dancing; and the Fourteen Step and the Ten Step lived on, but not on an international level.

By the end of World War I, then, figure skating had taken shape as a global form of entertainment and competition, shared by both men and women. The influence of intricate, English-style figuring still loomed large, though, and as the Jazz Age dawned, the romanticism of Jackson Haines began to seem a bit musty. The new, faster-paced world of the Roaring Twenties needed something stronger and shinier to keep its interest.

✳ ✳ ✳

What the world got was not just a skating star but a phenomenon. After the war and its vast restructurings, the world was ready to enjoy itself again. Interest in sports in general took off, and especially so in the United States, where the National Football League was founded early in the decade and baseball enjoyed what is now regarded as its glory period. Skaters across the country started clubs and established the sport well beyond its hub in the Northeast, although membership was based more on social interest than on ability. At this time, the sport of figure skating was governed, along with speed skating, by the International Skating Union of America, and the speed skaters had control of it. George Browne and other figure skaters wanted oversight of their sport in the hands of their fellow figure skaters, so in the spring of 1921 the United States Figure Skating Association (USFSA) was created to set standards for amateur skating in this country, and to promote and govern the growth of the sport. Seven charter clubs joined the USFSA, and the Association placed itself under the auspices of the ISU. The organization that figure skating in the United States needed was now in place. From this point on, skaters were required to pass proficiency tests and progress in competitive levels.

As important as this structural change was for skating in the United States, it was a small, beaming girl from Norway who transformed the sport throughout the world. Sonja Henie was the right person at the right time. Born in 1912 to a wealthy Oslo furrier and his wife, Henie took her first ballet lessons at age six and began skating at age eight. At ten she was the national champion of Norway and in 1924, at eleven, she made her first appearance in the first Olympic Winter Games in Chamonix. Clearly there was something special about Sonja Henie, and her combination of dance and youthful athleticism was eagerly received by a world looking for something fresh and fast and innocent. Though she finished last in Chamonix, she won the gold medal in Ladies' skating at the next three Winter

BRITISH SKATING ENTHUSIASTS SUCH AS EDGAR AND MADGE SYERS, PICTURED HERE IN DAVOS, SWITZERLAND, HELPED SPREAD THE POPULARITY OF WINTER SPORTS AND MADE RESORTS SUCH AS DAVOS DESTINATIONS FOR GENERATIONS OF TRAVELERS.

Olympics: St. Moritz in 1928, Lake Placid in 1932, and Garmisch-Partenkirchen in 1936—a record still unequaled. Henie turned professional in 1936 at the age of twenty-four and began a career as an entertainer, making a series of highly successful films and touring the world with her own ice shows.

Sonja Henie influenced figure skating in a number of important ways. First, she liberated not just women's skating but the sport as a whole. A bouncy, round-faced teenager, Henie was not an academic skater; she moved quickly and exuberantly and athletically. For Henie, skating was as much an athletic event as it was an artistic one—a new attitude especially on the women's side, where American skater Theresa Weld Blanchard had been scolded for trying a jump in her program. Henie's athleticism, as tame as it may seem to us today, paved the way for later moves and styles that emphasized the sport aspects of skating. By extension, her youth allowed her to wear short skirts, which remained her costume throughout her career despite the fact that she was expected to change into more conservative outfits as an adult. The physicality of her programs made a shorter, more fluid skirt seem necessary, changing the look of skating—costumes would now have to serve the athletic demands of the sport, not limit what was possible.

As a dancer trained by Anna Pavlova's teacher, Henie combined, as others had, dance with skating, but such was the force of her abilities and charisma that she fused the two into a new form of mass entertainment, one that fully exploited both its athletic and aesthetic potentials. Her films made her an estimated $76 million, which was on top of twenty years of sold-out ice shows around the world, dwarfing the overall earnings of other big sports names of the time such as Babe Ruth and Joe Louis. She took the idea of the "ice show," at which Charlotte Oelschlagel had been so successful, and, along with Arthur Wirtz, owner of the Chicago Stadium and the Blackhawks, created an entertainment institution by touring with it. Her appearances became an annual tradition in cities everywhere. She was romantic and glamorous, the highest-paid performer in show business, linked with Clark Gable and Tyrone Power. The fact that one of the world's biggest entertainment stars was a skater gave ice skating a prime place in American culture—an achievement especially important during a period when no Americans were among the leaders of world skating.

Her success also continued skating's emerging tradition of putting women forward. Sonja Henie was not just a well-paid performer; she was the most successful businesswoman and female athlete in the world, with stock in the New York Yankees and Madison Square Garden, as well as other businesses, and one of the world's most important collections of modern art. In 1969, Sonja Henie died of leukemia at age fifty-seven; her estimated net worth at the time of her death was $47 million.

Figure skating would never be the same.

Now that there was a regular demand for skating entertainment, skating could conceivably be considered an artistic profession, not just an amateur sport. At the same time, Henie increased

the physical demands of the sport, often staying on ice for nearly an hour of a two-and-a-half-hour show. Spectator skating would never again be a slow, romantic procession; skaters would now have to consider themselves athletes. Reflecting her times, Sonja Henie also brought sex appeal to the sport, and her short skirts not only allowed her to achieve jumps spectacular to their time, they allowed her to look spectacular doing it. The success of great American skaters who followed her—from Tenley Albright to Michelle Kwan—began after Henie took figure skating out of elite clubs, away from the unsettled politics of nascent national and international associations, and put it back among the people with her shows and movies. New rinks were built throughout the country, pushing all the way to California, where Henie made her home for many years. Skating had become a coast-to-coast activity, and there were plenty of rinks for young American skaters to perfect their art.

Up to this time, no matter how popular figure skating was in the United States, it was still very much an expertise of Europeans. From 1896 to 1938, the Men's World Championship was won by either an Austrian, a Swede, or a German; eleven times by Salchow, eight times by Austrian Karl Schafer. The women's side was slightly more global, with the presence at the top of Englishwoman Madge Syers in 1906 and 1907, and Hungarian skaters Lily Kronberger and Opika von Horvath from 1908 to 1914, and, of course, Norwegian Sonja Henie ten straight years from 1927 to 1936. The Olympics mirrored the World Championships: Out of eighteen medals awarded to men prior to World War II, seventeen went to Europeans, while non-European women fared a bit better. Theresa Weld Blanchard was the first American to take an Olympic medal in world figure skating, winning the bronze in Ladies' Singles in 1920, and in the next

Olympics, Beatrix Loughran achieved an as-yet unmatched feat when she won the silver medal in the Ladies' division in 1924, the 1928 bronze, and the silver in pairs with her partner Sherwin Badger in 1932, making her the only American woman ever to medal in two skating disciplines. Europeans also dominated pairs skating, with the French coupling of Andree and Pierre Brunet and the Hungarians Emilie Rotter and Laszlo Szollas each winning four World Championship titles between 1926 and 1935, and the Brunets also taking the Olympic gold medal in 1928 and 1932.

England's skating fortunes also rose just prior to World War II. Between the years immediately following World War I and the late 1920s, figure skating as a popular diversion in England suffered next to motion pictures and even its year-round cousin, roller skating. There was also a sense that since control of the sport had left England, a nation that prided itself on being the most "sporting" of all lands, it had fallen into some disrepute, what with no one treating it like a science anymore. How could a sport that Englishmen didn't dominate really be a sport? In reaction, English skaters began to take a very precise, exacting approach to skating, emphasizing technique over artistry. It was essentially a renaissance of old "English Style" skating, and it worked. Thirty-three rinks opened in England between 1927 and 1939 and for the three years leading up to World War II, the English excelled: Cecilia Colledge won the Ladies' Singles World Championship in 1937 and the Olympic silver in 1936; Megan Taylor won the World Championship in 1938 and 1939; and Graham Sharp won the Men's Singles at the World Championships in 1939.

The amateur ideals of the Olympics also helped skating's 1930s revival in England by providing a vital counterweight to the undeniable commercialism Sonja Henie had forever instilled in the sport. The border between amateur and professional was becoming increasingly porous as more opportunities beckoned to gifted skaters in the form of ice shows and even movies. Some big-name amateur skaters had reportedly signed professional contracts before retiring from competition, charges investigated at the time by the IOC. The IOC's oversight guaranteed skating's credibility as a sport.

FORGET SHIRLEY TEMPLE. SONJA HENIE WAS THE BIGGEST DRAW IN HOLLYWOOD IN THE LATE 1930S. AMONG HER MANY CONTRIBUTIONS TO SKATING WAS BLACK ICE, AS SEEN IN THE STILL ABOVE FROM *IT'S A PLEASURE* (1945), WHICH HELPED THE CAMERA BETTER CATCH HER INTRICATE FOOTWORK.

OPPOSITE. THE WINSOME HENIE CAPTURED THE HEARTS OF MILLIONS.

And then came World War II. Competitive figure skating, like so much else, was put on hiatus—no Olympic Games were held in 1940 and 1944; nor were the World Championships held from 1940 through 1946. The major controversy surrounding skating at the time involved Sonja Henie, who had been photographed with Hitler in the 1930s and entertained by him at Bertechsgaden. When the Germans invaded Norway in 1940, Sonja Henie, certainly the world's most famous Norwegian and one of the world's wealthiest, refused to offer her support to a Canadian training base for Norwegian fighter pilots, claiming that as an American citizen—as of that year—it would be improper given the neutrality of the United States. Many saw this as a cover for her Nazi sympathies or at least a case of tragic self-interest, and many Norwegians never again viewed her as a favorite daughter.

HAYES ALAN JENKINS (CENTER) WON THE WORLD CHAMPIONSHIP IN 1953. FELLOW AMERICAN JAMES GROGAN (LEFT) WON THE SILVER AND CARLO FASSI (RIGHT) OF ITALY, WHO LATER COACHED MANY GREAT SKATERS, FINISHED THIRD.

✳ ✳ ✳

The new, post–World War II world did not edge its way through the rubble—it blasted its way through with American abandon. America had come of age during the war, and the combination of prosperity and power was almost intoxicating. People couldn't get enough of big shiny American cars, American music, American everything. The GI Bill was in full swing, the baby boom had begun, and magazine ads led one to believe that the entire country was one big backyard barbecue, from Catalina, California, to Bangor, Maine. The massive change in skating after the war was a direct expression of that vibrant, optimistic, slightly out-of-control world.

Despite the popularity of Sonja Henie, figure skating was still not the first love of most New Jersey boys during the 1930s and 1940s. Dick Button, though, learned to skate on the ponds near his home wearing hand-me-down skates, never taking a serious lesson until he was twelve years old. During the next six years Button developed a style related more to the energy and action of American team sports and jazz than to ballet. He jumped as no other skater had before, using the whole ice surface to build up speed—adding elements of excitement and danger to a sport whose primary appeal had always been aesthetic. Until then, jumps and fast spins had been slightly suspect—Sonja Henie's competitive best was two single Axels in a row. Button's jumps were higher than the boards, and long. He was not just about aerial razzle-dazzle, though he raised the bar technically for every skater who would come after him. He and the other Americans working with him began to double jumps, and, in the 1948 Winter Olympics, Button became the first person to nail a double Axel in competition. An innovator as well, Button worked intensely with his coach, Gustave Lussi, to invent the flying camel and also to land the first triple jump, a loop.

Like Sonja Henie, Button changed the nature of the skating costume. Until he took to the ice in men's pants and a white military service jacket, men had worn tight leggings and bulky jackets in competition. Button's new, more masculine costume matched the athleticism of his skating and bolstered the sport's image in the United States.

The skating world had taken notice of Dick Button from the moment he leapt onto the world skating scene in 1947. After winning the U.S. Championship that year, he failed to win the gold at the World Championships strictly because Hans Gerschwiler of Switzerland had gotten higher marks in figures. Button was such a gifted—and technically proficient—skater that his second-place finish was a shock to ISU president Ulrich Salchow, who gave Button a trophy of his own. Button and the new American style introduced a way of skating so fresh, so meaty, that it pushed the already decimated European skating teams out of serious contention well into the 1950s. Button won the World Championship five straight years, from 1948 to 1952, and the Olympic gold medal in 1948 and 1952, becoming the first American to win Olympic gold in figure skating.

Through 1960, Americans such as David and Hayes Alan Jenkins, Carol Heiss, Tenley Albright and

CAROL HEISS WAS ONE OF MANY APPEALING AND TALENTED SKATERS PRODUCED BY THE UNITED STATES AFTER WORLD WAR II.

their American style ruled the figure skating world. From 1948 to 1960, U.S. men won seven out of twelve available Olympic medals, including a sweep at Cortina, Italy in 1956, and won the World Championship every year from 1948 to 1959. On the ladies' side, Albright and Heiss won seven out of eight World titles from 1953 to 1960 and with Barbara Roles won five out of nine Olympic medals from 1952 to 1960. Karol and Peter Kennedy won the first American gold medal in Pairs at the 1950 World Championships. The top non-American skaters, such as France's

Jacqueline du Bief and England's Jeannette Altwegg, succeeded by adopting the American style—they became proficient jumpers. Canadian Donald Jackson, winner of the Men's bronze medal at the 1960 Winter Olympics in Squaw Valley, not only adopted the American style, but surpassed it: He landed the first triple Lutz ever performed in competition at the World Championships in 1962. He later added a triple Salchow and a triple loop to his arsenal.

That the American style could so completely alter the performance and judging of figure skating was not proof that it was necessarily "better" than other, less

athletic styles of skating, or some new, predestined step in the evolution of the sport. The triumph of the American style was an expression of the global acceptance of American culture and American aesthetics. What had once been considered flashy and ostentatious now seemed to much of the world vigorous, free, and democratic. This vision, spread by American cultural influence after the war, was reinforced by the contrasting lack of openness behind the "Iron Curtain" of the late 1940s and early 1950s, a contrast that lasted until the collapse of the Soviet Union in the 1990s. The new American skating style was an escape from the old-fashioned lyrical style that would soon be abandoned by virtually all skaters except those from the Soviet bloc. The stylistic conflict so familiar to figure skating now assumed political overtones with the rise of communism.

The roots of the Soviet sports machine went as deep as the ideology of Lenin, who encouraged wide participation in athletics for reasons similar to those of nineteenth-century Englishmen such as Thomas Arnold: Sports build bodies and character; they impose a group spirit; they create team leaders who respect higher authority. All of those ends would serve the goals of Lenin as well as they had served Queen Victoria. Sports were also something of a novelty to a largely peasant culture, and their mass dissemination throughout Bolshevik Russia was born of the same impulse that tried to democratize the arts by giving over a bourgeois preserve to the workers. The Stalinist purges and World War II had given the Soviets more to think about than calisthenics, but in the late 1940s, as the physical and ideological battle lines of the second half of the century were being drawn, the Soviets saw the propaganda value of sports and began to cultivate a sporting elite who, it was hoped, would prove the superiority of the Communist system. That the revolutionary Soviets represented the more traditional side of figure skating may seem ironic, but Russian ballet tradition must be taken into account. For all the experiments of the early Russian avant-garde, it was the romanticism of Theatre Street in Leningrad that continued to speak most to the Russian soul.

And so the Cold War entered the world of skating. The first sign of change was dramatic: The Prague European Championships in 1948 ended just as the Communists took hold of Czechoslovakia, and Dick Button and Canadian Ladies' World Champion Barbara Ann Scott barely reached the airport before the borders were closed. Other effects were more long-lasting. Judging became a political issue and no longer simply a battle between styles, because the styles represented cultures, politics, and power. Regulations regarding international judging were put in place in 1927, but it was during the post–World War II era that they really came into play. Judges from both sides of the Iron Curtain were at times suspended for "national bias," including an ISU suspension in 1977 that barred all Soviet judges from international competition for that year.

Two events, one in 1961 and the other in 1964, signaled the end of the American era in figure skating. The first was tragic; the second, beautiful. By 1960, most of the important names in American skating had retired—Button, the Jenkins brothers, and Carol Heiss, to name a few—but a promising new generation was being groomed. Then, on February 15, 1961, a Boeing 707 carrying the entire young American team to the World Championships in Prague crashed while attempting to abort a landing in Brussels, Belgium. There were no survivors. Thirty-four of the seventy-two passengers were either skaters or coaches. The American figure skating program had been killed in one day, and a long reconstruction process began. In some ways, American skating has never fully recovered—the rousing American style of Button and the Jenkins never regained its influence, and the loss of both athletes and coaches left American skating behind the rest of the world. American Scott Ethan Allen did take the bronze at the Innsbruck Olympics in 1964 at age fourteen, but the "great" American skating era was over.

The other event took place at the 1964 Olympics in Innsbruck, Austria. In Pairs, the Soviet couple of Ludmila Belousova and Oleg Protopopov won the gold medal with a romantic, International-style program that caused a sensation. Though pairs skaters had integrated the American style into their discipline with

TOP. IN SOME WAYS THE OPPOSITES OF THE PROTOPOPOVS, IRINA RODNINA AND ALEXANDR ZAITSEV BROUGHT SPEED AND POWER TO PAIRS SKATING.

ABOVE. THE 1961 U.S. FIGURE SKATING TEAM PREPARES TO LEAVE ON THEIR FATAL JOURNEY.

lifts and other strength moves, Belousova and Protopopov used these new elements to serve their lyrical style. The fashion for high leaps and unbound athleticism gave way to aesthetics, especially so in pairs, where the Soviets now dominated, and continue to do so today. A Soviet or Russian pair has won every Olympic gold medal since 1964, and twenty-eight out of thirty-four World Championships. Belousova and Protopopov won two Olympic golds and four World titles, while Irina Rodnina won ten World titles (four with Alexsei Ulanov and six with Alexandr Zaitsev) and three Olympic golds (one with Ulanov and two with Zaitsev). Save for the British pairings of Diane Towler and Bernard Ford in the 1960s and Jayne Torvill and Christopher Dean in the 1980s, skaters from the Soviet Union and Soviet bloc countries also took control of ice dancing.

※　＊　❋

Another, larger power that came to bear on the 1968 Olympics would eventually overshadow politics as an influence in the future direction of figure skating. Television had already reshaped American sports by the late 1960s: The once sprawling system of minor-league baseball teams was reduced to a quarter of what it had been twenty years earlier, in large part because of televised baseball; and one televised game, the dramatic 1958 National Football League Championship, started football's rise toward sports supremacy. Similarly, the seventh game of the 1962 NBA finals, another televised overtime thriller, put the National Basketball Association on the map. The 1968 Winter Olympics would have a similar effect on figure skating.

After CBS had aired the 1960 Winter Olympics from Squaw Valley (introducing Dick Button as a color commentator) to no great success, the ABC television network paid $200,000 for the right to broadcast the Innsbruck Winter Olympics in 1964. That the network paid $91.5 million to broadcast the Calgary Winter Olympics in 1988 was thanks to what a nineteen-year-old named Peggy Fleming did in 1968. In the aftermath of the tragedy of 1961, many had believed that it would take years to reconstruct the American figure skating program. European coaches, John Nicks and Carlo Fassi among them, were brought over to work with the young American skaters, and their efforts had immediate results. Peggy Fleming, whose coach William Kipp had died in the crash, won the 1964 U.S. Championships at only fifteen years of age and took on Fassi as her new coach; after only two years, she had won the first of her three consecutive World Championships. While her immense talent and remarkable charm were well known in the skating world by 1968, the entire world would learn about Peggy Fleming on a February night in Grenoble, France.

Skating onto the ice that night for her free-skate program, Fleming already had a sizable lead from her strong performance in the compulsory figures. In truth, she had only to perform well—not brilliantly—to capture the gold medal, but what the viewers of the first live Olympic satellite broadcast saw was magic. What they saw was something new in skating, a demure young woman with a guileless brand of California cool. Figure skating seemed to be the natural expression of Peggy Fleming. Some labored at the athletics of the sport as others danced on ice, but watching Peggy Fleming that night was like watching a beautiful young woman alone on a pond, skating for the pure love of the sport. Everything wonderful about skating seemed to have been poured into this one teenager who made a very hard sport look easy. Fleming won the gold medal and overnight became the girl every girl wanted to be, the girl every boy wanted to go out with. She went on to do seven television specials which were viewed throughout the world, making her an international representative of the sport. If Sonja Henie became a star through movies, Peggy Fleming did it through television.

The triumph of Peggy Fleming's Grenoble magic vindicated the storytelling approach to televised sports pioneered by ABC's Roone Arledge. Figure skating lent itself particularly well to the "human interest" concept of shows like "The Wide World of Sports," and it began to attract a national viewing audience, launching its crucial growth as a spectator sport. To some, the tension between athletics and entertainment was again being strained by the "up close and personal" style the network employed in its skating coverage, but that blend perfectly expressed the uniqueness of figure skating. At the 1976 Winter Olympics in Innsbruck, Dick Button's easy going American style of explaining the finer points of skating to millions of viewers was

THOUGH SHE NEVER WON AN OLYMPIC GOLD MEDAL, JANET LYNN SUCCEEDED FLEMING AS AN INTERNATIONAL STAR.

THE TELEVISED BROADCASTS OF THE 1968 OLYMPIC WINTER GAMES WOULD CHANGE THE WAY THE WORLD WATCHED SPORTS. PEGGY FLEMING (OPPOSITE) WAS THE STAR OF THE SHOW.

as celebrated as Dorothy Hamill's gold medal.

Figure skating became the core event of each Winter Games, and with the instant attention provided by network television, at each Olympiad a new American star would emerge, with the promise of a lucrative professional touring deal after the Games. In fact, an American woman has medaled in figure skating at every Olympics since 1968: After Fleming came Janet Lynn in 1972, Dorothy Hamill in 1976, Linda Fratianne in 1980, Rosalynn Sumners in 1984, Debi Thomas in 1988, Kristi Yamaguchi in 1992, Nancy Kerrigan in 1994, and Tara Lipinski and Michelle Kwan in 1998. American men did well through these years too, with the "Battle of the Brians" between Canada's Brian Orser and American Brian Boitano at Calgary in 1988 making men's skating as glamorous and exciting as the ladies' competition. Americans Tim Wood, Scott Hamilton, Charlie Tickner, and Paul Wylie have also won Olympic medals.

TOP. TONYA HARDING (LEFT), KRISTI YAM-AGUCHI (CENTER) AND NANCY KERRIGAN (RIGHT) AT THE U. S. CHAMPIONSHIPS IN 1992. THESE THREE SKATERS WOULD HELP BRING THE SPORT TO NEW HEIGHTS OF INTER-EST AND POPULARITY, ALBEIT FOR VASTLY DIF-FERENT REASONS.

ABOVE. KRISTI YAMAGUCHI DURING HER SHORT PROGRAM AT THE 1992 OLYMPICS. SHE WENT ON TO WIN THE GOLD MEDAL.

American skaters have not been the only ones to profit from television's focused eye. What matters most on TV is charisma and looks—and East German Katarina Witt had both in great abundance. Though she represented what was then a crumbling Eastern European Communist system, Witt's expressive skating and mature beauty made her a star in the late 1980s as well as the 1990s.

On top of making personality a primary component of figure skating, television even altered the way the sport is judged. The legacy of the old English style held sway into the late 1960s, with compulsory figures judged as sixty percent of each skater's final score against forty percent for the free skate. But compulsories made for terrible television: Cutting figures in the ice is a slow, silent, careful process, with the difference between winning and losing measured in millimeters. In 1968 this ratio was evened to fifty/fifty, and in 1973 a short program was brought in which covered a number of required elements, with scores calculated at forty percent for compulsories, forty percent for the long program, and twenty percent for the new short program. Three years later, the balance was reset again at twenty/thirty/fifty, but the problem still remained: Millions of people would watch the long program and were left puzzled when the greatest freestyle skater did not win. Rather than a test of skill, the compulsories were beginning to seem like an obstacle or, at best, an anachronism. To a world that no longer skated figures on the ice for fun, compulsories no longer had any relevance. The decision was finally made in 1988 to eliminate compulsory figures from competition, and on March 7, 1990, at the World Championships in Halifax, Nova Scotia, Yugoslavian Zeljka Cizme sija skated the last figures in international competition.

Some argue that television coverage played a role in the decision to allow professionals to participate in the Olympics. Until 1988, strict rules governing amateur status kept many out of what was always billed as a meeting of the world's best athletes. The emergence of a global sports culture raised the question of whether it still made sense to keep out some of the best—and most popular—athletes out of the Games. The American boycott of the 1980 Summer Olympics, followed by the Soviet boycott of the 1984 Summer Olympics, left the integrity and the hallowed aura of the movement in need of some bolstering. The answer, it seemed, to the ultimate politicizing of the Games through the 1980s was to make them more commercial by allowing sports the right to send professionals to compete.

The world of figure skating had already set a similar change into motion, but for other reasons. Rules had been amended to broaden eligibility and to allow competitive skaters to earn money. Skaters who had turned professional prior to the change were allowed one chance to regain their eligible status under the new rules. This brought back to the 1994 Winter Olympics (now on an alternate schedule with the Summer Games) many of figure skating's greatest names who had left the Olympic-eligible ranks. Brian Boitano, Katarina Witt, Jayne Torvill and Christopher Dean, Viktor Petrenko, and Russian pairs skaters Ekaterina Gordeeva and Sergei Grinkov were among those who received reinstatement and participated in the Games, and their impact was not limited to glamour: Gordeeva and Grinkov took the gold and Torvill and Dean won the Ice Dancing bronze.

The stakes now were higher than ever for elite figure skaters. With the booming popularity of the sport, increased television exposure, professional circuits, and more, a gold medal–winning skater was virtually guaranteed millions of dollars in appearance fees and endorsements. Kristi Yamaguchi, American gold medal winner at the 1992 Olympics, was even modeling in major fashion magazines. Figure skating had become the second-most popular sport to watch on television behind football, and all those years of practice and all the money that went into developing an elite skater now actually could be viewed by some as a business investment, and not just as an investment in something they loved to do. The stakes were so high that, in

TOP. BRIAN BOITANO, ONCE AGAIN COMPETING IN THE ELIGIBLE RANKS, IS SURROUNDED BY THE PRESS AT THE 1994 OLYMPIC WINTER GAMES.

ABOVE. WITH HIS TOUGH-GUY, CROWD-PLEASING DYNAMICS ON ICE, ELVIS STOJKO IS A HERO IN HIS NATIVE CANADA.

1994, extreme means were used in an attempt to achieve that success. In Detroit, only months before the Lillehammer Olympics, Tonya Harding was allegedly involved in a conspiracy to bash her rival, Nancy Kerrigan, on the knee with a police baton. But the plan backfired. Kerrigan was placed on the American Olympic team and performed the best free skate of her life, winning the silver medal at the most-watched event in Olympic history. Though figure skating had already begun to surge in popularity, the Harding/Kerrigan debacle drew more people than ever to pay attention to the sport.

With figure skating now firmly locked into the sporting consciousness, the sport looked again for its new identity and found it in the same quality it had always turned to—youth. The advent of skaters like Michelle Kwan and Tara Lipinski marked the beginning of a new athleticism in the sport, but one closer to the gymnastic model than that of Dick Button in the 1950s. The athleticism of the 1990s was a combination of technical rigor that harkened back to English figures and an exuberance that had as much to do with the tender age of the skaters as it did with a love of the sport. A new attention to physicality, conditioning, and weight training began another period of testing limits, as all women skaters needed to land multiple triples to compete at an elite international level, and the first quadruple jump—a quadruple toe loop—was landed by Canadian Kurt Browning at the 1988 World Championships, opening a challenge to every other male skater. Figure skating news now made the front page of the sports section on a regular basis, not just

THE MOST RECENT GENERATION OF AMERICAN SKATERS HAS BEEN AMONG THE GREATEST: TWO-TIME WORLD CHAMPION MICHELLE KWAN (OPPOSITE); OLYMPIC GOLD MEDALIST TARA LIPINSKI (LEFT), AND FIVE-TIME U.S. MEN'S CHAMPION TODD ELDREDGE (ABOVE).

during the Olympics. As the twenty-first century nears, figure skating seems to be the perfect sport for our times: fast-paced; enjoyable to both men and women as a spectator sport and as a pastime; entertaining; glamorous; and just dangerous enough to be thrilling. ✳

CAROL HEISS JENKINS

"Being able to do it when it counts, that's intensely satisfying."

Carol Heiss Jenkins has two particularly cherished memories from her competitive career: the 1956 World Championships in Germany and the 1960 Olympics in Squaw Valley, California.

Sixteen-year-old Carol Heiss had just come back from the 1956 Olympics in Cortina, Italy with a silver medal when she and her mother boarded a plane bound for the World Championships in Germany. In those days school figures were almost everything—they accounted for sixty percent of a skater's overall score, while the free-skate program was worth just forty percent. Heiss's strength had been free skating, but in 1956 she managed to place first in figures—ahead of Tenley Albright, who had won the Olympic gold medal two weeks before.

"I had always been coming from behind in the free program, but this time I was ahead," Heiss Jenkins recalls. "I knew I had to skate a perfect program because Tenley had already skated, and skated well." But Heiss was flawless, and won her first World title. It would be the only World title she would ever win in front of her mother, who died of cancer less than a year later.

Four years later, the graceful young skater charmed the entire world in the first televised Winter Olympics (Squaw Valley). "I had the honor of being asked to give the athlete's oath during the opening ceremonies. I think I was just as nervous to say that oath as I was to skate," Heiss Jenkins remembers. "I memorized the whole thing. I had a card in my pocket in case I forgot any of it, but I just didn't want to look foolish and fumble in front of all those people."

By that time, Heiss had won the World Championship four years in a row. She was expected to win the Olympic gold medal, and she did. She was in first place after the figures, but she felt the pressure anyway.

"It was the first time the Olympics were on TV," she explains, "and I was very concerned about not falling on CBS television." Winning in the United States made it extra special. "I remember standing on the podium. They play the national anthem and the flag is raised in your honor. It's such a patriotic feeling, then when you step down, it's a very personal feeling. Being able to do it when it counts, that's intensely satisfying. It's a culmination of all the years of hard work, perseverance, and self-discipline." ✳

AS A COACH, CAROL HEISS JENKINS REMAINS AN ACTIVE
PARTICIPANT IN THE WORLD OF FIGURE SKATING.

Scott Hamilton

"Memories just get richer with time."

Scott Hamilton's most cherished memories are from his first trip to the Olympic Winter Games, in 1980. But the magic actually started for Hamilton a couple of months earlier at the U.S. Championships.

He was friends with a number of other skaters competing in various disciplines that year, and before the championships they had fantasized about the team they would like to see go to the Olympics—a team that, not surprisingly, would include all of them. When every one of them did make it, they dubbed themselves the "Dream Team."

The 1980 Olympics were made even more special for Hamilton because they were held in Lake Placid, New York—a city he knew well—and because his girlfriend had also

FOUR YEARS AFTER HIS FIRST APPEARANCE AT THE OLYMPICS IN 1980, SCOTT HAMILTON WON THE GOLD MEDAL FOR MEN'S FIGURE SKATING IN SARAJEVO.

made the team, so they were able to experience all the excitement and nervousness together. And to top it all off, he had been chosen to carry the American flag in the opening ceremonies.

Hamilton enjoyed living in the Olympic Village and meeting athletes from all over the world.

"We just had the best time," he says. "They had concerts to entertain all the athletes. I got to watch the U.S. hockey team win, and see Eric Heiden win his five gold medals. It was really quite amazing. To have a first Olympic experience like that was just awesome. And then to have been able to skate as well as I did was even better."

Although Hamilton didn't win a medal that year, he gave two good performances of which he is quite proud.

"During the long program, the crowd was standing before I even finished," he recalls. "The sound of the crowd was unbelievable—they were so incredibly loud."

The members of that figure skating Dream Team have now gone in many directions, but Hamilton still sees many of them each year and works with some of them on a regular basis. He had a brilliant competitive career—and is still one of the most respected ambassadors of the sport—but the friendships and the memories from his first Olympic experience endure. Says Hamilton: "Those memories just get richer with time." ❋

JANET LYNN WITH HER COACH, FRENCH PAIRS GREAT PIERRE BRUNET

CHAPTER TWO

PERSONALITIES

The goal of figure skating is not to score points or sneak a ball past an opponent. While sports such as baseball and basketball certainly feature creativity and beauty, these qualities are splendid afterthoughts in these games, signs of greatness. A home run that just clears the fence is worth the same one run as a towering shot that clears the stadium. Only figure skating requires beauty. Other sports may have room for the individual to shine—a wide receiver outrunning the coverage, a goalie making a point-blank save—but once the play is over, the star of that moment melts back into his team and so does the player he beat. Without helmets or pads, with no dugout or bench or huddle to hide in, a singles skater steps onto the ice as the whole focus for the length of her program. Her job is to shine as an individual. The jumps and spins and delicate footwork—these make up the language of figure skating, and the athlete must combine them with music and dress, and perform them—perfectly— in a way that expresses who she is.

As a sport of self-expression, figure skating's history is not a story of strategies or coaches or teams, but of fascinating, talented individuals. The thirty skaters and skating teams that follow all advanced the sport in their own way. Some, such as Dick Button, Irina Rodnina, and Elaine Zayak, raised the bar with new technical achievements. Others, such as John Curry, Toller Cranston, the Brunets, and the Protopopovs, created programs that blurred the line between sport and art. And a few changed more than just skating. The seemingly effortless work of Sonja Henie, Peggy Fleming, and Madge Syers transformed the movies, television, and sports themselves. The popularity of Henie and Fleming and the achievements of Syers not only brought skating into the mainstream of popular culture, but helped shape how we view sports.

Much of figure skating is subjective, and these thirty profiles help explain why. This is not a sport of systems; it is a sport of faces we can watch smile and cry and beam in triumph. It is a sport of styles, individual ways of moving and assembling movements that one can identify without ever seeing the face of the performer. The passion and energy that infuse the finest skaters can only come from personal dreams and inspiration. Figure skating is, above all else, a sport of great personalities.

MADGE SYERS

THE MOTHER OF LADIES' SKATING

LITTLE KNOWN OUTSIDE OF SKATING CIRCLES, SYERS
BROKE GROUND FOR WOMEN ATHLETES.

The "mother of figure skating," Madge Syers was the ladies' figure skating champion before ladies' competition even existed. Born Madeline Cave in 1881, she was raised in an upper-class British family and had become an expert in the stiff, formal English style of skating when her future husband, Edgar Morris Wood Syers, introduced her to the new International style. She quickly mastered that, too. The couple married in 1900 and pursued individual careers in singles competition while they developed as a pairs team. Both were active in the development of skating competitions and clubs, particularly the National Skating Association of Great Britain.

From the first ISU–sanctioned World Championship held in St. Petersburg, Russia, in 1896, singles competition had included only men. Mrs. Syers shocked the staid British sporting world by filing an official entry application for the 1902 World Championship in London amid a flurry of protest. It was considered highly improper for a woman to compete in an athletic event with men, but since no specific rule prevented it, Syers was allowed to participate. She exasperated her male competitors by winning the silver medal, second only to defending champion Ulrich Salchow of Sweden.

The lady's success did not amuse the gentlemen who governed the sport, and in response, the ISU immediately passed a rule prohibiting women and men from competing against each other. Great Britain, however, continued to allow the practice in its national championships, which Syers won in 1903 and 1904, defeating her husband in the latter year. Finally, in 1906, Syers and Britain's NSA convinced the ISU to hold a Ladies' World Championship, which she won its first two years.

The indomitable Syers seemed never to run out of ways to astound the sports world. When figure skating was first recognized as an Olympic event in 1908, the Games were to take place on her home turf—London—at the Prince's Skating Club Rink. Syers won the first Olympic Ladies' gold medal as well as the bronze medal (with her husband) in the Pairs competition. She remains the only woman ever to win two figure skating medals at the same Olympics.

The competition was to be her last. Her health began to fail after giving birth to a daughter on August 22, 1917. The child lived only twelve hours; Madge Syers died of heart failure and blood poisoning eighteen days later, on September 9, at age thirty-six. Her husband withdrew from all skating activity for the remainder of his life.

Madge Syers was elected to the World Figure Skating Hall of Fame in 1981.

MADGE SYERS
GREAT BRITAIN
BORN: 1881
OLYMPIC LADIES' GOLD: 1908
OLYMPIC PAIRS BRONZE: 1908
WORLD SILVER: 1902
LADIES' WORLD CHAMPION: 1906-07
BRITISH CHAMPION: 1903-04
FIRST WOMAN TO ENTER
THE WORLD CHAMPIONSHIPS
FIRST LADIES' WORLD CHAMPION
FIRST LADIES' OLYMPIC CHAMPION

THE BRUNETS

ELEGANT CHAMPIONS AND INSPIRING COACHES

THE BRUNETS FEATURED A SMOOTH, ELEGANT STYLE.

*S*ome of today's figure skating fans may be more familiar with the legendary students of Andrée and Pierre Brunet—including Carol Heiss and Dorothy Hamill—than with the charismatic French couple who dominated both singles and pairs skating for more than two decades.

Andrée was the French Ladies' champion for eleven consecutive years and competed in two Olympic Winter Games, in 1924 and 1928. Pierre, a former engineering student with a passion for inventiveness, was seven time French national champion and also competed in Men's singles in the 1924 and 1928 Olympic Games. As a pair, they earned the Olympic bronze medal in 1924, and later took gold at both St. Moritz in 1928 and Lake Placid in 1932. No one knows why they entered World Championships only in even-numbered years, but they won all three times they competed (1928, 1930, and 1932) and captured the European title in 1932.

The innovative husband-and-wife team was famous for spectacular routines that incorporated challenging elements from their days as singles champions. They invented new spins and dazzled judges as well as audiences with their mirror skating, jumps, and lifts. Nothing could stop them. Even after Andrée broke her back while skiing in St. Moritz in 1933, she returned to the ice the next year.

When they turned their focus to coaching, the legends continued. The Brunets guided their foremost student, Carol Heiss, to four U.S., two North American, one Olympic and five World. Andrée's teaching career ended when she was hit by a New York taxi and her back was broken a second time. She assisted as best she could, but Pierre remained the genius of invention and teaching technique, coaching Dorothy Hamill, Canadian World Champion Donald Jackson (the first man to land a triple Lutz), French World Champion Alain Giletti, and Alain Calmat, Janet Lynn, Gordon McKellen, Nancy and Bruce Heiss, Patrick Pera, and others.

Their only son, Jean-Pierre, was born in 1930 and won the U.S. Junior Pairs Championship in 1944 and the national title in both 1945 and 1946 with partner Donna Pospisil. He was killed in an auto accident in 1948, shortly before he was to begin studying at the Massachusetts Institute of Technology. He was eighteen years old.

The Brunets were inducted into the World Figure Skating Hall of Fame in 1976 and Pierre was awarded France's highest citation, the Legion of Honor, in 1989.

ANDRÉE AND PIERRE BRUNET
FRANCE
ANDRÉE: SEPTEMBER 16, 1901
FRENCH LADIES' CHAMPION: 1921-31
PIERRE: JUNE 28, 1902
FRENCH MEN'S CHAMPION: 1924-30
OLYMPIC GOLD: 1928, 1932
OLYMPIC BRONZE: 1924
WORLD CHAMPIONS: 1928, 1930, 1932
WORLD SILVER: 1925
EUROPEAN CHAMPIONS: 1932
FRENCH CHAMPIONS: 1924-35

SONJA HENIE
THE CREATOR OF MODERN SKATING

SONJA HENIE IN 1927, SHOWING OFF SOME OF HER FIRST AWARDS

Every sport has its legend. Someone almost bigger than the sport itself. Someone who forces the world to make space at center stage for what he or she does. Baseball has Babe Ruth, basketball has Michael Jordan, and figure skating has Sonja Henie.

Sonja Henie's story is a lot like the Hollywood fantasies that made her a movie star. Born the daughter of a wealthy furrier in Oslo, Norway, Henie was on skates when she was five years old and Norway's national champion by the time she was nine. At eleven, she was the youngest competitor ever in the Olympics; at fourteen, she won the World Championship; and at sixteen she won both the Olympic gold medal and the World Championship. With her fresh style merging balletic form with youthful vigor, this always effervescent teenager became a global phenomenon.

She totally dominated the sport for more than a decade, winning ten consecutive World Championships between 1927 and 1936 along with three Olympic gold medals, records that will probably never be surpassed.

By the time she was twenty-four, Sonja Henie had not only conquered her sport, she had reinvented it. Her short skirts, a holdover from her days as a child skater, set a totally new style for women on the ice. Her speedy, athletic approach pushed figure skating into the world of active sport, while her dance background set a serious choreography standard. Henie's tremendous popularity brought into the public spotlight a sport that had been largely a pastime for the wealthy.

In 1936, she turned professional with a Twentieth Century-Fox movie contract. Her first film, *One in a Million*, was a hit, and between 1937 and 1948 she starred in nine more movies that made her one of the top female stars in Hollywood. At the same time that she was making headlines in Hollywood—including rumored love affairs with Tyrone Power and Clark Gable, plus two marriages, to rich celebrities Dan Topping, then-owner of the Brooklyn football Dodgers, and Long Island real estate heir Winston Gardiner—Sonja Henie created the first modern ice show, with which she toured when she wasn't shooting films. She was the highest-paid star in show business and sports; her skill, energy, and unstinting demands for perfection were both admired and feared.

The only serious dent to her popularity occurred during World War II, when her previous acquaintance with Adolf Hitler in the 1930s led to suspicions that she did not fully support the Allied cause or the plight of occupied Norway. Her last years were spent with her third husband, Norwegian shipbuilder Niels Onstad, whom she had married in 1956 and with whom she had amassed an impressive collection of modern art. When she died of leukemia in 1969, she left a fortune estimated to have been in the neighborhood of $50 million. She was inducted into the World Figure Skating Hall of Fame in 1976.

SONJA HENIE
NORWAY
BORN: APRIL 8, 1912
OLYMPIC GOLD: 1928, 1932, 1936
WORLD CHAMPION: 1927-36

COURTNEY JONES
THE ICE DANCING MASTER

JONES AND MARKHAM WON TWO WORLD TITLES.

Through its long relationship with the sport of figure skating, from the earliest skating socials of the nineteenth century to Torvill and Dean today, England has thrived most consistently in ice dancing. Of all the ice dancers England has produced, Courtney Jones stands out, not just for his performances on the ice, but for his contributions to the sport of ice dancing, in particular, and skating, in general.

In 1955, Courtney Jones moved to London to train for pairs with Gladys Hogg at the Queens Ice Rink; instead, Hogg moved him into ice dancing, and for a time worked with him as a partner. Jones was familiar with ballroom dancing, having taken lessons some years before, and he soon found that the face-to-face style and intricate footwork of ballroom dance transposed well to the ice. Later that year, illness forced Hogg to partner Jones with June Markham, another of her students. Jones and Markham were a perfect match. Both strong skaters in their own rights, they placed second in the 1955 British Dance Championships after only two months together, then placed second at both the European Championships and the Worlds.

Jones was a tireless worker. By day he worked in the fashion industry, so his practice time was limited but constantly observed; he skated with Markham at the Queens Ice Rink six nights a week from 11 P.M. until 2 A.M. The straight-backed, precise style of Jones proved unbeatable. Having had a

year as a team, Jones and Markham swept through the British, European, and World championships in 1957, winning all three, and then repeated the same feat in 1958. As the list of their titles grew, Jones also extended himself artistically, creating two ice dancing patterns—the Silver Samba and the Starlight Waltz—that are now among the thirty-one patterns in use competitively by the ISU.

After two years of success, Markham left the team to teach skating. Jones took a new partner, Doreen Denny. Picking up where he had left off, Jones, with Denny, swept the British, European, and World championships in 1959 and 1960, and they probably would have repeated a third time if not for the cancellation of the 1961 World Championships due to the tragic plane crash that killed the entire U.S. team.

Both Jones and Denny left competition but chose not to turn professional. Instead, Jones became an ice dancing judge and referee, receiving his first international appointment in 1962. His energies also went into the National Skating Association of Great Britain, where he was president in 1985. Jones's influence was not purely organizational, though. Through the 1970s and 1980s, he helped skaters such as Toller Cranston and Torvill and Dean craft their groundbreaking routines.

Courtney Jones was elected into the World Figure Skating Hall of Fame in 1986.

> **COURTNEY JONES**
> GREAT BRITAIN
> BORN: 1936
> WORLD CHAMPION: 1957-58 (WITH JUNE MARKHAM),
> 1959-60 (WITH DOREEN DENNY)

DICK BUTTON

SKATING TAKES TO THE AIR

BUTTON'S ATHLETIC STYLE CHANGED THE SPORT.

For as long as most skating fans can remember, televised figure skating competition has been synonymous with the voice of Dick Button. Since the 1960 Olympics in Squaw Valley, his engaging commentary has taught millions of viewers about triple toe loops, double Axels, and all the other jumps and spins that make up a spectacular figure skating program.

And he certainly should know. He was the first skater ever to perform a double Axel, a triple jump (the loop), a double jump combination (two loops), and a flying camel (his own invention). As the star pupil of coach Gustave Lussi, Dick Button broke all barriers and helped usher in an energetic, athletic approach to skating.

His unmatched competitive record, which he compiled while he was a full-time high school and college student, included a remarkable series of firsts. In 1948, at age eighteen, he won the U.S. and European championships, then became the first American to win the World Championship, which he did for five consecutive years—more than any other American man. Also in 1948, he became the first North American man to win Olympic gold, and he remains the youngest Olympic Men's champion in history. (After he won the European Championship, the event was closed to all non-Europeans, so no one will ever be able to equal his 1948 grand slam of U.S., European, World, and Olympic titles.)

In 1952, the twenty-two-year-old phenomenon from Englewood, New Jersey, won the U.S. Championship for the seventh consecutive time—a feat accomplished by only two men: Button and Roger Turner (1928–34). He also repeated his Olympic victory, becoming the only men's singles skater ever to win two Olympic gold medals.

Dick Button's accomplishments, which also include winning three North American Championships and being the first skater to receive the coveted Sullivan Award as the country's outstanding amateur athlete, continued after he retired from competition. For a short time he skated as a professional performer; then he returned to school, eventually graduating from Harvard Law School. He also developed numerous skating events while continuing to be the country's primary commentator and spokesperson for figure skating.

For all of those achievements and his dedication to the sport, Dick Button was inducted into both the U.S. Olympic Committee and the World Figure Skating halls of fame.

DICK BUTTON
UNITED STATES
BORN: JULY 18, 1929
OLYMPIC GOLD: 1948-52
WORLD CHAMPION: 1948-52
EUROPEAN CHAMPION: 1948
NORTH AMERICAN CHAMPION:
1947, 1949, 1951
U.S. CHAMPION: 1946-52
FIRST TRIPLE JUMP AND FIRST DOUBLE
AXEL IN COMPETITION
YOUNGEST MALE FIGURE SKATING
OLYMPIC GOLD MEDALIST IN HISTORY

HAYES ALAN AND DAVID JENKINS

CHAMPIONS AND BROTHERS

DAVID (LEFT) AND HAYES ALAN JENKINS

Following Dick Button's stellar career, Hayes Alan Jenkins and David Jenkins continued America's domination of men's international skating, winning all major titles from 1953 to 1960. The Jenkins were the second and third American men to win World and Olympic gold medals. Between them they won eight consecutive U.S. Championships, seven consecutive World Championships, and two consecutive Olympic Championships.

Only three years apart in age, Hayes and David were encouraged throughout their careers by their mother, Sara, an ice dancing judge. In 1954, she convinced them to give up working with Walter Arian's and Button's famous coach, Gustave Lussi, in order to train with Edi Scholdan, who successfully guided their development and careers. (Scholdan was later killed in the 1961 plane crash along with the U.S. world figure skating team.) Like Button, both brothers continued as full-time students, graduating from Colorado College with honors.

Most remarkable among their achievements is that they are the only brothers ever to share the podium at the U.S. Championships, Worlds, and Olympics, and were part of three American sweeps in Men's medals. At the 1954 and 1955 U.S. Championships, Hayes won the gold medal and David stood beside him with the silver. In 1956, while Hayes again took the gold, David won bronze. But it was at the 1955 and 1956 World Championships that U.S. men for the first time swept the medals, with Hayes in first, legendary spinner Ronald Robertson in second, and David in third, both years. The three men then finished in the same order at the 1956 Olympics in Cortina, a feat that has never been repeated.

Hayes retired from the sport in 1956 and, like Dick Button, graduated from Harvard Law School. David then took over the men's skating world. His athletic style earned him three World titles and four U.S. titles between 1957 and 1960, as well as the Olympic gold medal at Squaw Valley. Hayes married the 1960 Olympic Ladies' Champion Carol Heiss shortly afterward; between the two of them, they hold eighteen national, ten North American, twelve World, and three Olympic medals. After retiring, David Jenkins went on to become a doctor. Both brothers were inducted into the World Figure Skating Hall of Fame in 1976.

HAYES ALAN JENKINS
UNITED STATES
BORN: MARCH 23, 1933
OLYMPIC GOLD: 1956
WORLD CHAMPION: 1953-56
WORLD BRONZE: 1950, 1952
NORTH AMERICAN CHAMPION: 1953, 1955
NORTH AMERICAN BRONZE 1949, 1951
U.S. CHAMPION: 1953-56
U.S. SILVER: 1950
U.S. BRONZE: 1949, 1951-52

DAVID JENKINS
UNITED STATES
BORN: JUNE 29, 1936
OLYMPIC GOLD: 1960
OLYMPIC BRONZE: 1956
WORLD CHAMPION: 1957-59
WORLD BRONZE: 1955-56
NORTH AMERICAN CHAMPION: 1957
NORTH AMERICAN SILVER: 1955
U.S. CHAMPION: 1957-60
U.S. SILVER: 1954-55
U.S. BRONZE: 1956

CAROL HEISS

AMERICAN SKATING GLAMOUR

THE BEAUTY AND SUCCESS OF HEISS INSPIRED A GENERATION OF SKATERS.

When television first brought the Olympics into millions of American homes, Carol Heiss was on center stage. The year was 1960, and Heiss's gold medal at Squaw Valley made her an instant star. But her success had not come overnight.

The only American woman to win five World titles along with Olympic gold and silver medals, Carol Heiss had been skating since she was six years old and growing up in Queens, New York. Though her brother and sister also skated, Heiss showed unusual promise. Famed French skater and coach Pierre Brunet took her as his student and within five years she won the U.S. Novice title; the following year she brought home the U.S. Junior title.

When she progressed to the championship level, finishing fourth at the 1953 World Championships, one of the greatest national rivalries in skating history developed, between Heiss and Tenley Albright, four years her senior. The competition was always tough and exciting, and pushed both skaters to their very best performance levels.

One of America's most charismatic skaters, Heiss finished a close second behind Albright at four U.S. Championships, at the 1955 North American Championships, and in the 1956 Olympics. She finally succeeded in beating Albright at the 1956 World Championships in Garmisch, West Germany, the first of five consecutive World titles for Heiss. She also went on to win four consecutive U.S. titles and two North American Championships before the television cameras captured her winning the gold at the 1960 Olympics.

Sharing the international spotlight at Squaw Valley was Men's gold medalist David Jenkins, whose brother, four-time World and Olympic champion Hayes Alan Jenkins, would become Heiss's husband later that year.

Carol Heiss won the last of her five World and four U.S. titles that same year, then retired from competition. She turned professional and had a brief career in ice shows and in Hollywood, but decided to leave the ice to devote herself full-time to raising her three children.

After eighteen years away from figure skating, the charming ladies' champion who had won America's heart at the first televised Olympics returned to the sport—this time as a coach. Following in the footsteps of her own teacher, Pierre Brunet, she has become one of the top U.S. instructors, whose champion students include Tonia Kwiatkowski, Ryan Hunka, Timothy Goebel, and David Liu, among others.

Carol Heiss Jenkins has been inducted into the U.S., Olympic, Women's Sports Foundation, and World Figure Skating halls of fame, and has served on both the U.S. Olympic Committee and the USFSA Board of Directors.

CAROL HEISS
UNITED STATES
BORN: JANUARY 20, 1940
OLYMPIC GOLD: 1960
OLYMPIC SILVER: 1956
WORLD CHAMPION: 1956-60
WORLD SILVER: 1955
NORTH AMERICAN CHAMPION: 1957, 1959
U.S. CHAMPION: 1957-60
U.S. SILVER: 1953-56

TENLEY ALBRIGHT

TRIUMPH ON AND OFF THE ICE

ALBRIGHT'S RECOVERY FROM POLIO WAS DRAMATIC.

Tenley Albright secured her place in figure skating history when she became the first American woman to win the World Championship and an Olympic gold medal—but her biggest victory had come long before that.

In 1946, when the promising Junior skater from Newton Center, Massachusetts, was just eleven years old, she was stricken with polio. The onset was sudden and severe. One day she was well; the next she could not walk. But Albright was fortunate, and recovered rapidly. She returned to the ice for both physical and psychological therapy, and within four months had won not only her battle against polio but the Eastern U.S. Junior Ladies' title as well.

From that point on, Tenley Albright's skating career blossomed with one success after another. At age thirteen she won the U.S. Novice Ladies' Championship, at fourteen she captured the U.S. Junior title, and at sixteen she won the first of five consecutive U.S. Championships.

She was seventeen when she won her first Olympic medal (silver) in 1952, and still just seventeen when she became the first American woman ever to win the World Championship, in 1953. Then she won her second U.S. title and quickly captured the North American title.

The world wanted to see more of this gifted skater, who had become known for creating new and unusual variations on standard moves, and for

balancing the artistry and athletic skills of skating in a harmonious whole. So Albright completed an international exhibition tour before entering Radcliffe College as a pre-med student. She took her studies seriously, but managed to skate full-time as well, successfully defending her U.S. title in 1954 and 1955 and adding a second World Championship title in 1955.

By then, a talented rival had appeared on the scene: Carol Heiss. Heiss was a tough, charismatic competitor, so Albright took a break from school in order to focus on her training for the 1956 Olympics. During a practice session, she fell and slashed her ankle, but she refused to let the injury stop her. Two weeks later, she became the first American woman to win the Olympic gold medal for ladies' figure skating.

Within a few weeks, however, Carol Heiss took over the World title. Even though Albright won the U.S. Championship the following month, it had become Heiss's turn to delight the world as America's leading lady on the ice. Albright retired from figure skating after the U.S. Championship and finished her academic studies, eventually graduating from Harvard Medical School in 1961. She joined her father and brother in practice, specializing in general surgery.

Tenley Albright has been inducted into the U.S., Olympic, the World Figure Skating, and the Harvard University Halls of Fame.

TENLEY ALBRIGHT
UNITED STATES
BORN: JULY 18, 1935
OLYMPIC GOLD: 1956
OLYMPIC SILVER: 1952
WORLD CHAMPION: 1953, 1955
WORLD SILVER: 1954, 1956
NORTH AMERICAN CHAMPION:
1953, 1955
U.S. CHAMPION: 1952-56

THE PROTOPOPOVS
THE QUINTESSENTIAL PAIRS SKATERS

THE PROTOPOPOVS' DEVOTION TO SKATING WAS AS INFLUENTIAL AS THEIR STYLE.

At a time when young skaters are achieving greater prominence than ever in the world of figure skating, it is good to remember the benefits that maturity can bring to a sport and an art form. A perfect example is Ludmilla and Oleg Protopopov, who were thirty-two and twenty-nine, respectively, when their lush, gold-medal performance electrified the 1964 Winter Olympics in Innsbruck. Perhaps the most admired pairs team in history, the elegant couple didn't even begin skating competitively until they were at an age when many of today's pairs consider retirement. Yet the Protopopovs were far from a novelty or a moving story of overcoming the odds. Their elegance and beauty on the ice established a standard for pairs skating so high that it remains unchallenged.

Unlike most pairs under the Soviet system, the Protopopovs chose on their own to skate as a team. Oleg Protopopov took up skating when he was fifteen, emerging like the rest of the Soviet Union from the rubble of World War II. Despite his late start, he showed great talent and, after a stint in the Soviet navy, the Leningrad native began serious training in Moscow, where he met Ludmilla Belousova. Like Protopopov, she had started skating at a relatively advanced age—in her case sixteen—and now, at nineteen, she teamed up with him.

The results were stunning. Left to their own inspiration, Protopopov and Belousova created a style of pair skating at once romantic, stately, and graceful. While speed defines the upper reaches of pairs skating today, they skated with a sure, deliberate flow that seemed to defy time. This was not a matter of pretty hand moves tacked onto landings. Great strength was necessary to skate with such lyrical slowness. With no balletic background, they skated in a way that approached the heights of the Bolshoi and Balanchine, yet showed a deep understanding of the artistic possibilities of skating.

The Protopopovs soon began realizing those possibilities. After they wed in 1957, the couple finally broke through, winning the silver at the European and World championships in 1962. Then, defying the athletic skating style that dominated the sport at that time, the Protopopovs mesmerized the world at the 1964 Olympics. Though they did not win the Worlds that year, they would win every major competition they entered for the next four years, culminating in their second Olympic gold medal in 1968. Their signature performance, to Liszt's "Liebestraum," became a much-loved routine, highlighted by swooning death spirals and perfect unison.

In 1973, with Soviets Rodnina and Ulanov now at the top of pair skating, the Protopopovs left competition and skated with a touring Soviet company until 1979, when they defected to the West. They skated professionally until 1992, inspiring fellow skaters with their love of the sport.

LUDMILLA AND OLEG PROTOPOV
SOVIET UNION
LUDMILLA: JULY 16, 1932
OLEG: NOVEMBER 22, 1935
OLYMPIC GOLD: 1964, 1968
WORLD CHAMPION: 1965-68

CARLO FASSI
COACH OF CHAMPIONS

CARLO FASSI (LEFT) AND JOHN CURRY AT THE
1976 OLYMPIC WINTER GAMES

The tragic 1961 airplane crash that killed the entire U.S. Figure Skating team also claimed the lives of many coaches, among them Edi Scholdan of the prestigious Broadmoor program in Colorado Springs. With so much American talent gone, The Broadmoor replaced Scholdan with Carlo Fassi, one of the few Europeans who had been able to crack the dominance of American skaters during the 1950s by winning the bronze medal at the 1953 World Championships. It was a brilliant move. Fassi's profound influence on the sport during the next thirty-five years was as full of joy and success as the circumstances that brought him were tragic.

Only thirty-one when he began at The Broadmoor, Carlo Fassi developed a reputation as a tough coach, especially effective working with skaters on their school figures. It was his expertise on the compulsories that led him to his first great student, Peggy Fleming. Fleming's coach William Kipp had died in the crash; after placing sixth in the 1964 Winter Olympics, Fleming and her family decided to move to Colorado so that she could work with Fassi, particularly on her figures. The strategy paid off: Peggy Fleming had such a lead after the compulsories at the 1968 Olympics in Grenoble that she had the gold medal virtually locked even before her legendary free-skating program.

With the spotlight so bright on Fleming, it was inevitable that it would shine on Fassi, too. He left The Broadmoor to coach on his own, guiding a list of champions from around the world. In 1976, he achieved the pinnacle of coaching success: Both the Men's and Ladies' gold medal winners at the Olympics—Dorothy Hamill and John Curry—were Fassi's students. Robin Cousins, 1980 Olympic champion, was his pupil as well, as were Caryn Kadavy, bronze winner at the 1987 Worlds, and Jill Trenary, three-time U.S. champion and 1990 World champion.

What drew skaters to Fassi was not just his ability to bolster them in compulsories (which were abandoned in 1990), but also his very human approach to coaching and to the sport in general. Fassi and his wife, Christa, seemed to be as interested in creating good people as they were in making champions. They introduced many skaters to their competitors and built friendships, not rivalries.

Fassi returned to The Broadmoor in 1980 for ten highly productive years, then went to Italy for a short stint before coming back to the United States to work at Lake Arrowhead, California. His last student was Nicole Bobek, who flourished under his direction.

Carlo Fassi was inducted into the World Figure Skating Hall of Fame in 1997. He died of a heart attack during the 1997 World Championships in Lausanne, Switzerland.

CARLO FASSI
UNITED STATES/ITALY
BORN: DECEMBER 20, 1929
WORLD BRONZE: 1953
PUPILS: PEGGY FLEMING, DOROTHY
HAMILL, JOHN CURRY, ROBIN COUSINS,
JILL TRENARY, CARYN KADAVY, PAUL
WYLIE, NICOLE BOBEK
COACHED 4 OLYMPIC GOLD MEDALISTS
COACHED 6 WORLD CHAMPIONS

PEGGY FLEMING

THE SPIRIT OF AMERICAN SKATING

When someone completely expresses the time in which they live, they become timeless. And so it was that in 1968 Peggy Fleming, then a shy nineteen-year-old girl, seemed to put in one place everything good about the new generation making themselves heard across America. When she won the Ladies' Olympic gold medal on a memorable February night in Grenoble, France, she became the first overnight television sensation and inspired the next wave of American skaters.

FLEMING'S ELEGANT STYLE SET A NEW STANDARD.

entire world of figure skating. The ladies' long program that night was broadcast live via satellite, and though she had built an insurmountable lead with her strong showing in the compulsories, there was still drama when Fleming strode forward to Tchaikovsky's Sixth Symphony in a chartreuse dress sewn by her mother, Doris. Compared to the jumping pyrotechnics of today's women skaters, Fleming's routine was low to the ground and not very fast, but in beauty and expression it was beyond compare. Fleming wasn't happy with her performance, but

Peggy Fleming began skating along with her three sisters in San Jose, California, at the age of nine. A reserved child, Fleming found the ice a place of quiet and grace where she could excel at something she enjoyed. Her talent was spotted early, and soon she was working with coach William Kipp. In 1961, Kipp was killed in the plane crash that took the entire U.S. figure skating team. In 1964 she won the U.S. title and finished sixth at the Innsbruck Olympic Winter Games. Despite their modest means—Fleming's father was a printer—the family moved to Colorado Springs so she could train with Carlo Fassi. Fleming blossomed under Fassi's eye, and when her father died in 1966, skating became the focus of her life.

By 1968 Peggy Fleming had won five U.S. titles and two World titles, but though she was the clear favorite going into the Olympic Winter Games, the world did not yet really know her. That would change in Grenoble, as would the

everyone else was in love. For one night the world sat and watched a young woman become a star. Peggy Fleming became an enduring sign of what was possible: She was the first Baby Boomer star, and, as the first prominent figure skater to come out of California, an early hint that the West Coast would soon have a strong hand in directing American culture. Peggy Fleming's magical night also displayed the immense power that television could, and would, wield in the world of sports.

After winning the World Championships later that year, Fleming retired from competition to start a successful career in the Ice Follies and on television. She married dermatologist Greg Jenkins in 1970 and had two sons. Aside from joining ABC as a commentator in 1981, Fleming has concentrated most on her family since then, returning to professional touring in 1990. Peggy Fleming was inducted into the World Figure Skating Hall of Fame in 1976.

PEGGY FLEMING
UNITED STATES
BORN: JULY 27, 1948
OLYMPIC GOLD: 1968
WORLD CHAMPION: 1966-68
U.S. CHAMPION: 1964-68

TOLLER CRANSTON

THE COURAGE TO CREATE

CRANSTON INTRODUCED NEW FORMS TO SKATING.

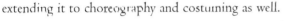

Every skater's performance must be artistic, but rarely has the word *artist* applied to a skater as well as it does to Toller Cranston. His unorthodox style in free skating, which delighted audiences but often vexed conservative judges, kept the innovative Canadian from winning a cache of international medals. Still, he won the Canadian title every year from 1971 to 1976 and left a profound mark on the sport, not only by applying his unique aesthetic vision to skating itself but by extending it to choreography and costuming as well.

Growing up in Hamilton, Ontario, Cranston thought at age six that he wanted to be a dancer, but one ballet class and a visit to a skating rink with his sister put him on ice. Though he showed exceptional talent and expressive abilities, even as a young skater he sometimes found himself out of step with the judges. While developing his skating skills, Cranston was encouraged by his parents to pursue his artistic career, and was accepted at age eighteen to the exclusive Ecole des Beaux-Arts in Montreal. Two years later, in 1969, he left school, briefly moved to Lake Placid, New York, and then went on to Toronto, where he began to work with coach Ellen Burka.

Cranston won his first Canadian Championship in 1971, but his scores on the free program ranged from 4.2 to 5.9—a reflection of the effect his unconventional style had on the judges. His consistent strength in the compulsory figures always kept him within striking distance of medals, but

it was his controversial freestyle skating that made Cranston's name. Where other skaters emphasized rounded lines and smooth movements from classical dance, Cranston was a bold modernist, forming unusual angles with his limbs and body, à la Merce Cunningham, and skating to modern music. Traditionalists were at best puzzled by the artistic Canadian's performances, but audiences loved his deep understanding of dance and his emotional programs. Cranston's costuming was also a timely burst of energy; his fitted, colorful outfits, decorated with sequins and rhinestones in an era when formal wear was still common, introduced an exuberance to men's skating that others eagerly carried forward.

Cranston's highest achievement at the international level was the bronze medal at the 1976 Olympic Games in Innsbruck, where he followed John Curry's gold and Vladimir Kovalev's silver. After finishing fourth in the World Championships that year, he left competitive skating to begin a career as a professional. Outside of the competitive structure, his interpretive strengths flourished. In the two decades since, his work on ice has garnered critical acclaim all over the world. He has also created choreography, coached, and designed costumes for world-class skaters and done skating commentary for the Canadian Broadcasting Corporation. Since his retirement, Cranston has also found critical success with his career as a painter.

TOLLER CRANSTON
CANADA
BORN: APRIL 20, 1949
OLYMPIC BRONZE: 1976
WORLD BRONZE: 1974

JOHN CURRY

THE FINE ART OF FIGURE SKATING

FIGURE SKATING WAS A FORM OF DANCE TO CURRY.
RIGHT. IN "TANGO TANGO"

A true champion is one who forever leaves his mark on the sport. John Curry left his stamp on figure skating by transferring the art and interpretive skills of ballet to singles skating in a way that had never been done before. He also used his consummate technical skills to win British, World, and Olympic championships.

Born in Birmingham, England, Curry wanted to be a dancer from the time he was a little boy, but his family disapproved. So seven-year-old John Curry took up the more athletic pastime of figure skating. He seldom spent more than an hour a week on the ice until he was thirteen, when he began studying more earnestly.

Three years later, in 1965, his father died, and Curry moved to London to study skating with coach Arnold Gershwiler and dance with several teachers—he was all of sixteen. Curry focused on skating as a way to interpret music, as dance does, while other skaters focused on jumps and revolutions with music merely as a background.

Curry's interpretative style went against the trend, and it was not easy for him to find a sponsor—or judges who were not somewhat mystified by his routines. Eventually, though, he was able to move to the United States to train with Gustave Lussi and Carlo Fassi, who coached him to his amateur triumphs.

He was twenty-one—supposedly too old for a competitive career in skat-

ing—when he won the British Championship in 1971, a title he would own from 1973 through 1976. Despite his crisp technical execution, the fact that he used jumps as part of his interpretive choreography—and not as a matter of athletic prowess, like the other skaters—was still not fully appreciated by the judges. It was not until 1975 that Curry took a medal—the bronze—at the World Championships. In 1976, to satisfy the judges, this dancer at heart simplified his skating choreography, emphasizing jumps for their technical merit and making them less an extension of the music, and went on to win the British, European, World, and Olympic Championships.

Having conquered the world of competitive skating, Curry then turned professional, forming his own company to pursue his dream of truly merging skating with dance. His signature piece, *L'Après midi d'un Faune (Afternoon of a Fawn)*, debuted on BBC-TV in 1976. The John Curry Theatre of Skating produced shows that enchanted dance and skating audiences alike, performing Curry's own pieces as well as works choreographed for the ice by Twyla Tharp, Lar Lubovitch, J.P. Bonnefous, and Peter Martins. Curry also brought the full-length ballet, *Les Patineurs*, originally created for dancers, back to the ice.

John Curry was inducted into the World Figure Skating Hall of Fame in 1991, and died from complications resulting from AIDS at age forty-four.

JOHN CURRY
GREAT BRITAIN
BORN: SEPTEMBER 9, 1949
OLYMPIC GOLD: 1976
WORLD CHAMPION: 1976
WORLD BRONZE: 1975
EUROPEAN CHAMPION: 1976
EUROPEAN SILVER: 1975
EUROPEAN BRONZE: 1974
BRITISH CHAMPION: 1971, 1973-76

IRINA RODNINA

A TALE OF TWO PARTNERS

RODNINA WITH HER FIRST PARTNER, ALEXSEI ULANOV

The Protopopovs' velvet lock on pair skating in the 1960s was broken by another Soviet team, one whose style differed enormously from the Olympic champions of 1964 and 1968 but which was no less influential. Irina Rodnina and Alexsei Ulanov were a splash of very cold water after the lulling beauty of the Protopopovs. From her first World Championship in 1969 with Ulanov and on to her later triumphs with her next partner, Alexandr Zaitsev, Rodnina continued to bring pair skating into the jet age with speed, power, and impact, dominating her division for a decade. By the time she retired from skating in 1980, she had won more medals than any other figure skater in history.

A native of Moscow, Rodnina began skating at six and was quickly selected as a young athlete of promise. She was paired with Alexsei Ulanov in the mid-1960s during the reign of the Protopopovs, but under the coaching of Stanislav Zhuk, the two developed a style that was full of the energy of their changing times. Using jumps, lifts, and loud music, Rodnina and Ulanov muscled aside their more classical competitors and won the World Championship in their first appearance in 1969, heralding a change in pair skating. No more Protopopovs—Rodnina and Ulanov won the World Championship every year from 1969 to 1972.

Their pairing reached a dramatic climax in 1972 when Ulanov fell in love with Ludmila Smirnova, a member of a competing Soviet pair team. Despite speculation that Rodnina herself was in love with Ulanov, and the mutual distraction of the intrigue that led to public tears more than once, the two won both the Olympic gold medal in Sapporo and the World Championship that season before splitting up.

An audition was held to find a new partner for Rodnina. Already a world champion, this pair would be Rodnina's, so she chose someone who would complement her great abilities. The winner was Alexandr Zaitsev. A foot taller than his new partner, he concentrated on weight lifting to be able to take full advantage of the differential. Soon they could land difficult jumps with remarkable unison, incorporating flashy twists and lifts that some still under the sway of the Protopopovs found overdone. The judges disagreed. As strong as Rodnina and Ulanov were, Rodnina and Zaitsev were even better, taking the World Championship six straight years, from 1973 to 1978, and winning the Olympic gold medal in 1976 and 1980.

The pairing of Rodnina and Zaitsev also held, for a time, off the ice. They were married in 1975 and had a son in 1979. The two retired after winning the 1980 Olympic title and Rodnina began a new career as a coach. After divorcing Alexandr Zaitsev, she remarried and moved to the United States in 1990, where she has continued coaching. She was inducted into the World Figure Skating Hall of Fame in 1989.

IRINA RODNINA
SOVIET UNION
BORN: SEPTEMBER 12, 1949
OLYMPIC GOLD: (WITH ALEXSEI
ULANOV) 1972, (WITH ALEXANDR
ZAITSEV) 1976, 1980
WORLD CHAMPION: (WITH ULANOV)
1969-72, (WITH ZAITSEV) 1973-78

JANET LYNN

THE ESSENCE OF FREE SKATING

For expressive power and grace on ice, no one has surpassed Janet Lynn, one of the most beloved skaters America has ever produced. Without ever winning an Olympic gold medal or a World Championship, Lynn captivated skating fans everywhere through her seemingly boundless charm and love of the sport.

Born Janet Nowicki and raised in south suburban Chicago, she took to the ice early. By the time she was in first grade, her parents were driving her more than a hundred miles twice a week for lessons at the Wagon Wheel Ice Palace in Rockton, Illinois. A year later she moved in with another skater who lived near Rockton, and her family soon followed.

While studying with coach Slavka Kohout, Nowicki took her mother's maiden name—Lynn—for simplicity, and began moving rapidly up the ranks of American skaters. In 1966, at age thirteen, she won the U.S. Junior Ladies' title. Janet Lynn had blossomed into an exceptional skater with remarkable technical skill. As a Junior she was able to land triples, which only elite skaters were performing then. She was also acclaimed for her artistry by the time she was fifteen, when she finished third at the 1968 U.S. Championships.

Lynn's weakness, from a competitive standpoint, was the compulsory figures. Although she won five consecutive U.S. titles, from 1969 to 1973, she suffered in international competition, where her consistently low marks in the school fig-

JANET LYNN'S FREE SKATING WAS UNMATCHED.

ures put her too far back for rescue by her incomparable free skates. Lynn failed to make the top three at Worlds from 1969 to 1971.

Her most famous moment on ice was a triumph of personal grace, when she fell during a sit spin in her free-skate program at the 1972 Winter Olympics in Sapporo and got back up smiling. She ended up with a bronze medal, but the world had seen what those inside the sport already knew: Janet Lynn was the most elegant, joyous free-skater around. That such a remarkable skater, whose grace and athletic abilities were unchallenged, could be pushed down to a third-place finish because of a relatively poor showing in the compulsories, caused a huge uproar. Soon after, the short program in singles skating was added as a way to show technical proficiency apart from school figures.

Despite her disappointing finish at the Olympics, Lynn became a star. After finishing second at the 1973 World Championships, she signed a three-year contract with the Ice Follies for $1.45 million, which made her the highest-paid female athlete in the world. She skated professionally for two years until exercise-induced asthma forced her to quit. She married and had three sons, and in 1980 went back to skating professionally for three more years. After that she had two more sons, and she now devotes her full attention to her family. Beloved in Japan since the 1972 Olympics, she was an honorary chairman of the 1998 Nagano Olympic Games.

JANET LYNN
UNITED STATES
BORN: APRIL 6, 1953
OLYMPIC BRONZE: 1972
WORLD SILVER: 1973
WORLD BRONZE: 1972
U.S. CHAMPION: 1969-73
U.S. BRONZE: 1968

DOROTHY HAMILL

SOPHISTICATION AND GRACE

WITH CARLO FASSI AT THE 1974 WORLDS.
LEFT. WINNING THE GOLD MEDAL IN 1976.

While Peggy Fleming and her California cool epitomized the late 1960s, Dorothy Hamill's wedge haircut and simple pink knit dress became cultural icons of the 1970s. Her polish on the ice projected the combination of idealism and savvy that characterized that post-Watergate era, and Hamill's Olympic gold medal and 1976 World title further anchored figure skating in the American mind.

A native of Connecticut, Hamill began skating when she was eight. She quickly displayed talent and drive, and within three years she was studying with Gustave Lussi, the great Swiss coach who had also worked with Dick Button and Tenley Albright. After winning the U.S. Novice Championship, she turned her full focus to skating, moving to New York to facilitate her training. Hamill took the U.S. Junior silver medal in 1970 and then moved again, this time to Colorado Springs, where Carlo Fassi brought her under his wing. The two became a strong unit, and in years to come the sight of both of them in the "kiss and cry"—Fassi reading the scores aloud to a squinting Hamill who hadn't worn her glasses—would become almost a tradition.

Having made such a fuss over Peggy Fleming in 1968, many were disappointed when Janet Lynn did not win the Olympic gold medal in Ladies' figure skating at the Sapporo Winter Games in 1972. America wanted a new skating star. As Hamill moved up in the rankings, finally winning the first of three U.S. Championships in 1974, she began to draw attention with her athleticism and intelligence. By the eve of the 1976 Olympics at Innsbruck, Hamill and her distinctive haircut were already the story of the Games.

A student of Fassi, Hamill did well in the compulsories and the short program, and wearing a homemade dress that cost just $75, she won the gold medal with an excellent free skate. As with Peggy Fleming, millions in the United States shared Hamill's triumph as they watched on television. Wedge haircuts were soon appearing everywhere. Hamill won her only World Championship soon afterward in Gothenberg, Sweden, where she defeated Dianne de Leeuw of the Netherlands and East German Christine Errath, just as she had in the Innsbruck Olympics.

The swirl of publicity that had surrounded Hamill at the Olympics and the World Championships helped launch her into a professional career. After the Worlds, Hamill retired from competition and signed a multiyear, seven-figure deal with Ice Capades. She married twice, to Dean Martin, Jr., and Dr. Kenneth Forsythe, but both ended in divorce, though she did briefly own the Ice Capades with Forsythe. She continues to skate in tours and exhibitions.

Dorothy Hamill was inducted into the U.S. Figure Skating Hall of Fame in 1991.

DOROTHY HAMILL
UNITED STATES
BORN: JULY 26, 1956
OLYMPIC GOLD: 1976
WORLD CHAMPION: 1976
WORLD SILVER: 1974–75
U.S. CHAMPION: 1974–76
U.S. BRONZE: 1973

TAI BABILONIA & RANDY GARDNER

TWO LIFETIMES OF SKATING

Most discussions of Tai Babilonia and Randy Gardner focus on one night in the winter of 1980 when they were unable to skate. What gets lost is just how wonderful they were nearly every other night they skated. Only one of two American pairs ever to win a World Championship, Babilonia and Gardner broke through thirteen years of Soviet dominance in the discipline by returning to the lyrical style of skating made popular by Oleg and Ludmilla Protopopov. While disappointment is part of the story of Babilonia and Gardner, so is great success and beauty.

Tai Babilonia and Randy Gardner were paired as children—at ages eight and ten, respectively—and they made their mark young, winning the 1973 U.S. Junior title at just thirteen and fifteen. They rose rapidly: After finishing second at the senior level in 1974 and 1975, they won the 1976 U.S. title and started to advance in the world of international skating as well, coming in fifth at both the World Championships and the Olympics.

These were the prime years of Irina Rodnina and Alexandr Zaitsev and their powerful, high-energy style, but Babilonia and Gardner took a different tack. Though they were both of average height, they presented a much longer, elegant line, and they played to this strength, stressing artistry and unison more than the jumping of the Soviets. Their coach, former English pairs skater John Nicks, guided them toward greater

BABIILONIA AND GARDNER HAVE SKATED
TOGETHER SINCE THE EARLY 1970S.

athleticism, and the pair did eventually land the first throw triple Salchow in competition, but they remained best known for their smooth and flowing style. While not as classically inclined as the Protopopovs, the young American pair's theatricality did share with the Soviets a sense of dance movement and romance.

In 1977 and 1978, Babilonia and Gardner took the bronze at the World Championships, and when Rodnina took time off in 1979 to have a child, the Americans won the gold, setting up a contest of champions for the 1980 Winter Games in Lake Placid. Just before the short program, though, a groin injury Randy Gardner had sustained a few months earlier flared up and he was unable to make it through the warm-ups. Babilonia and Gardner were forced to withdraw from the competition, allowing Rodnina to win her third Olympic gold medal.

The missed opportunity hit both partners hard, but Tai Babilonia was particularly distressed. The pair left competitive skating and toured internationally with major skating companies, becoming much-beloved attractions. Gardner began choreographing and producing for skaters and companies, but Babilonia still seemed to regret the Olympic disappointment and in 1988 admitted to substance abuse problems. After a year of treatment, she returned to the ice where she had left off, rejoining Randy Gardner. They continue to skate as a professional team, together now for more than thirty years.

> ### TAI BABILONIA AND RANDY GARDNER
> UNITED STATES
> BABILONIA: SEPTEMBER 22, 1960
> GARDNER: DECEMBER 2, 1958
> WORLD CHAMPION: 1979
> WORLD BRONZE: 1977-78
> U.S. CHAMPION: 1976-80
> U.S. SILVER: 1974-75

ELAINE ZAYAK

ALWAYS REACHING NEW HEIGHTS

ZAYAK PUSHED LADIES' SKATING INTO THE AIR.

Most champion figure skaters say they took up the sport for fun when they were children, but Elaine Zayak started skating on doctor's orders. More than pleasure, skating was meant at first to be therapy for a childhood foot injury, but pleasure soon won out. Zayak used skating not just to walk better but to fly: As women skaters in the early 1980s began landing triple jumps, she became an expert. Zayak's great jumping exhibitions and energetic programs earned her the World and U.S. championships, and a place in American skating history.

When she was three years old, a lawn mower accident claimed two toes of Elaine Zayak's right foot. As a sport of balance, skating seemed an appropriate way for young Elaine to deal with the walking problems caused by the injury. The therapy worked beyond anyone's expectations, and Elaine excelled at her new sport, though not by doing what everyone else had done. Following the example of four-time U.S. Champion Linda Fratianne, whose ability to land triple jumps had placed her among the leaders of women skaters, Zayak made jumping her strength and used it to great effect. At thirteen, she won both the World and U.S. Junior championships, and at fourteen, she finished fourth as a senior at the 1980 U.S. Championships.

In 1981, Zayak won the U.S. title and finished second at the World Championships. A year later, while still only sixteen, she defeated Katarina Witt

for the World Championship at Copenhagen. Though such an accomplishment was remarkable at Zayak's age, it was how she won that made the most news. Zayak landed six triples in her free skate, a record at that point for ladies' skating. She performed only the same two types of triple jumps that Fratianne did, but she repeated them again and again in her program. Her achievement presaged the movement toward jump-oriented young skaters at the elite level, but it also led the ISU to some rule changes intended to prevent ladies' skating from becoming purely jumping exhibitions. Passed in 1983 and called by some the Zayak rule, the primary change limited the number of triple jumps a woman could repeat in her free-skate program.

The emergence of Rosalynn Sumners and the rise of Katarina Witt, injuries, and the effect of the new rules kept her from reaching those championship heights again, though she did win the bronze at the 1984 World Championships. She retired from competitive skating afterward and toured as a professional until 1994, when she applied for reinstatement for the U.S. Championships. Where she had once been the youngest skater, Zayak was now the oldest. At twenty-eight she was given little chance of doing well against skaters almost half her age, but she proved everyone wrong. To the appreciation of the skating world, Zayak finished fourth, adding a happy coda to a career full of surprises and innovations.

> **ELAINE ZAYAK**
> UNITED STATES
> BORN: APRIL 12, 1965
> WORLD CHAMPION: 1982
> WORLD SILVER: 1981
> WORLD BRONZE: 1984
> U.S. CHAMPION: 1981
> U.S. SILVER: 1974-75
> U.S. BRONZE: 1982, 1984

SCOTT HAMILTON

THE COMPLETE PACKAGE

HAMILTON'S GOLD MEDAL VICTORY AT THE 1984 OLYMPICS ENERGIZED AMERICAN MEN'S SKATING.

The world of sports loves an underdog, but Scott Hamilton has been so good for so long, and so visible a spokesman for figure skating, that the story of his long struggle to the top has been overshadowed.

When Hamilton was a toddler in Bowling Green, Ohio, he was diagnosed with Schwachman's syndrome, a rare intestinal disease that prevents the body from absorbing nutrients, and thus growing. Throughout his childhood, he was kept alive by feeding tubes and other intense medical treatments. When he was nine, he took his first steps on the ice after watching his sister skate. Competing in most sports was out of the question given the disease's effect on his size, so Hamilton decided to pursue skating seriously. Practicing on the ice regularly actually helped stop the disease, and soon Hamilton was free of symptoms and competing on the junior level.

His advancement was not overnight. During the early years of his career many skating insiders said he was too small and frail. At one point in 1978, after his mother died of cancer, Hamilton was so discouraged he considered leaving the sport altogether. He did not give up, but despite a good training environment in Denver and coaching from the legendary Carlo Fassi, Hamilton continued to bounce between third and fifth in the nation for two more years. When Fassi left Denver in 1980, Hamilton went to Don Laws, who intensified the level of training. The result was a breakthrough.

Against a superlative field at the 1981 U.S. Championships, Hamilton took the lead into the free-skate program, where a flawless performance netted his first American title and his first perfect 6.0 mark. After that, Scott Hamilton became invincible. Over the next four years he won every U.S. Championship, every World title, and his ultimate ambition, the 1984 Olympic gold medal at Sarajevo.

Hamilton was the last of the great international champions who didn't have to master the triple Axel jump in order to reach or remain in the highest echelon. He did conquer all the other triples, building and sustaining a reputation for being solid with every jump in every program, and his proficiency in compulsory figures gave him an early edge over his rivals going into the short and free-skate programs.

Through the early 1980s, Hamilton became a role model for his entire sport with his incredible consistency, unwavering work ethic, and even his push for male skaters to wear less gaudy outfits in competition. When he turned professional, he kept the same standards and became one of the most popular ambassadors of figure skating, leading to a new role as a television commentator on the sport.

In 1997, Hamilton learned he had testicular cancer. He was overwhelmed by a massive outpouring of support from skating fans around the globe, and less than a year later he was back on the ice—and in front of the camera—winner of yet another tough fight.

SCOTT HAMILTON
UNITED STATES
BORN: AUGUST 28, 1958
OLYMPIC GOLD: 1984
WORLD CHAMPION: 1981-84
U.S. CHAMPION: 1981-84
U.S. BRONZE: 1978, 1980

TORVILL & DEAN

THE GREATEST STARS OF ICE DANCING

TORVILL AND DEAN CONSTANTLY CHALLENGED THE LIMITS OF ICE DANCING.

One was raised in Nottingham, England, in public housing, the daughter of a bicyclemaker. The other was the son of an electrician in a small town outside of Nottingham. She was an insurance clerk. He was a policeman. From these working-class roots, sunk deep into the north of England, Jayne Torvill and Christopher Dean became the most popular—and maybe most influential—ice dancing team ever.

As the two began their slow climb up the ice dancing ladder, they continued their jobs in Nottingham. But in 1978 they hired famed coach Betty Callaway, and results came quickly. Torvill and Dean won their first British title that year, quit their day jobs, and focused on skating.

The team now looked to Callaway and legendary English ice dancer Courtney Jones to help them reach a higher level. No longer willing to be constrained by the complex rules of ice dancing, Torvill and Dean began the experimentation that would characterize their career. Dean especially, as the creative force on the team, wanted to elevate ice dancing from the realm of sport to the world of art. Rather than imitate ballroom dancing, Torvill and Dean created programs that told stories, that communicated with the audience, that were truly performances. They won the European and World championships in 1981, and broke new territory in 1982 with their "Summer-

time" original dance and "Mack and Mabel" free dance. They continued to win the World and European championships through 1984, making them heroes in England and the center of a swirl of press.

The climax of their competitive career came at the 1984 Olympics in Sarajevo, where their free dance to Ravel's "Bolero" earned them straight 6.0s for artistic merit—and the gold medal. No other skaters have as many perfect 6.0s as Torvill and Dean. The team turned professional shortly afterward, parlaying their fame and skills into a lucrative touring business. Dean created unusual pieces using music as diverse as Philip Glass and pipe music from the Andes, and choreographed for other skaters. Torvill married sound technician Phil Christensen in 1990, while Dean married ice dancer Isabelle Duchesnay in 1991, divorced her two years later, and married skater Jill Trenary in 1994.

To the skating audience's delight, Torvill and Dean requested reinstatement for the 1994 Olympics. Their brilliant efforts were clearly the crowd's favorite throughout the competition, but they were awarded only a bronze medal. Their third-place finish raised many eyebrows and questions about the judges' decision. After that, the couple returned to their professional careers, and continue to draw a massive following to their unique interpretation of what is possible on ice.

JAYNE TORVILL & CHRISTOPHER DEAN
GREAT BRITAIN
TORVILL: OCTOBER 7, 1957
DEAN: JULY 22, 1958
OLYMPIC GOLD: 1984
OLYMPIC BRONZE: 1994
WORLD CHAMPIONS: 1981-84
EUROPEAN CHAMPIONS: 1981-82
1984, 1994
BRITISH CHAMPIONS: 1981-1984, 1994

KURT BROWNING

ARTISTRY AND POWER COMBINED

BROWNING EXCELLED AT PLAYING CHARACTERS.

*W*ith their sport a rare amalgam of athletics and art, most great figure skaters advance either one aspect or the other, but Canadian Kurt Browning, four-time World champion, pushed skating ahead on both fronts. After literally leaping onto the scene in 1988 with the first quadruple jump ever landed in competition, he ended his competitive career six years later with a free-skate program that broke new ground in artistic interpretation. During a period of great depth in men's skating, Browning will be remembered as one of the very best of his time.

Browning made his first mark on the international scene at the 1988 World Championships in Budapest. While he finished out of the medals, the lanky Canadian hit a quadruple toe loop—the first quad ever in competition. Suddenly a whole new level had been added to the sport; it was the skating equivalent of Roger Bannister's first four-minute mile. Competitions could be won without quads, but to make history, skaters would now have to land one.

Both Brian Boitano and Brian Orser retired after the 1988 season, leaving room for Browning, who quickly took advantage. He won three consecutive Canadian and World championships from 1989 to 1991, and seemed a lock for the 1992 Olympic gold medal. But a back injury forced him to stay off the ice and he did not even enter the Canadian Championships that year. Still recuperating from his back injury, he performed poorly at the Olympics in

Albertville and finished sixth. He won the silver medal at the Worlds that year, but as defending champion, a second-place finish was no consolation.

While he had planned to move out of competitive skating after the 1992 Olympics, Browning now chose to stay eligible for the 1994 Games. He again won both the Canadian and World titles in 1993, but Elvis Stojko won the Canadian Championship in 1994 and Browning's concentration seemed at times to flag. In the short program at Lillehammer, Browning, the man to hit the first quad, missed a triple toe loop and came in twelfth in the event. He could be seen mouthing the words, "I'm sorry," to the television cameras as he finished his program.

In the end, though, he had nothing to apologize for. His free skate, created with choreographer Sandra Bezic, featured Browning in a white dinner jacket, skating to music from the film *Casablanca*. Rather than just using a character as a focus for his program, Browning truly portrayed Humphrey Bogart. While it pulled him up only as high as fifth place, the routine became an instant classic and was an important addition to the dramatic potential of the sport.

Having made his last run at Olympic gold, Browning left competitive skating and began to expand upon his interpretive abilities. The new kind of entertainment being created by noncompetitive skaters—led in no small part by Browning—will surely allow him to continue exploring all the possibilities of figure skating.

KURT BROWNING
CANADA
BORN: JUNE 18, 1966
WORLD CHAMPION: 1989-91, 1993
WORLD SILVER: 1992
CANADIAN CHAMPION: 1989-91, 1993

KATARINA WITT
INTERNATIONAL ELEGANCE

WITT WON HER FIRST OLYMPIC GOLD MEDAL IN 1984, IN SARAJEVO.

Katarina Witt's first appearance in America was a forgettable ninth-place performance at the 1979 Norton Skate, an international event held to test Lake Placid's new figure skating rink built for the 1980 Olympics. That was the last time anyone would be able to forget the only woman since Sonja Henie to win two Olympic gold medals in Ladies' singles, or to tie Henie's record of six consecutive European Championships.

Born and raised in the political strife of a divided Germany following World War II, she was fascinated by the skaters at the Kuchwald rink near her East German home and started skating at age five.

At nine, Witt was assigned to Jutta Mueller, esteemed coach of World Champion Jan Hoffman, and mother and coach of two-time World Champion and Olympic silver medalist Gabriele Seyfert. The relationship continued, for better or worse, with Mueller in total control of all aspects of Witt's competitive career. Witt's challenge was to follow in the footsteps of East Germany's international champions Seyfert, Christine Errath, and Anett Poetzsch (who later married Witt's brother, Axel).

Her breakthrough came in a stunning upset of America's reigning World Champion Rosalynn Sumners for her first Olympic gold medal at the 1984 Games in Sarajevo, and a World title the following month. Witt captured the hearts—and media attention—of two continents with her striking beauty as well as her artistry and technical skill on the ice. The only threat to Witt's supremacy came from America's Debi Thomas, who beat the German skater at the 1986 Worlds but later lost to her at the Calgary Olympics in the "Battle of the Carmens", when both skated to music from Bizet's opera.

The East German government at first denied Witt permission to leave the country to skate professionally, but with the fall of the Berlin Wall and the East German regime in 1989, Witt was free at last. She appeared with Brian Boitano in his television special *Canvas of Ice* and toured with his skating shows for three years. After that she starred with Boitano and Brian Orser in *Carmen on Ice*, a full-length ice ballet filmed in Spain and Germany. The film was released in theaters throughout Europe and shown on HBO in the United States; all three skaters won Emmys for it.

In 1993, at twenty-eight, she was reinstated and entered the Olympics in Lillehammer. She finished out of the medals but thrilled the audience as she skated last to "Where Have All the Flowers Gone?" in tribute to the people of war-torn Sarajevo.

Katarina Witt was inducted into the World Figure Skating Hall of Fame in 1995, and remains one of the sport's most popular personalities, just as alluring as the youngster of 1984 who ignited the world.

KATARINA WITT
GERMANY
BORN: DECEMBER 3, 1965
OLYMPIC GOLD: 1984, 1988
WORLD CHAMPION: 1984-85, 1987-88
WORLD SILVER: 1982
EUROPEAN CHAMPION: 1983-88
EUROPEAN SILVER: 1982
EAST GERMAN CHAMPION: 1981-88

DEBI THOMAS

POWER SKATING RETURNS TO AMERICA

THOMAS MERGED BEAUTY AND GREAT STRENGTH.

ebi Thomas was one of the first modern American power skaters, gaining international prominence with World and Olympic medals when the full arsenal of triple jumps first became an expected part of free skating and when compulsory figures were on the decline as part of the competitive structure.

Born in San Jose, California, Thomas took to the ice as a girl, after seeing an ice show with a fascinating trick skater named Mr. Frick. Her initial interest was strictly recreational, but she was a strong, athletic child and showed promise as a skater. She began to train seriously with Alex McGowan, even though financing such a program was a struggle for Thomas's single mother, Janice, a computer programmer.

Debi Thomas's determination was as strong as her talent, though, and by the time she was fifteen, in 1982, she had reached the Senior level of the U.S. Championships. In 1985, she won two international events, finished second at the U.S. Championships, and placed fifth at her first World Championships.

The following year, she won the U.S. title and was not only the first woman to beat East Germany's Olympic gold medalist, Katarina Witt, but also the first African-American ever to win the Worlds. Fellow Californian Brian Boitano won the Men's title, and the two became instant favorites to capture the gold at the 1988 Olympics.

Witt, however, was not about to be written off, and she proved her tenacity by regaining her World title at the 1987 event in Cincinnati, where Thomas finished second. The tight competition set up what would be called the Battle of the Carmens at the upcoming Olympics: By chance, each had chosen music from Bizet's *Carmen* and neither would back down and change. Like the Battle of the Brians between Boitano and Brian Orser, the face-off of Witt and Thomas turned into a media frenzy, exploiting the dramatic political element of East meets West.

Thomas's program was challenging and difficult; she was the only skater to attempt a triple toe/triple toe combination during the Games, but she failed to land it, and ended up with the bronze medal. Witt was confident and flawless as she claimed her second Olympic gold. Elizabeth Manley of Canada took silver. It was a huge disappointment for Thomas, one that would be repeated at the ensuing World Championships in Budapest: Witt finished first, Manley second, Thomas third.

That summer, Thomas turned professional and went on tour, but not for long. Throughout her skating career she had been a dedicated student at Stanford University, where she resumed her studies. She continued to make occasional special appearances on the ice, but her priority now was her work at the Northwestern University School of Medicine.

DEBI THOMAS
UNITED STATES
BORN: MARCH 25, 1967
OLYMPIC BRONZE: 1988
WORLD CHAMPION: 1986
WORLD SILVER: 1987
WORLD BRONZE: 1988
U.S. CHAMPION: 1986, 1988
U.S. SILVER: 1985, 1987

BRIAN BOITANO

JUMPING UP TO STARDOM

BOITANO'S EXCITING VICTORY AT THE 1988 OLYMPIC WINTER GAMES MADE HIM A STAR.

Many top-caliber skaters must leave home to find the right training base, and they often have multiple coaches along the way to gold medals and World Championships. Brian Boitano stayed home. At one rink, one coach, Linda Leaver, developed him from a raw beginner into a champion. The native of Sunnyvale, California, achieved his dreams from his own backyard, capturing an impressive string of U.S. and international titles, all capped by the 1988 Olympic gold medal at Calgary.

Boitano started skating when he was eight, first on roller skates, then on ice at a rink minutes from his home. After only a few months, Linda Leaver took him on as a student and he began jumping, imitating his hero, Terry Kubicka, who had landed the first and only back flip in international competition. Boitano won the U.S. Junior Championship in 1978, and was soon challenging at the senior level, finishing second to Scott Hamilton in the U.S. Championships in 1983 and 1984.

Boitano possessed a powerful variety of athletic talents, and by the 1984 Olympics, he had developed into the best jumper in all of skating. His chance finally came when Hamilton retired, but an injury stopped him short of pulling off the U.S. and World sweep in 1985. He settled for the American title, with Alexandr Fadeev of the Soviet Union claiming the World crown. The next year, 1986, Boitano at last conquered every

challenge, national as well as global. But in 1987, Brian Orser of Canada, who had chased Hamilton as well as Boitano through the 1980s, won the World Championship in Cincinnati, setting the stage for a confrontation at the 1988 Winter Olympics in Orser's homeland.

With the crowds cheering wildly, Orser pushed Boitano to the limit, and Boitano pushed himself to new heights. Despite heavy precompetition debate over whether he should try a quadruple jump, Boitano decided to concentrate on triple Axels and his own personalized version of the triple Lutz, called a 'Tano, performed with a hand held above his head. The decision proved right. His flawless long program at Calgary brought him the gold medal. It was also an artistic triumph. After losing the 1987 World Championship, Boitano had enlisted choreographer Sandra Bezic to add fresh drama and style to his routines. Boitano won the 1988 World gold skating to music from Abel Gance's film *Napoleon*, dressed in military garb and assuming a character to go with his unquestioned athletic abilities. The combination was unbeatable.

Boitano turned professional in 1989 and also starred in two television shows: *Canvas of Ice* and the Emmy-winning ice ballet *Carmen on Ice*. Reinstated in 1994, he came in second to Scott Davis in the U.S. Championships and finished sixth at the Olympics. Boitano was inducted into the World and United States Figure Skating halls of fame in 1996.

BRIAN BOITANO
UNITED STATES
BORN: OCTOBER 22, 1963
OLYMPIC GOLD: 1988
WORLD CHAMPION: 1986, 1988
WORLD SILVER: 1987
WORLD BRONZE: 1985
U.S. CHAMPION: 1985-88
U.S. SILVER: 1983-84, 1994

GORDEEVA & GRINKOV

TRUE PARTNERS

GRINKOV'S POWER PERFECTLY BALANCED GORDEEVA'S GRACE.

*I*t was the Central Red Army Club in Moscow, not love, that first brought Ekaterina Gordeeva and Sergei Grinkov together, but it was love and ultimately tragedy that made them perhaps the best-known pairs skaters in history.

The petite and already beautiful Gordeeva was eleven when she was matched on the ice with fifteen-year-old Grinkov in 1982. The daughter of a dancer with the Moiseev Dance Company, she had been admitted to the prestigious Central Red Army Club at the age of four; Grinkov, the son of two Moscow police officers, had been in the club since he was five. Neither had exhibited the superior jumping skills needed to compete as elite singles skaters, so they were groomed for pairs. The wisdom of that decision was quickly apparent when they won the World Junior Championship in 1984, having skated together for little more than a year.

Working with choreographer Marina Zueva, Gordeeva and Grinkov began creating a style of pairs skating at once youthful and elegant, a combination of Soviet athletic skills and the Russian ballet tradition. Though only teenagers when they won their first World Championship in 1986, they skated with unusual maturity. The team defended its World title in 1987, then went on to win the gold medal at the 1988 Winter Olympics in Calgary.

They had fully meshed as a skating team, and by 1989 they had become a couple off the ice as well. In April 1991,

nine years after they had begun skating together, Gordeeva and Grinkov were married in Moscow. The breakup of the Soviet Union created new opportunities for the couple, who turned professional that same year. Through 1991 they skated professionally, until they learned that Gordeeva was pregnant. Shortly after the birth of their daughter, Daria, in September 1992, they were back on the road, skating with a passion and an intimacy that was now a genuine expression of their affection. On ice, they seemed to work as one. The 1994 ISU reinstatement of professionals allowed them to compete in the Lillehammer Olympics, where they won their second gold medal for Pairs with a memorable performance to Beethoven's "Moonlight Sonata."

Gold medals, World Championships, a happy and romantic marriage, and a healthy child—it all seemed perfect, until Sergei Grinkov collapsed on the ice during a practice session in Lake Placid, New York, on November 20, 1995. Within hours he was pronounced dead of heart failure. The world mourned the loss of not just a great skater but a beloved husband and father. Gordeeva's bestselling book *My Sergei*, published in 1996, told the story of their love and their career.

Ekaterina Gordeeva returned to professional skating in 1996, competing and touring as a single skater. Her dignity and strength have made her a legend and an inspiration to millions, even outside the sport of figure skating.

EKATERINA GORDEEVA
SERGEI GRINKOV
SOVIET UNION
GORDEEVA: MAY 22, 1971
GRINKOV: FEBRUARY 4, 1967
OLYMPIC GOLD: 1988, 1994
WORLD CHAMPION: 1986-87, 1989-90
WORLD SILVER: 1988

KRISTI YAMAGUCHI

A DIFFICULT CHOICE FOR THE GOLD

YAMAGUCHI WAS THE FIFTH AMERICAN WOMAN TO WIN AN OLYMPIC GOLD MEDAL IN LADIES' SINGLES.

It is hard enough to master one ice skating discipline, but Kristi Yamaguchi was among those rare athletes in the history of the sport to excel at two. To simply excel, though, wasn't enough. Before she became Ladies' world champion in 1991 and 1992, and won the Ladies' gold medal at the 1992 Olympics, Yamaguchi had to make a tough decision that would affect many lives.

Kristi Yamaguchi began skating as a six-year-old in Fremont, California, where she was raised. When she was nine, she began working with Christy Ness, who remained her coach throughout her competitive career. While she developed as a singles skater, Yamaguchi, in 1983, began skating pairs with Rudy Galindo, and in 1986 they won the U.S. Junior title. Yamaguchi finished fourth in Novice Ladies' the same year. Her training schedule was relentless. Yamaguchi crammed in every hour she could to her two styles of skating, and it was worth it: She and Galindo won the 1988 World Juniors, and she won the Ladies' 1988 World Juniors. Some began to ask if she might be even better if she concentrated on only one discipline.

The next year Yamaguchi nearly pulled off what everyone said was impossible, taking the U.S. Pairs title with Galindo, and finishing second to Jill Trenary for the U.S. Ladies' title. In the United States, only Joan Tozzer in 1938 and Maribel Vinson in 1933 had won golds in both disciplines, and those were in the years before pair skating involved jumps and throws. At the 1989 Worlds, Yamaguchi came tantalizingly close: fifth place in Pairs and sixth in Ladies' singles.

Then came a turning point. Jim Hulick, her pairs coach, died. For a time, Yamaguchi and Galindo worked with pairs coach John Nicks in Southern California, but when Christy Ness moved to Edmonton, Alberta, Yamaguchi followed her across the Canadian border to continue training in singles. The stress on Yamaguchi and her partnership with Galindo increased, as did the voices who counseled her to focus on one discipline.

Although she and Galindo won the U.S. title again in 1990, and finished fifth again at the Worlds in Halifax, her fourth-place finish in Ladies' singles pushed her to the decision to finally skate completely on her own after six years with a partner. The championships soon followed. After another second-place finish in the U.S. in 1991, she broke through at the Worlds, leading an American sweep with Tonya Harding in second and Nancy Kerrigan in third. She won her only U.S. title in 1992, then went on to Albertville, where she surprised many with a gold medal only two years after she had settled on singles. Her choice had paid off.

Yamaguchi retired from competitive figure skating after the 1992 season. She is now a popular fixture on the professional touring circuit, and was inducted into the U.S. Figure Skating Hall of Fame in 1998.

KRISTI YAMAGUCHI
UNITED STATES
BORN: JULY 12, 1971
OLYMPIC GOLD: 1992
WORLD CHAMPION: 1991-92
WORLD SILVER: 1989
WORLD BRONZE: 1990
U.S. CHAMPION: 1992
U.S. SILVER: 1989-91

TODD ELDREDGE

SKATING FOR MORE THAN GLORY

ONLY ROGER TURNER AND DICK BUTTON WON MORE
U.S. MEN'S TITLES THAN TODD ELDREDGE.

orn the son and grandson of commercial fishermen on Cape Cod, Todd Eldredge first hit the ice at age five, using hockey skates his parents, Ruth and John, had given him for Christmas. Within two weeks, he declared he had to have figure skates so he could jump and spin. His parents had no idea how long this fascination would last, but they bought the new skates anyway, and a future champion was born.

Ruth Eldredge recalls waking up in the morning and finding her son standing beside the bed, waiting to go skate before he went off to kindergarten. That drive and determination was matched by talent and unusual competitiveness; within a few years he was traveling to workshops for advanced training.

At a summer camp, Eldredge met Richard Callaghan, who would be his only coach—an unusual relationship in a sport where most champions work with several coaches during a career. When Callaghan moved to Philadelphia to teach, Todd, who was just ten years old, left home to train with him. He would later follow Callaghan to Colorado Springs, San Diego, and Detroit.

As training expenses mounted, Eldredge was almost forced to quit skating. His mother had returned to work as a nurse, but the family's income relied on the seasonal catch from the sea. To make sure that their local boy could continue his quest for greatness, the small Cape Cod village that was Eldredge's home

town came to his aid, holding fundraisers and summer barbecues—even the local hockey team played benefit games.

Eldredge finally gained prominence by winning the U.S. and World Junior titles and followed with the U.S. Championship. His rise, however, came to an abrupt halt when a spine injury kept him from competing at the 1992 U.S. Championships. He went on to the Albertville Olympics, where the injury was aggravated and he finished out of the medals. In 1993, facing burnout, his development declined. The next year at the U.S. Championships, he came down with the flu and, after fainting in the morning with a high fever, skated an uncharacteristically flawed program. He missed the 1994 Olympic team, and almost quit figure skating.

But the extraordinary determination that had always motivated Eldredge came through again, and he came back in 1995 with new resolve, regaining his national title. From there, he went on to win the U.S. Championship in 1995, 1997, and 1998, the World title in 1996, and a total of twenty-five international medals.

In the 1990s, a change in ISU rules allowed skaters to accept prize money and appearance fees, and Eldredge's financial burden was finally lifted. Remembering those who gave him his start, he repaid his family, who had mortgaged their home, and built a community athletic field in his hometown.

TODD ELDREDGE

UNITED STATES
BORN: AUGUST 28, 1971
WORLD CHAMPION 1996
WORLD SILVER 1995, 1997-98
WORLD BRONZE: 1991
U.S. CHAMPION:
1990-91, 1995, 1997-98

ELVIS STOJKO

SKATING SUPERSTAR

QUADRUPLE JUMPS AND CHARISMA ARE TRADEMARKS OF
THE ENERGETIC STOJKO.

*E*very great figure skater has a personal vision of the sport. Some have viewed it as a cousin to dance, adapting ballet, modern, and even ballroom dancing to a more treacherous surface. Others have seen skating as a sport that rewards perfect athletic performance. To Canadian Elvis Stojko, figure skating is not far from his other passion, martial arts, which not only informs his explosive skating style but also casts a fresh light on the concept of figure skating.

While still a teenager, Stojko realized his great promise in both sports, studying skating with successful coaches such as Ellen Burka while at the same time earning his black belt in karate. Though seemingly very different, skating and martial arts both necessitate great body control and intense concentration, and both exist in the place where sport and art meet. While developing as a skater, Stojko transferred much of what he learned in the kendo to the rink. Unlike many other elite men skaters, Stojko's body is thick and his limbs short, and while this may have held him back from the aesthetic form to which most in the skating world were accustomed, he turned it to his advantage and became one of the world's best jumpers. Before he had won even his first Canadian Championship, Stojko landed the first quadruple/double combination ever performed in competition at the 1991 World Championships.

That record jump launched him onto the world stage. When an injury kept Kurt Browning out of the 1994 Canadian Championships, Stojko stepped in and won the first of his four national championships and took the bronze at the Worlds. He and Browning traded the Canadian title back and forth in 1993 and 1994, and he finished second behind Browning in 1993 at the Worlds, but it was Stojko who went into the 1994 Olympics with the edge. A major reason for this was his artistic development, which came to the fore in Lillehammer, where he skated two programs that drew deeply from his personal interests. His short program was a technodance piece that featured Stojko in leather, while the free skate was crafted around martial arts themes. Though crowd-pleasing, the routines earned him only the silver, behind Alexei Urmanov.

Stojko won the World title a few months later, defended it the next year despite an ankle injury, and won again in 1997. That same year, he landed the first quad/triple combination in competition at the ISU Champions Series Final. The persistence he learned from martial arts has served him well; at the 1998 Winter Games, he skated while suffering from a groin injury. With only an outside chance at catching Ilia Kulik for the gold, Stojko performed a memorable long program, coming off the ice in visible pain and winning more admirers along with the silver medal.

Stojko's powerful jumping abilities and pop-culture aesthetics—after all, he was named after Elvis Presley—have made him a superstar.

ELVIS STOJKO

CANADA

BORN: JANUARY 22, 1972
OLYMPIC SILVER: 1994, 1998
WORLD CHAMPION: 1994-95, 1997
WORLD SILVER: 1993
WORLD BRONZE: 1992
CANADIAN CHAMPION: 1994, 1996-98

MICHELLE KWAN

GROWING UP A CHAMPION

KWAN'S PERFORMANCES AT THE 1998 U.S. CHAMPIONSHIPS ARE ALREADY LEGENDARY.

Though she grew up in Southern California, near the glow of Hollywood stars, all Michelle Kwan ever wanted to be was a figure skater. Sure, movie stars were nice, but Brian Boitano was her idol. Since those first dreams in the late 1980s, Kwan has become the figure skating star she always wanted to be. Twice U.S. and World champion and a silver medalist at the 1998 Olympics, Michelle Kwan is one of the premier women skaters of her time, and among the youngest ever to make an impact on the sport.

Kwan's early entrance into world figure skating was due in large part, of course, to her talent, but also to the Harding/Kerrigan affair of 1994. With Kerrigan out of the U.S. Championships that year due to her knee injury, Harding took back the title she had won in 1991 and Michelle Kwan won the silver. Although Kerrigan did go to the Olympics that year, she did not compete at the World Championships and so Kwan was named in her place. Only thirteen at the time, it gave her a taste of what could be hers.

After finishing second again in the 1995 U.S. Championships, this time to Nicole Bobek, she altered her image going into the 1996 season. Once Kwan was the youngest competitor in the field, but the appearance of Tara Lipinski took away that distinction; now Kwan showed how she had grown out of that role by portraying Salome for her free skate wearing a bare midriff outfit.

The new look and her maturing skating abilities earned Kwan, still only fifteen, both the U.S. and World titles. She was favored to repeat the double in 1997, but she fell three times in her free skate at the U.S. Championships, allowing Tara Lipinski to take the gold medal. Confidence shaken, she also performed below her potential at the Worlds and again Lipinski won.

Going into the 1998 U.S. Championships it seemed that Kwan would not have the chance to regain her title. A stress fracture had forced her off the ice for two months prior to the January competition and even up to the day of the short program, there was speculation about whether she would compete. What happened instead has quickly become figure skating legend. Skating to Rachmaninoff piano music, she performed what many said afterward was one of the greatest programs they'd ever seen, and her free skating program two days later was just as good. For artistic merit, she received seven perfect 6.0s on the short program and eight on the free skate, reclaiming the U.S. Championship with style.

Kwan entered the Nagano Winter Games as the favorite, leading one of the strongest American figure skating teams ever. After a solid short program, though, she performed a conservative free skate and once again lost the gold to Tara Lipinski. Two months later she reclaimed the World Championship, closing an exciting season and claiming her stake at the top of ladies' figure skating.

> **MICHELLE KWAN**
> UNITED STATES
> BORN: JULY 7, 1980
> OLYMPIC SILVER: 1998
> WORLD CHAMPION: 1996, 1998
> WORLD SILVER: 1997
> U.S. CHAMPION: 1996, 1998
> U.S. SILVER: 1994-95, 1997

TARA LIPINSKI
The Youngest Star Ever

WINNING THE OLYMPIC GOLD IN 1998 CAPPED
LIPINSKI'S COMPETITIVE CAREER.

*S*ome very good things come in very small packages. At four-foot-ten, Tara Lipinski is indeed a small package, but she may prove to be one of the greatest figure skaters of all time. She burst onto the world of skating at the age of twelve and has broken two records held by the legendary Sonja Henie: Lipinski is now the youngest skater to win the World Championship and, at age fifteen, the youngest ever to win the Olympic gold medal for ladies' figure skating.

The road to becoming the leading skater of her time began early for Lipinski, and not just on the ice. When she was only two, she held a mock gold medal ceremony for herself while watching the 1984 Olympic Winter Games on television. At age three, she got her first skates—roller skates, like Brian Boitano's first pair—and she quickly showed herself to be a prodigy, winning championships and competing on an all-boy roller hockey team. At six she took up figure skating and learned to perform her roller skating jumps and spins on ice. Lipinski was now skating seven days a week; her mother, Pat, drove an hour each way from their home in Philadelphia to the ice rink in Delaware. In 1991, Lipinski's father, Jack, was promoted to a new job in Texas. The Lipinskis moved, but the effort to keep Tara skating was enormous. To get ice time before school, she woke up at 3 A.M. every day, then returned to the rink after school. That summer, the family decided to divide and conquer: Her father would stay in

Texas while Tara and her mother returned to Delaware to continue training.

The sacrifice paid off in 1994, when Lipinski won the gold at the U.S. Olympic Festival and placed fourth at the World Junior Championships. In 1996, Todd Eldredge's coach Richard Callaghan came aboard as Lipinski's coach, and the talented young skater's prodigious athletic ability and energy began to be shaped into world-class performances that were as satisfying artistically as they were technically. After finishing fifteenth at the Worlds in 1996, she pushed the envelope the next season, landing the first triple loop/triple loop combination in competition by either a man or a woman. She won both the 1997 U.S. Championship and the Worlds, becoming the youngest-ever World champion and defeating the favorite, Michelle Kwan.

Kwan fought back in 1998 when she recaptured the U.S. title and took the lead after the short program of the Ladies' final at the Olympics in Nagano, Japan. In the long program, though, Kwan skated conservatively—some say even tentatively—and Lipinski took advantage. Her unmatched jumping, combined with her growing maturity and expressiveness, resulted in a powerful and nearly flawless program that overshadowed her fellow American and brought Lipinski the gold medal.

Following the Olympics, Lipinski chose to leave the eligible ranks in order to spend more time with her family, and to concentrate on her studies.

TARA LIPINSKI
UNITED STATES
BORN: JUNE 10, 1982
OLYMPIC GOLD: 1998
WORLD CHAMPION: 1997
U.S. CHAMPION: 1997
U.S. BRONZE: 1996

DEBI THOMAS

"When Everyone Said I Couldn't"

Debi Thomas is most proud of her free-skate program at the 1986 U.S. Championships. Unlike most skaters, who take a break from college or work to train full-time, Thomas was determined to skate competitively and to complete her education without interruption. Most people told her that she couldn't possibly handle a full college course load at Stanford University and train for the U.S. Championships at the same time.

At the U.S. Championships, Thomas skated well in both figures and the short program. Although she was in first place going into the free skate, Thomas knew she still had to win there in order to take the title. But in practices that week, she had been having trouble landing all five of her planned triple jumps.

"I spent the entire day of the long program pacing back and forth in my hotel room trying to convince myself that I could do it," Thomas recalls. "I told myself, 'You can do these jumps. You've done them before—not all in one program, but you can do them.' "

That evening in the warm-up Thomas fell each time she tried her triple loop. Her coach advised her to take the jump out of her program, but she felt she needed it to win. And when she took the ice for her performance, Thomas knew she had made the right decision.

"When they announced my name, the crowd roared," she says. "It was an amazing feeling, the first time I had a sense of what it might be like to do something outstanding." That confidence helped Thomas focus on her jumps one at a time. "I could practically hear the crowd talking to me...." she says. "I knew they were pulling for me."

The audience had seen her miss the triple loop during the warmup, and when she set up for that jump, it was as if the whole arena held its breath for her. "Then I landed it," Thomas recounts proudly. "It wasn't the best one in the world, but everyone went wild."

Debi Thomas won the title, but she also learned an important lesson before she ever got to the podium to receive her gold medal.

"I learned that your attitude is the most important component for performing well. . . . What made the 1986 Nationals so important was not that I won, but that I got my act together and skated so well. And doing it when everyone said I couldn't—that was special." ✳

DEBI THOMAS MANAGED TO ATTEND STANFORD UNIVERSITY FULL-TIME AS WELL AS SKATE COMPETITIVELY AT THE HIGHEST INTERNATIONAL LEVEL.

KYOKO INA AND JASON DUNGJEN

"It meant so much to have him there."

Although Jason Dungjen has enjoyed tremendous success with Kyoko Ina in the last several years of his eligible career, his favorite memory goes back to a time years before he and Ina gained national recognition as U.S. pairs champions.

"There are so many wonderful memories that I could draw from," Dungjen recounts. "Making the World and Olympic teams, winning the national championships, skating at the Olympics. But the memory that stands out the most is from back in 1981. I was skating pairs with my sister back then, and it was the first time we skated at the Junior Pairs sectionals."

Jason's father had been involved in a very serious automobile accident several weeks before the competition, and doctors didn't know whether he would fully recover from his extensive injuries.

"But my father was able to be there at sectionals," Dungjen recalls. "They brought him into the arena in a wheelchair and just wheeled him right up to the side of the boards. It meant so much to have him there, and for us to win."

Dungjen says the experience helped him maintain perspective during the many ups and downs and years of hard work that followed. "It made me realize what's really important in life. No matter what you do in sports, there's nothing more important than family."

Ina has had many extraordinary moments, from the first time she landed a difficult jump to competing in the 1998 Winter Olympics in Japan, where she was born. But the experience that stands out most for her is the first time she and Dungjen won the U.S. Championship—1997—after having finished second three times before. Their coach, Peter Burrows, had lost his wife to cancer just two weeks earlier.

AFTER COMING IN SECOND FOR MANY YEARS, KYOKO INA AND JASON DUNGJEN WON BACK-TO-BACK U.S. PAIRS CHAMPIONSHIPS IN 1997 AND 1998.

"I was really close to her, and it was tough mentally and emotionally," Ina says. "But it made me realize that skating is skating, and as long as we have our health and our life and our happiness, nothing else really matters."

Ina and Dungjen were first after the short program in 1997, but they had been in that position before, and Ina had learned not to take it for granted.

"We had been first after the short the year before too, and even though we skated clean in the long, we didn't win," Ina explains. "So after we skated the long program in 1997, I couldn't watch the rest of the competition. I sat in the locker room. Then after a while Jason and Peter came in and broke the news that we had won. It was really special. I learned that eventually things do work out the way they should." ✳

CHAPTER THREE

THE SKATE

*N*obody cared about triple toe loops—or any other fancy jumps and twists, for that matter—when the first pair of ice skates was made four or five thousand years ago. Skates were, quite simply, transportation. Skates of a sort were invented by the primitive people of the Scandinavian region, who had to cross icy fjords and frozen lakes as they hunted wild animals, then brought them to villages where they could barter—and occasionally plunder. These first skates were made of animal bones, ground to a smooth finish and drilled with holes in the front and back to hold leather thongs (*talares*) that were used to tie the skate to the foot and ankle, like Hermes' winged sandals. Most of the skates were made from shank, rib, or jaw bones of elk, reindeer, or horses, but some skates excavated in Sweden—now in the National Museum of Ethnology in Leiden, Holland—were made from walrus tusks.

Since the bones were flat, without sharp edges to cut into the ice, these first skates had to be greased with lard or animal fat to improve glide, and long pointed poles were used to help push the skater along. In this respect, skating on ice was not unlike cross-country skiing on snow, which probably began on wooden slabs around the same time. Other samples of early skates excavated in England date back about two thousand years, to the era of the Roman conquests. These skates were attached to simple, leather-strap sandals. Early native North Americans used similar skates for transportation and hunting long before Columbus or any other Europeans "discovered" America.

As with all inventions, skates went through numerous alterations—some good and some not so good—before they became anything like what we have today. Wooden skates were one short-lived development that fit soundly into the "not so good" category. Originally about the width of one's foot, they were carved from hard woods, like tiny skis. But they wore down and broke easily. Very few examples

TOP. WOODEN SKATES FROM 1867. LEATHER STRAPS WERE PULLED OVER THE SHOES AND THEN THROUGH SLOTS ON THE SKATES.

ABOVE. THE CAST-STEEL SKATES (ABOVE) DATE FROM 1860. EACH WEIGHS 1½ POUNDS. (THE EDDIE SHIPSTAD COLLECTION).

A GOOD PAIR OF SKATES IS THE ONLY EQUIPMENT A FIGURE SKATER REALLY NEEDS.

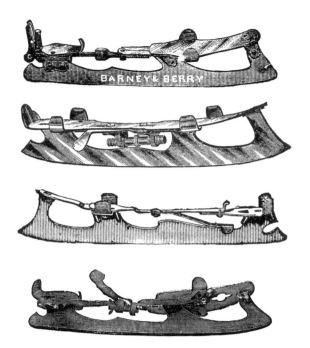

As the skate evolved in the nineteenth century, a wide variety of styles became available to the general public. Clamp-on skates such as these could be bought and enjoyed even by members of the working classes.

of these skates still exist, but the ones that do show an eventual refinement from the flat-bone skates toward a narrower bottom. Embedding small strips of iron into the wood helped their strength, but did little to improve maneuverability.

Finally, around the fourteenth century, the Dutch are believed to have invented the first metal skates from iron. The hand-forged blades were wide and embedded into—or attached to—a wooden platform to hold the shoe. They still had to be tied to the feet with thongs or cords, which could cut off circulation and be extremely painful if worn for long periods of time, but the first signs of sharpening the outside edges for better grip began to appear. The primary purpose for these uncomfortable, utilitarian skates remained practical, not recreational.

Then, around 1550, a Dutch blacksmith apparently misunderstood his client's directions and made a set of blades that were thin, with narrow runners and sharper edges. These new blades, it turned out, allowed for greatly increased control and speed, and as this style of skate reached a wide audience, recreational skating became more popular. Various refinements of this style continued for many years, such as the addition of a large curl at the front of the blade, called a prow, to help cut through the snow, and the addition of a spike on the rear of the platform to hold the heel of the boot firmly in place. These early styles were transported to countries throughout the world and copied by immigrants, traders, and military personnel.

Besides adding to the development of the skate itself, the Dutch also brought the word into the English language. To the Danes, it was a *skoite*, and to the Dutch, a *schaat*, which later became known as simply a "skate" in English.

Though native North Americans already had skates, American colonists brought their own version with them, as did English, French, and Dutch soldiers. As skating became more of a recreational pastime, heavily decorated and ornamental skates were made, but it was not until the early 1800s that steel was first used to make blades that clamped onto street shoes and boots and did away with the troublesome straps and ties.

The first skate designed specifically for figure skating was developed in 1837 by an Englishman, Henry Boswell. He shortened the front of the blade and added a longer heel, which gave greater stability and control. But more important, he forged a groove—then called a "flute," now called a "channel" or "hollow," down the middle of the blade—giving it an edge on each side to better cut into and grip the ice. This improvement allowed for sharp turns, reverse directions, and increased speed. The blades were made of iron with steel welded to the bottom, which allowed for the innovative flute.

Eleven years later, American E. V. Bushnell of Philadelphia made the first pair of all-steel skates. He did away with the wooden platform, instead welding the blade directly onto a footplate, which made the skates lighter and stronger. Sometime later he incorporated the fluted edges. He and other manufacturers also began to make a closed toe, doing away with the prow. The front of the blade, either curved or pointed, was welded directly onto the footplate. Many different varieties of straps and screw clamps were devised to fasten the skate onto the shoe, with varying degrees of success. But the problem of how best to attach the blade to the shoe or boot remained unsolved.

Jackson Haines was one of the first to screw the blades permanently to his boots and not to a wooden platform, thereby removing any need for special attachments, but this was not practical for the casual skater or those of moderate means who could not afford separate skating and street boots. In 1864, the Barney & Berry Company of Springfield, Massachusetts, patented the first locking clamp-on skates that could be attached directly to street shoes without straps, but were also removable. No extra pair of boots was necessary. That did it—the "skating craze" took off. B&B manufactured as many as 600,000 pairs of skates a year. In 1919, the company was purchased by the Winchester Repeating Arms Company, which made recreational skates emblazoned with the same logo that adorned their famous rifles.

Meanwhile, in 1867, John Martin, also an American, added a single "diamond point" or metal spike on the prow of the skate, which allowed skaters to perform toe steps and small spins or pirouettes. It was later adapted to closed-toe blades. In the United States alone, more than 200 patents for different skate designs were issued in the 1870s. There were flat and fluted bottoms, orthopedic-like metal leg supports, different curved prows, and elegant engraved blades.

It was in the 1890s that the first "rake-toe" skate came from Sweden. The front of the blade had a sawtooth edge that for the first time began to allow for what were known as "fancy" moves. This "rake," which later evolved into "toe picks," became the major advancement that allowed figure skating technique to develop at full speed. And as a result, new complicated figure tracings, spins, jumps, and original movements were being invented throughout the world, many borrowed from the traditions of formal dance.

Skating was no longer a means of transportation. It had become a popular recreational winter pastime for both men and women, which in turn led to the development of contests and a competitive sport that involved elaborate, precise figures traced into the ice, a distinctive style of movement, rules, and eventually specific spins and jumps.

NEARLY EVERYONE SUCCUMBED TO THE VICTORIAN RAGE FOR SKATING, INCLUDING QUEEN VICTORIA HERSELF. HER MAJESTY AND PRINCE ALBERT OWNED THEIR OWN CUSTOM SKATES WITH WHICH THEY TOOK THE (VERY) OCCASIONAL REGAL OUTING.

AN ADVERTISEMENT FROM THE 1960S FROM
SKATING MAGAZINE

THE BOOTS

The only actual pieces of "equipment" used in the sport of figure skating are the boots and the blades. Throughout the nineteenth and early twentieth centuries, both men and women skated in black boots, which were usually just their everyday street shoes. Sonja Henie was one of the first to break that tradition and wear special white boots, a shocking change at the time. It was not long before the style became a fashionable status statement. Today, almost all women wear light-colored boots; the most recent fashion is a flesh-colored leather, which is thought to give the appearance of a longer leg line. Men generally have stayed with the traditional black.

As the athletic aspects advanced, specially designed boots were developed to meet the demands of the sport. In 1906, Gustave Stanzione, an Italian shoemaker, opened the first shop on Columbus Avenue in New York City, "specializing in the making of fine skating boots for ladies and gentlemen." He crafted a selection of boots designed just for skating from the finest leathers in custom, made-to-fit styles. A soft, suede leather model was the most popular, used even by Sonja Henie. For well over half a century Stanzione boots were the choice of champions.

The high-button boot style with a stable heel, though no longer a standard street shoe, is still used to give the foot and ankle support. Through the years, there have been many changes from the original flexible soft sides, though up to the 1950s the leather used for boots was a little thicker than that used for street shoes, offering the skater a little extra support. Today, elite skaters usually wear boots that are custom made, heavily reinforced with thick, stiff leather interiors, extra ankle bracing, and wide tongues with a rubber or sponge padding to allow for foot flexibility. Insulation, additional padding at the ankle bones, and a heel notch that can reduce stress on the Achilles tendon and enable easier pointing of the toe are also found. The sole is thick and flat to allow for proper attachment to the blades. Different skaters prefer different heel heights; some ice dancers wear a high heel, which pushes their body weight forward onto the ball of the foot for deeper edges and better control.

The custom-made boots used today by major competitive and professional skaters often weigh well over two pounds each and range in price from $500 to $800 a pair. Top-level skaters usually go through at least two pairs a season. Beginning- and intermediate-level skaters do not need such special boots and can find many other choices within a more moderate price range—stock boots are available in sizes like shoes.

To save the high expense of different colored boots to match different outfits, skaters frequently wear boot covers that blend with their costumes. These are simple stretch-fabric covers that slip snugly over the boot and are held in place with elastic or hook closures.

Research has been under way for several years to design new boots and blades to meet the high technical demands of today's sport and to reduce the great force exerted on the feet, ankles, and body during multiple triple and quadruple jumps. Several styles are now being tested that may absorb, or at least reduce, the immense shock of repeated jumping. These new skates may include retractable blades or boots constructed of elasticized leather.

THE BLADE

Today's skate blades are made of high-quality polished steel. The bottom of a modern blade is not flat, as it may appear. It has a very slight curve to it, equal to the radius of approximately a six- or seven-foot arc. Also, there is a groove down the middle—called the hollow—that is finely ground with razor-sharp edges on each side, allowing for faster speed and control, quicker turns, and certain jumps and spins.

Each blade has an inside and an outside edge: Weight can be placed on either the front or the back of either one. Different jumps and spins are done from different edges; the Axel, for instance, takes off on a front (or forward) outside edge and is landed on a backward outside edge.

Only the bottom quarter-inch of the blade is made from fine-tempered steel to maintain a sharp edge. After many sharpenings, blades must be replaced, as the tempered steel eventually wears away. Blades need to be sharpened frequently, usually at least once a month—more often for those who prefer really sharp edges. Sharpness is a matter of personal preference, but as a general rule, if the edges are too sharp, they will cut too deeply into the ice to allow good movement. Conversely, if not sharp enough, they will slip off the ice and not hold.

Basic blades come in many different styles and designs. Some men and women at the championship level prefer blades with longer heels for stability; some like higher stanchions (the upright pieces connecting the blades to the footplate) for added lift in jumps; some like large toe picks or a certain depth to the channel and arc of the radius of the blade. As skaters advance in skills and technique, they develop a preference for the blade that they find most comfortable and serviceable.

One easily noticed variation in skate blades is on ice dancing skates. Since spins and jumps are not part of ice dancing, and since ice dancers skate very close together and want to avoid getting their blades caught and tripping one another, the heel-length of a dance blade is much shorter than those worn by most singles or pairs skaters.

The high-quality blades used by elite skaters, most of which are crafted in England, generally cost about $350 to $400 a pair; most high-level competitors use two pairs a season. Blades and boots can easily cost more than $2,000 a year, not counting the expense of sharpening and general maintenance.

Perhaps more changes have taken place in the development of the boot and blade in the last fifty years than in the previous two hundred. Much of this is due to the changing requisites of the sport. With the increasing technical difficulty of skating, researchers are only now learning about the wear and tear of regular triple and quadruple jumps on the body. As science continues to study the bio-mechanics of skating and sports medicine investigates the body's functions and its potential, expect many more changes in boots and blades in the near future. ✳

TOP. EDGES AT WORK, NICOLE BOBEK GOES INTO AN AXEL JUMP BY GLIDING ON THE OUTSIDE EDGE OF HER LEFT SKATE.

ABOVE. HER FOOTWORK PLACES HER ON THE OUTSIDE EDGE OF HER LEFT SKATE AND THE INSIDE EDGE OF HER RIGHT SKATE.

THE FIRST PAIR OF SKATES

Getting that first pair of figure skates is a lot of fun, but it can also be confusing if you don't have all the facts beforehand. Here are a few basic shopping tips:

COST
Budget skates: Strap-on double-edge "runners" for kids start at about $25; molded plastic skates start at about $35; vinyl or leather boots with vinyl soles and nickel blades already attached range from $35-$60 for kids and $50-$75 for adults.

Mid-range: Leather boots with single-layer leather soles sold with inexpensive blades attached range from $90-$160 for kids and $125-$180 for adults.

High-end: Leather boots with double-layer leather soles sold separate from the blades range from $160-$400 for the boots (excluding custom-made boots) and $35-$500 for a pair of blades.

SELECTION
It's generally a good idea to avoid molded plastic skates and the runners. The molded plastic will not allow proper knee and ankle bend. The runners, which have two blades and are almost like training wheels on a bicycle, do not teach the beginner to balance on one blade. It's best to stick with traditional boots and blades.

Adult beginners should not purchase the least expensive skates; the flimsy material these skates are made of is no match for an adult's height and weight, and ankles may buckle from the lack of support. At best, these cheap skates are uncomfortable; at worst, they may lead to injuries. Small children may use them for a while, but stronger skates will definitely be needed for lessons.

Seasonal skaters should plan on spending at least $70 for children's skates and $125 for adults'; those taking lessons should plan on at least $150 for kids and $200 for adults. For an adult, $200 will get a decent-quality beginner boot with an inexpensive beginner blade.

For a beginner it is more important to get a good boot than an expensive blade. But the top-of-the-line stock boot is not appropriate for a beginner—it will be too stiff to break in, which could cause the skater to give up in pain and frustration. A good mid-level stock boot with a beginner pair of blades is more practical.

FIT
It's best to have a professional at the pro shop fit the skates. Figure skates are not supposed to fit like sneakers. They must be extremely snug in order to provide support—as tight as possible without causing pain. The proper skate size is actually a size to a size and a half smaller than regular shoe size. A skate that is too large will cause poor control over moves; also, the ankle area leather will "break down"—lose support—faster. A child can get away with no more than an extra half-size of "growing room."

WHERE TO BUY
The best place to buy entry-level skates is at a rink's pro shop. These shops specialize in skating equipment and know all about proper equipment care. General sporting goods stores are less well informed about the special requirements of figure skates; they may not know, for example, that new figure skate blades need to be sharpened before the skater takes to the ice or that the proper skate size is not the same as shoe size. New skaters might end up with skates that are much too large, and find themselves unable to stand up on the ice because no one told them they had to have the blades sharpened first.

TIPS
1. Don't wear thick socks; thin socks allow more control. Some advanced skaters wear no socks at all.

2. Protect blades with terry cloth "soakers" and rubber or plastic guards when not in use. After skating, dry the blades with a cloth, then put on the soakers. These absorb the condensation that develops as the blades warm to room temperature and prevents them from rusting. Use the guards when walking in your skates—the rubber matting in a rink is covered with dirt that can damage blades—but never leave the guards on overnight or the blades will rust. Guards also protect other people from injury in case they are accidentally stepped on or kicked.

3. Sharpen inexpensive blades more often than expensive blades. About once every ten hours of skating is average for inexpensive blades, as opposed to once every thirty to forty hours of skating for expensive blades. A pro shop can usually sharpen blades.

THE SKATE

Today's elite skaters usually wear boots that are custom made for each foot and heavily reinforced with thick, stiff leather interiors and extra ankle bracing. Pleasure skaters don't need the same level of quality as competitors, but they should still pay close attention to how much support the boot offers their ankles.

Wide tongues with a rubber or sponge padding allow for foot flexibility. Skates should be tied tightly to afford maximum control, a good idea for both artistic and safety reasons.

A heel notch can reduce stress on the Achilles tendon. Additional padding can also help avoid tendinitis, a common ailment among figure skaters.

Skating boots were originally street boots, so heels were naturally attached. Different skaters today prefer different heel heights; some ice dancers wear a high heel, which pushes their body weight forward onto the ball of the foot for deeper edges and better control of quick steps and changes of direction.

The first "rake-toe" skate, which evolved into the toe pick, was invented during the late nineteenth century and allowed complicated spins and jumps. The toe pick is used for pushing off in jumps and as the pivot point in spins.

A modern blade has a very slight curve, equal to the radius of approximately a six- or seven-foot arc. The "sweet spot" of the blade is usually below the ball of the foot.

Only the bottom quarter-inch of the blade is made from fine-tempered steel to maintain a sharp edge.

The groove down the middle of the blade is called the hollow. It has finely ground edges on each side, which offer the skater control and speed.

CHAPTER FOUR

HOW TO SKATE

The descriptions, illustrations, and photographs in this chapter show how some of the many moves in figure skating are performed. Skaters building their skills can see what's ahead as they grow in the sport, and review what they've already learned. Enthusiasts at home—even if they'll never get any closer to the ice than their kitchen freezer—can follow step-by-step through the moves that make skating magic.

These moves are the fundamentals, the basic skills that figure skaters use to create programs. Just as a classically trained dancer, a boxer, or a painter has a certain vocabulary of moves, so does a skater, and it is how the moves are executed, interpreted, and placed within the context of an entire program that defines a skater's ability. Great skaters also create new moves by adding their own style to a spin or a jump or a step sequence. So while this section give us a full round-up of the basics, it would take a whole book (or two) to catalogue every variation that has been added to the vocabularies of all five disciplines.

Despite the sport's emphasis on personal expression, figure skating definitely mandates a right way of doing things, a progression of standards that must be met before a skater can begin to think about innovations. A brand new spin will not help a skater if she can't land an Axel, nor will some exciting new way of performing an Axel be accepted if it's just a way to hide the fact that the performer actually can't do the standard one. This chapter shows how these moves are done correctly.

What this chapter is not meant to do is substitute for competent, professional instruction. Don't prop the book up rinkside and think you'll be Kristi Yamaguchi or Scott Hamilton in a few days, or even a few years. The only safe, smart, and effective way to learn how to skate—be it simple stroking or triple jumps—is under the attentive eyes of a coach or instructor. As beautiful as skating is and no matter how effortless the great skaters make it seem, falling down is part of the game. These pages provide a reliable resource for how moves are done, but nothing in this chapter should be attempted without being in the presence of an instructor and with available first aid.

JOHN CURRY ELEVATED THE ELEMENTS OF FIGURE SKATING TO AN ART.

BEGINNING STROKING SKILLS

Stroking skills consist of methods of moving forward and backward across the ice. These are the fundamental steps connecting all elements of a freestyle program and are used to maintain speed or accelerate.

FORWARD STROKING

1. Bend both knees and bring the feet together simultaneously, with the future (here, left) skating foot held slightly off the ice. Observe good upright posture with the shoulders relaxed and the arms extended outward.

2. The push starts off on the inside edge of the right foot with your weight beginning on the middle/back of the blade and progressing to the ball of the foot by the end of the

push. As you finish the push, the free (right) leg will extend fully to the completion of the stroke and the body weight is balanced over the new (left) skating foot.

3. Glide and rise out of the skating knee as the free leg extends to the back and turns out.

4. Repeat from Step 1 on the opposite foot.

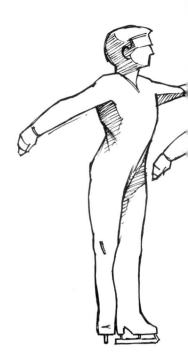

START   1

1
START

2

3

4

5

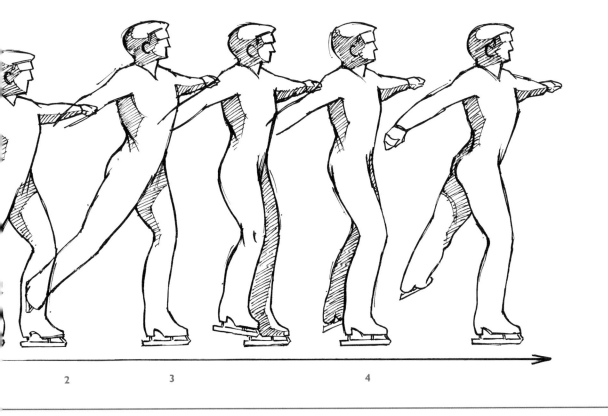

2   3   4

FORWARD CROSSOVERS

Crossover stroking is comprised of two power pushes of equal strength and rhythm, done on a curve.

1. As you move in a counter-clockwise direction, the preparation for the first push begins as the knees bend and the feet come together. With the future (left) skating foot held slightly off the ice, increase the right inside edge ankle pressure against the ice to begin the push.

2. The push starts off the inside edge of the right foot with your weight beginning on the middle/back of the blade and progressing to the ball of the foot by the end of the push. As you finish the push, the free leg will extend fully to the completion of the stroke and the body weight is balanced over the new (left) skating foot.

3. The extended free (right) leg now crosses in front of the skating foot.

4. The second push commences on the outside edge as the left foot pushes under and to the outside of the circle.

5. As the left foot completes the underneath stroke, the body weight shifts again to the right skating side as the left knee and ankle extend smoothly into a fully stretched position for the completion of the stroke. Use the curvature of the blade to rock from the middle/back to the front of the blade on each stroke, but never push with a toe pick.

6. Reverse all instructions for crossovers in a clockwise direction.

START

1   2   3   4

BEGINNING EDGE SKILLS

Edge quality is a fundamental component of skating. All spins, jumps and footwork are initiated and finished on edges. There are eight basic edges, each named for their position on the blade and the lean of the body weight (inside or outside) and defined by the balance of the foot on the ice (left or right) and the direction in which you're moving (forward or backward). The body's weight should lean into the circle in a straight line from the blade to the top of the head. When skating consecutive basic edges on an axis line, a key technical point in achieving a good edge is starting each edge by stepping perpendicular to the long axis and maintaining the body's balance over the skating side.

FORWARD OUTSIDE EDGE (LEFT OR RIGHT)

1. Begin in a standing position, with the feet in a "T" position. The skating foot and arm (here, right) should be in front with the knees and ankles bent in preparation for the push. The upper body maintains good upright posture.

2. Push off the back foot (top of the "T") and lead with the skating side. At the end of the push the body weight transfers and balances over the new skating side.

3. The free side is held back with the free foot held behind over the skating print.

4. Once balance is achieved and rotation controlled, the arms exchange positions as the free foot passes closely to the front and points over the skating print.

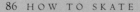

4

BACKWARD CROSSOVERS

1. In preparation for each stroke, the knees bend as the feet come together with the future (left) skating foot held slightly off the ice. The ankle pressure of the skating foot increases, which gives more pressure against the ice to begin the push.

2. Your weight is balanced on the middle/front of the right blade. Now push against the ice from a backward inside edge with a semicircular motion in a clockwise direction.

3. At the end of the push, transfer the weight to the new (left) skating foot.

4. Now the right foot (which should not leave the ice) draws across in front as the left leg begins its push from the left backward outside edge. This second push fully extends as it pushes toward the outside of the circle. The sound you should hear during back crossovers should be the rumble of the edge, not the scratch of the toe picks.

5. Reverse all instructions for crossovers in the counter-clockwise direction.

SCOTT DAVIS USES A BACKWARD CROSSOVER TO LEAD INTO A SPIN.

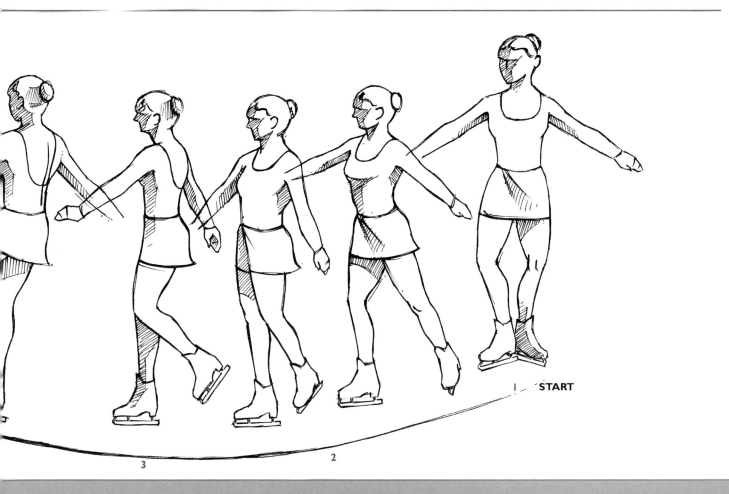

START

3   2

FORWARD INSIDE EDGE (LEFT OR RIGHT)

1. Begin in a standing position with the feet in a "T" position. The arm opposite the skating foot (here, the right foot) leads and the knees and ankles bend in preparation for the push. The upper body maintains good upright posture.

2. Now push, transferring your weight to the skating foot at the end of the push.

3. Achieve balance by controlling the free foot behind over the print (the line left by the skate), leading with the free arm and checking the skating arm to the back.

4. Once balance is achieved and rotation is controlled, the arms exchange positions as the free foot passes closely by the skating foot to the front and points over the skating print.

START

2

3

4

Backward Outside Edge (Left or Right)

1. Begin in a standing position, with the feet parallel and the body facing the direction of travel. Distribute weight evenly over both legs, with the knees bent and the upper body maintaining good upright posture.

2. Now your body weight transfers to the pushing foot (here, right). The push against the ice from a backward inside edge begins and progresses in a semicircular motion.

3. At the end of the push, the weight shifts to the new skating side. The new skating arm leads with the free foot held strongly in front and the head turned toward the direction of travel to help control rotation.

4. Once balance is achieved and rotation controlled, the arms exchange position as the free foot passes through and extends to the back. The head rotates toward the outside of the circle, as you maintain weight over the skating side.

JENNIFER BLOUNT PRACTICES HER BACKWARD OUTSIDE EDGE, ONE OF THE BASIC MOVEMENTS IN FIGURE SKATING.

START 1 2 3 4

BACKWARD INSIDE EDGE (LEFT OR RIGHT)

1. Start in a standing position, with the feet parallel and the body facing away from the direction of travel. Distribute weight evenly over both legs, with the knees bent and the upper body maintaining good upright posture.

2. Your body weight now transfers to the pushing foot (here, right). The push against the ice from a backward inside edge begins and progresses in a semicircular motion.

3. At the end of the push, the weight shifts to the new skating foot (here, the left foot), which is on a backward inside edge. The new skating arm leads strongly behind with the free foot held firmly in front and the head turned toward the outside of the circle to help control rotation.

4. Once balance is achieved and rotation controlled, the free foot passes close to the skating foot in back and the arms exchange positions while the head turns toward the inside of the circle. Maintain balance over the skating side.

TURNS

Turns link forward and backward movement throughout the program, provide entry and preparation for jumps and spins, and serve as a major part of the movement vocabulary for a skater's footwork. Turns are also basic elements of choreography, adding interest and appeal to programs. Both three-turns and Mohawks (p. 92) allow you to turn from forward to backward, or backward to forward. All the edges mentioned previously in the "Beginning Edge Skills" are used in these turns. Three-turns and Mohawks are the most common turns, while others include brackets, counters, rockers, and choctaws (not pictured).

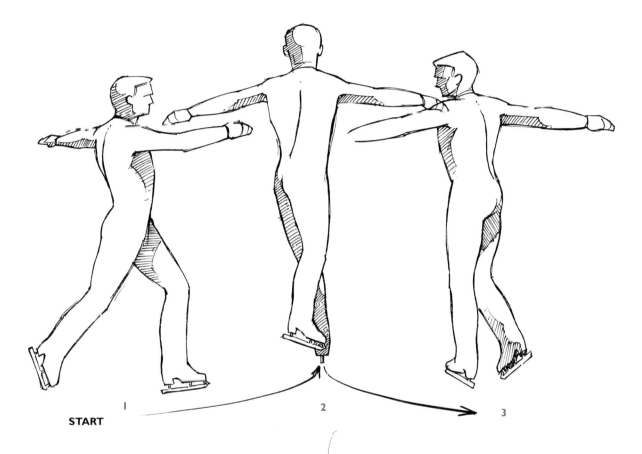

START　　1　　　　　　　　　2　　　　　　　　3

THREE-TURN

This move is named "three-turn" because the marking left on the ice looks like the number three. There are four forward three-turns and four backward three-turns, depending on the edge and the foot used. The three-turn changes from one edge to another edge, that is, outside to inside or inside to outside, the edge before and after the turn being on the same curve. The common principles include keeping the weight of the body on the skating side, with the free foot held firmly over the skating print and control of body rotation before and after the turn. Remain on the same foot as you change directions.

1. To initiate the rotation for three-turns, the arms and shoulders rotate while the hips remain square to the skating foot.

2. As the upper body rotates, the twisting pressure between the hips and shoulders increases and the curve of the edge tightens. Now change the weight on the same skating foot with a rocking action of the blade (back to front on forward three-turns, and front to back on backward three-turns).

3. At the actual moment of turning, the hips and skating foot quickly twist against the shoulder pressure and the turn reverses the direction in which the skate is traveling from backward to forward or forward to backward. The exit edge continues on the same curve as the entry edge.

MOHAWK

Unlike the three-turn, at the moment of turning in the Mohawk, you change feet. The change of foot is from the inside edge to the inside edge, or the outside edge to the outside edge. There are both inside and outside Mohawks.

1. The body weight is balanced over the skating side (here, right in outside Mohawk, left in inside Mohawk). To initiate the turn, the arms and shoulders rotate, and the hips follow as you change from one foot to the other.

2. Just before the moment when you transfer weight and change feet, the free leg moves into position within the width of the hips, with the free foot turned out, ready to complete the turn.

3. Lastly the hips reverse and the weight transfers from one foot to the other as the step of the Mohawk is completed. The exit edge continues the curve of the entry edge.

OUTSIDE MOHAWK

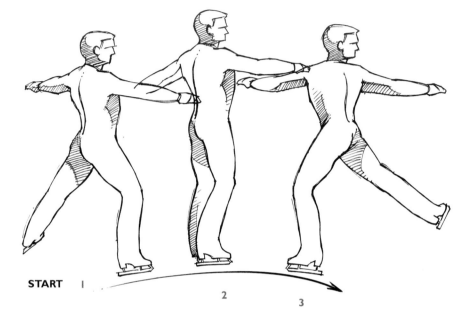

START   I   2   3

INSIDE MOHAWK

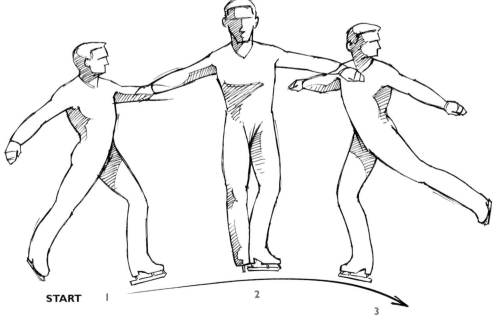

START   I   2   3

SPINS

The components of a good-quality spin are: a) centering (maintaining balance in one spot on the ice surface), which will create small circles on the ice instead of loops, b) accelerating and then maintaining good speed of rotation to create as many rotational turns per second as possible; c) using flexibility of the body to achieve interesting and pleasing positions. Generally, spins are executed skating backward on the ball of the foot, usually on a backward inside edge, with the weight on the front of the blade. The spin should remain inside the initial entry circle. Forward spins begin from a forward outside edge, culminating in a three-turn. However, even spins termed "forward" are skated with the skate traveling backward while spinning. Once you're spinning, you will see two tracings on the ice, one from the ball of the blade and a light tracing from the toe pick. Rotational speed is gained by moving the arms and legs from an open position to a tighter position closer to the axis of rotation.

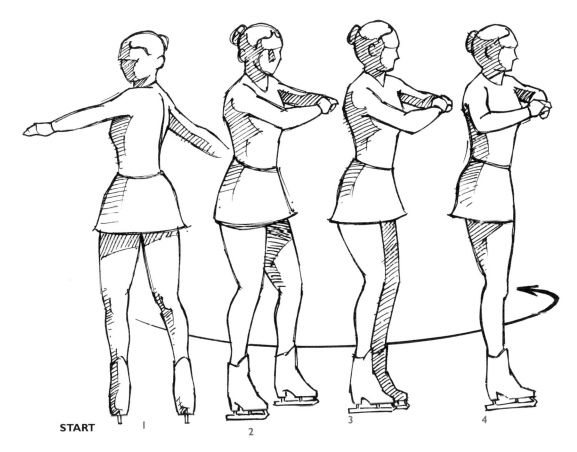

START   1   2   3   4

Two-Foot Spin

1. For a counterclockwise spin, stand in one spot, with the knees bent slightly, the feet at shoulder width, and the hips square. Then rotate the upper body strongly clockwise.

2. Start spinning by releasing the upper body and arms in a counterclockwise rotation until the hips and shoulders are square. The arms are held out to the side with the right foot making a small circular forward push.

3. Once momentum is created, spin on two feet with the right foot gliding forward on an inside edge and the left foot backward on an inside edge, continuing with level shoulders and the body in an upright and balanced position.

4. As rotation progresses, straighten the knees slowly, and to increase speed, gradually bring the arms close to the torso as the feet draw closer together.

5. To exit the spin, shift the weight to the left foot with the left knee bent and commence a semicircular push as the arms open outward.

6. At the end of the push transfer the weight to the right back outside edge, finishing the glide.

FORWARD SCRATCH SPIN

1. The preparation is done on a right back inside edge, generally after taking a backward crossover, with the skating knee bent. The upper body rotates outside of the circle and the weight is balanced over the skating hip.

2. Step into the circle of the right backward inside preparation edge, onto the left forward outside edge. The free leg will now be extended behind, the skating knee bent and the body weight leaning strongly into the new left forward outside circle.

3. The edge deepens as it reaches the point of the three-turn.

4. At the point of the three-turn the free leg swings in a wide arc to create momentum for the spins. The spin begins on small backward inside circles no larger in diameter than the length of the blade, spinning counter-clockwise on the ball of the foot. The arms and free leg are now in an open and extended position, slightly in front of the body. Take time in this position to relax and achieve balance.

5. Accelerate gradually by drawing the free foot in toward the top-front of the skating knee, then the arms reach forward and clasp around an imaginary tree trunk.

6. The arms pull in close to the body, and move with the free leg downward to the final fast spinning position.

7. Tighten the stomach and buttock muscles to achieve maximum speed of rotation toward the end of the spin.

8. To exit the spin, the right free leg uncrosses as the left skating knee bends. The left arm moves forward and the right arm extends slightly back to prepare for a powerful back inside thrust out of the spin. Glide out onto a right backward outside edge.

This spin can be used as an additional finish to the forward camel and forward sit spins. There are variations with arms raised above the head or the head tilted back (the "headless spin"). Also, because the skater can accelerate so much on this spin, it often makes an exciting finish to a program.

ELONGATING THE BODY WITH A STRAIGHT BACK AND TIGHTENED MUSCLES ACCELERATES A SCRATCH SPIN.

MICHELLE KWAN FINISHES THIS ROUTINE EARLY IN HER COMPETITIVE CAREER WITH A FORWARD SPIN.

THE ARMS AND LEGS SHOULD BE HELD CLOSE TO THE BODY IN A BACKWARD SCRATCH SPIN, A POSITION ALSO USED IN JUMPS.

THE GREAT SPEED OF MICHELLE KWAN'S SPIN MAKES THE MOVE A DRAMATIC ELEMENT OF HER PROGRAM.

BACKWARD SCRATCH SPIN

1. Stand with the body weight lined up over the right side, with the left toe touching the ice for balance at shoulder width to the side of the right foot. With the right knee slightly bent, the upper body winds up in a clockwise direction, with the hips staying square to the skating foot.

2. Start spinning by releasing the upper body and arms in a counterclockwise rotation until the hips and shoulders are square. Then, with a slight push off the left toe, the spin begins on small backward outside counterclockwise circles.

3. The free foot is crossed neatly in front of the ankle of the skating foot, with the arms rounded and the hands in front of the chest. To accelerate, draw the arms close to the body.

4. To exit the spin, the left knee lifts to uncross the free foot and the free foot passes backward into a fully extended position as the skater glides onto a right backward outside edge with the arms opening outward.

The upright backward scratch spin can be done after a backward sit spin or backward camel spin, and may be used in variations as an exciting finish to many combination spins. Also, the basic backward scratch spin teaches the air rotational position for double and triple jumps.

KEEPING THE TORSO STRAIGHT ADDS SPEED TO A SIT SPIN.

SIT SPIN

1. Begin with the same first three steps as in the scratch spin.

2. The free leg swings in a wide arc to the side, and a three-turn initiates the spin. The speed of rotation is created by the deepening entry edge and the swing of the free leg.

3. Move quickly into a sit-spin position by bending the body forward from the hip joint and bending the left skating knee. Simultaneously, the free leg draws into its position in front with the foot turned out, and the arms reach forward in front of the skating knee. To achieve the correct sit-spin position, the back should be straight (not hunched) with a sharp angle of the torso to the skating leg, and the skating leg from the knee to the hip should be parallel to the ice.

4. To finish the spin, slowly rise into an upright position with the same finish as for the scratch spin.

TARA LIPINSKI TUCKS INTO A BACKWARD SIT SPIN AT THE 1998 UNITED STATES CHAMPIONSHIPS.

CAMEL SPIN

1. Begin with the same first three steps as in the scratch spin, but as you step into the entry edge, the body extends forward more into an arabesque position, with the free leg stretched behind you and turned out.

2. To help create rotation and center the spin, move the left arm in a gradual counter-clockwise circular motion, maintaining balance over the skating foot as the entry edge deepens and approaches the three-turn.

As the three-turn is executed to initiate the spin, keep the skating knee bent until balance is established.

3. Lift and extend the free leg beyond a parallel to the ice as the body arches into an ideal camel spinning position, with the skating leg straightened. The body and free leg should reach the final spinning position simultaneously.

4. To finish the spin, slowly rise into an upright position and exit as in the scratch spin.

STACEY RENSGEN ADDS A PERSONAL VARIATION TO THE CAMEL.

START   1

2

3

LAYBACK

The basic layback spin is done with the free leg in a ballet attitude position, although one lovely variation on this position is done with the free leg stretched straight.

1. Begin with the same first three steps as in the scratch spin.

2. With the skating leg straight, the upper body turns away from the free leg as the free leg bends into the ballet attitude position. The knee and foot of the free leg must be turned out and held behind the skating leg with the knee held slightly higher than the toe.

3. Now the backward leaning position starts, with the hips moving slightly ahead of the skating foot as the upper body arches backward. (When the hips move forward, it provides a counterbalance for the body arching backward.)

4. Exit as in other spins. You may use a variety of arm and hand positions to interpret music and gain speed.

FLYING SPINS

Flying spins are a combination of a jump and a spin. The basic flying spins are flying camel, flying sit, flying reverse sit, death drop, and butterfly into a spin.

FLYING CAMEL

1. After preparing with either a forward inside three-turn or a back crossover, step forward onto the entry edge with the body extending forward in an arabesque position. Skate the entry edge with the skating knee deeply bent and the free leg stretched strongly behind.

2. To help create rotation and center the spin, move the left arm in a gradual counter-clockwise circular motion as the entry edge deepens and approaches the point of takeoff.

3. The timing of the takeoff phase starts when you rock forward to the toe pick. Then the free leg takes a wide swing to the side followed by jumping off the left leg's toe pick. The body will fly parallel to the ice, which is also known as a layout position. The landing of the flying phase and the centering of the backward camel spin should take place outside the circle of the spin's takeoff edge.

4. As you land, the free (left) leg continues into an immediate lifted and extended position to the back as the body arches into an ideal camel spinning position. The body and free leg must reach the final spin position at the same time. The beauty of the camel spinning position is determined by the arch of the body, the stretch and turnout of the free leg, and the extension of the arms and head. When the spin is centered, the weight is balanced on the ball of the foot creating small circles on the backward outside edge.

5. To finish the spin, rise into the upright backward spin position ending with either a backward scratch spin or gliding immediately onto a right backward outside edge.

In these images, Nicole Bobek shows how the layback can be a high point in a woman's routine.

4   3   2   I   **START**

FLYING SIT SPIN

This is an explosive jumping entry spin taking off from a forward outside edge, reaching an airborne sit-spin position and landing in a forward sit-spin position on the initial jumping leg. Remember, the term "forward sit spin" refers to a spin on the left foot in the counter-clockwise direction, not the direction the blade is traveling on the ice. The blade travels backward on all basic spins.

1. In preparation for this spin, skate a backward crossover, step forward onto a left forward outside edge, with the body in an upright position. The arm and free (right) leg draw back in preparation for the lift into the air.

2. The free (right) leg moves with a wide swing and a continuous motion helping to lift the skater into the air. As the free leg passes to the side, the actual jump begins in a coordinated effort between the jumping (left) leg, free leg and arms that lift forcefully into the air.

3. At the top of the jump, the left leg tucks immediately as the arms and free leg reach into a sit-spin position. This jump will essentially go up and down vertically, landing close to, and just ahead of, the point of takeoff.

4. After the air position is achieved, and in preparation for the landing, the left leg reaches down and extends toward the ice. As the left toe pick touches the ice, the knee bends to absorb the force of landing. The arms and free leg then quickly and simultaneously move into the forward sit-spin position to center the spin.

5. To finish the spin, rise into an upright position using any variation of a scratch spin.

3

2

5

4

3

2

1

START

1

START

BUTTERFLY

A butterfly, sometimes called an arabian cartwheel, is an acrobatic flying spin. The air position is horizontal rather than vertical. The unique look of the butterfly can add a dramatic effect and choreographic interest to a skating program. There are several different entrances to a butterfly and they can also be performed consecutively, a very difficult move.

1. Skate a right forward outside edge on a deeply bent skating leg with the left arm leading and the shoulders winding up clockwise. Trail the left foot behind the right on a left backward inside edge with the feet wide apart, similar to an inside edge spread eagle. Skate three-quarters of a circle in this position.

2. Now bend the trunk of your body sharply forward from the hips and shift your weight from the right foot to the left foot for takeoff. With the right arm now in front and the body parallel to the ice, catch the right toe pick in the ice and jump into the air from the left leg while you kick the right leg high into the air behind you. Follow by kicking the left leg into the air behind you with a scissor action. Now arch your body into a full layout position in the air parallel to the ice with the head up, arms outstretched and the legs a little higher than the head.

3. Land on your right toe pick briefly in a camel position, then move immediately into a backward sit spin or a backward scratch spin to complete the maneuver.

5   4   3

COMBINATION SPINS

These spins are achieved by combining the traditional basic spin positions plus doing changes of feet. These spins will have unique and various sequences in the positions of the arms, legs, torso and head. When executing combination spins, remember:

1. Maintain rotational forces;

2. Remain centered and balanced;

3. Create interest by using a variety of positions and changes of feet.

There are two key parts of a "combo" spin: changing positions and changing feet.

In position changes, wide motions of the arms and free leg moving from open to closed positions help to accelerate and maintain the rotational speed of the spin.

When changing feet, the arms will reach out from the center axis of the first spin before resisting the centrifugal forces as the skater steps into the second side of the spin. Each position should be held for a minimum of three revolutions to receive credit in a competition for the position and also add artistic appeal to the spin itself. There are mandated minimum revolutions in short programs and for testing purposes.

AN EXAMPLE OF A COMBINATION SPIN

Camel - Sit - Layback to a Backward Sit - Backward Headless:

1. Follow the first two steps of the forward camel spin. After reaching the balance and rotational speed of the camel spin, and in preparation for the change of position, the free leg does a wide swing to the side to increase speed as the skating knee bends and the body, arms and free leg reach forward and draw into a sit-spin position.

2. In transferring to a layback, rise out of the skating knee keeping the arms and free leg in front for balance. With the skating leg straight, shift the hips slightly forward over the skating foot as the free leg takes the classical ballet attitude position to the back and the upper body and head arch backward. Many variations of

arm positions can be used for beauty, speed and balance.

3. To prepare for the foot-changing portion of this spin, the body rises to an upright position with the arms reaching out into an open position as the free leg reaches to the side.

4. At the end of a semicircular push from the skating leg, transfer the weight to the new skating foot and move the arms, free leg, skating knee and body quickly into the basic backward sit-spin position.

5. While there is still adequate rotational force left in the backward sit spin, rise to an upright backward spin and tilt the head backward into the "headless" position.

6. Move the head to an erect position and exit the spin as in any backward scratch spin.

2

1   START

DEATH DROP

The takeoff of this jump-spin is a combination of the powerful jump takeoff of a flying sit spin and the swing into a flying camel. The move's dramatic name comes from its very risky appearance.

1. Begin with the first two steps as in the flying sit-spin.

2. The takeoff is a coordinated effort between the extension of the jumping (left) leg, the swing and kick of the right free (right) leg and the lifting of the arms and torso to the top of the jump.

3. Once you are airborne, the left leg kicks to the back as the legs split and extend in oppo-site directions and the body achieves a layout position parallel to the ice.

4. As the death drop begins to land, the right leg reaches straight toward the ice and you land briefly in a camel position.

5. Then draw the arms, body and free leg quickly into a backward sit-spin position.

6. The exit of the spin is similar to that of a backward scratch spin.

THE TRANSITIONS BETWEEN ELEMENTS OF MOST COMBINATION SPINS REQUIRE SLIGHT BUT GRACEFUL CHANGES OF FEET AND POSITION — HERE, A MOVE FROM CAMEL TO SIT TO LAYBACK.

ARTISTIC MOVES

SPIRAL

The spiral is a body position for forward or backward movement designed after a ballet arabesque position. It can be done on straight lines or large bold curves, skating on any of the four basic edges, forward or backward. The beauty of this move is shown with the arched position of the body and the stretch and turnout of the free leg, which require considerable flexibility and body strength from the skater. Both the free leg and the upper body are extended up and away from the skating leg and the surface of the ice. The torso should remain somewhat upright and not collapsed downward, and the head should maintain an upright position following the natural curve of the rest of the upper body. The free leg should be straight, turned out and extended at the level of the hip or preferably higher. The arms can be positioned as the skater chooses.

START

SPREAD EAGLE

A running edge move done with the feet in ballet's second position. This requires the athlete to have extreme turn-out flexibility of the legs as one skate glides forward and the other glides backward. Your knees should be in a straight and locked position as you lean into a circle. Varied arm positions can be added as well as changes of edges. Spread eagles can be done on outside or inside edges.

INA BAUER

In the 1950s, Ina Bauer, a creative skating champion from Germany, added a variation to the spread eagle by deeply bending the front leg which is gliding forward on an outside edge as she arched and leaned the upper body into a back bend position. The back leg was stretched and positioned to skate on an inside edge. Today, this move also known as the "Bauer" has become one of the most dramatic and lovely long gliding edge moves in a skater's repertoire.

JUMPS

All good jumps require accuracy in the following components: a) preparation, b) takeoff position, c) lift into the air, d) airborne position, and e) landing. There are two types of jumps, the edge takeoff jumps (Axel, Salchow, and loop) and the toe-tapping takeoff jumps, also known as vaulting jumps (toe loop, Lutz, and flip). Other ways to help the spectator identify jumps are the setup patterns and placement of jumps on the ice during a program. The Axel is the only jump that takes off moving forward with no assisted turn. Usually, skaters prepare for the Lutz jump on a long backward glide into a corner of the rink, which makes the move easily recognizable. The toe loops and flips are generally done from a straight-line entry pattern with a three-turn before takeoff. The Salchows and loops usually are choreographed in a slightly larger circular pattern. Loops take off directly from a backward outside edge and Salchows require a three-turn or Mohawk before the backward inside edge takeoff. A rule of thumb for all jumps is that the liftoff occurs before the rotation, and remember — all double and triple jumps look the same once they are rotating in the air.

WALTZ JUMP

The waltz jump is a jump with a half revolution turn in the air, which takes off from a forward outside edge and lands on the backward outside edge of the opposite foot.

1. Begin by skating on a right backward outside edge with the free (left) leg slightly extended to the back. The body weight is balanced over the skating side.

2. Step forward onto the left forward outside edge, bending the left knee and slightly leading with the left shoulder. Both arms are held behind and close to the sides of the body. Stand solidly over the skating hip, with the free (right) leg held solidly behind to control any pre-rotation.

3. The free leg begins the continuous motion that will help lift you into the air. As the free leg passes the skating foot, the actual jump begins in a coordinated effort between the jumping leg, free leg and arms to lift forcefully into the air. Just before the moment of takeoff, there is a greater curve on the outside edge prior to your hitting the toe pick and lifting into the air. At the moment of takeoff, the left knee and ankle straighten while the right leg and both arms move sharply upward.

4. As the body rises into the air, the legs stretch outward, creating a floating arc, and the body rotates counterclockwise a half-revolution.

5. In preparation for landing, the right leg extends toward the ice with the left leg moving backward. Land solidly over the right side with the left arm slightly forward and the right arm directly out from the side of the body, as total body alignment is achieved on a backward outside edge.

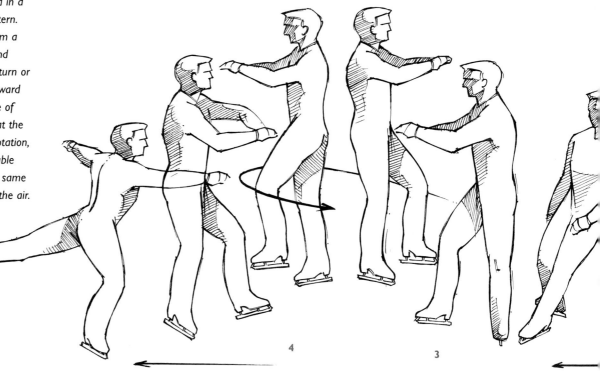

5   4   3   2

5   4   3   2   1   **START**

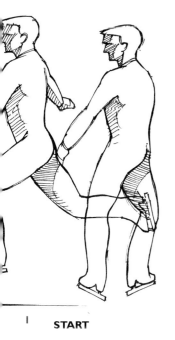

1   **START**

SINGLE AXEL JUMP

After a single air turn jump such as a single loop or single flip, the Axel is the first jump of higher difficulty, being one and a half revolutions in the air. The takeoff is forward and the landing is backward. The one-foot, forward takeoff presents many challenges.

1. The preparation begins on the right backward outside edge, the same as for the waltz jump. Now step forward into the takeoff position on the left forward outside edge, bending the left knee. The left shoulder should slightly lead with both arms pressed behind and close to the body. Stand solidly over the skating hip with the head facing the direction of travel and with the free (right) leg held solidly behind to control any pre-rotation.

2. The free leg begins the continuous motion that will help lift you into the air. As the free leg passes the skating foot, the actual jump begins in a coordinated effort between the jumping leg, free leg and arms to lift forcefully into the air. Just before the moment of takeoff, there is a greater curve on the outside edge prior to your jumping into the air from the toe pick.

3. As the left outside edge rocks toward the toe pick, the right leg begins its accelerating step into the air while the arms pass close by the body and lift forcefully.

4. After stepping into the air, the weight of your body transfers over the right leg. At that moment, the arms pull in close to the body with the hands in front of the chest as you continue rotation over the right leg. The left knee bends and is held directly in front of the right leg.

5. In preparation for landing, the right leg extends toward the ice with the left leg uncrossing to prepare for moving backward. The landing is solidly over the right foot after one and a half revolutions with the left arm slightly forward and the right arm directly out from the side of the body. Total body alignment is achieved on a backward outside edge.

DOUBLE AXEL

1. Repeat the same first three steps as in the Axel jump, but with greater energy in the takeoff leg and with quicker air rotation.

2. At the moment of takeoff, there is greater jumping force off the left leg, as the right leg makes a quick, short, angular step upward.

3. After stepping into the air, the weight of your body transfers over the right leg as the left foot crosses in front with a tighter rotation position than for the single Axel, and the arms pull powerfully toward the chest. This jump requires two and a half revolutions, with the body maintaining a balanced rotational axis over the right side.

4. The left leg initiates the preparation for landing by lifting slightly and then passing close to the skating foot in a powerful backward motion, with the arms simultaneously extending outward. Strong control of the right side of the body will help control rotation after impact.

5. As you land over the right foot, the skating knee bends to absorb the force of landing. Achieve a solid right backward outside edge with the free leg extended fully and turned out.

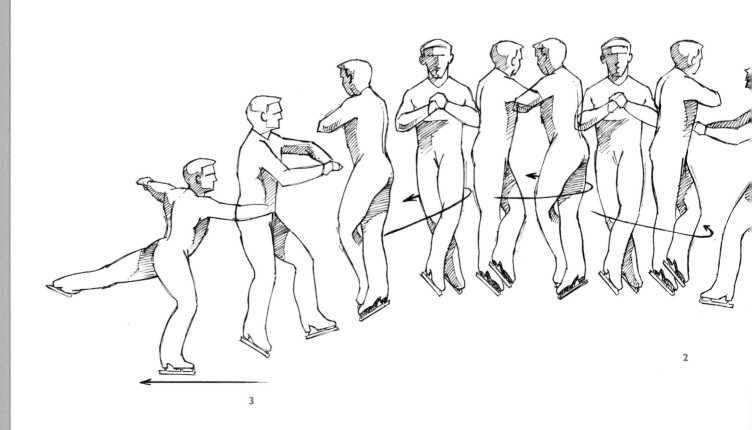

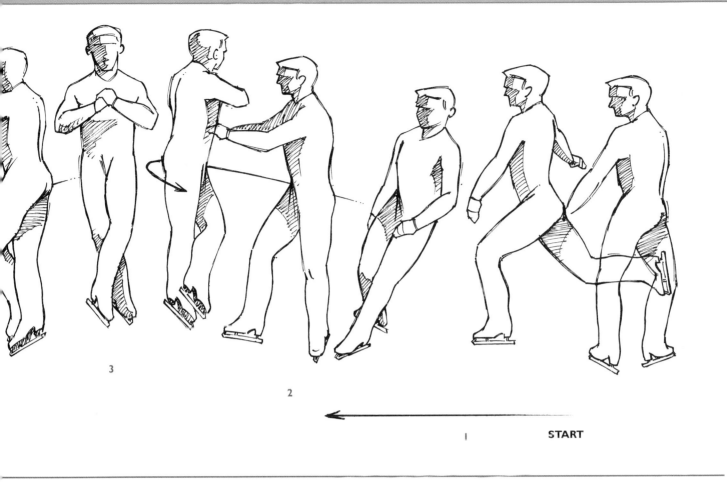

3

2

←

1   **START**

1   **START**

Triple Axel

The components are very similar to the double Axel, but require even more jumping energy, greater rotational speed, quicker reflexes, and a tighter body position. The skater spends the same time in the air as in the double Axel, but the jumping distance from takeoff to landing is shorter.

1. The preparation is similar to the double Axel but, once airborne, the arms and free leg must move more quickly and strongly into the rotational position.

2. The axis of rotation should remain over the right side keeping the body as straight as possible without the slightest tilt.

3. Land after three and a half revolutions on the right backward outside edge, with the arms opening and the knee bending to absorb the force of landing and help achieve balance as in the double Axel

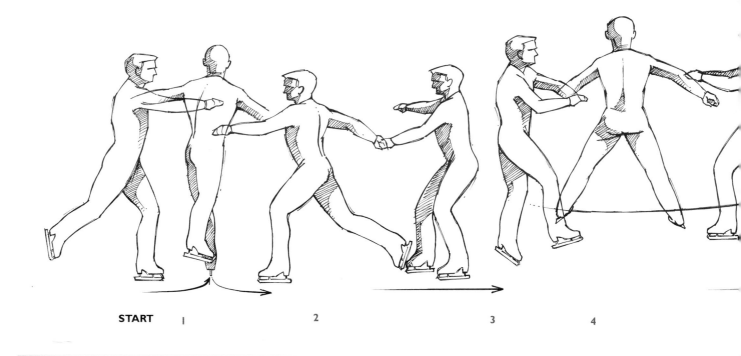

START   1   2   3   4

DOUBLE SALCHOW

1. Start with a left forward outside three-turn or a right forward inside Mohawk onto a left backward inside edge, as in the single Salchow. Repeat the first two steps of the single Salchow, but with greater knee bend, foot and ankle pressure against the ice and with particular attention to balancing over the left skating hip and increasing the curve and force of the backward inside edge.

2. Take off as in a single Salchow. At the moment of takeoff, as the right leg steps into the air, the left leg and foot explode off the ice.

3. After stepping into the air, the weight of your body transfers over the right leg. At that moment, the arms draw close to the body with the hands in front of the chest. The free (left) leg is crossed neatly in front of the skating leg as you continue rotating over the right leg.

4. In preparation for landing, the free foot uncrosses and passes closely to the back as the arms extend outward, allowing the body weight to balance over the right foot at landing after two revolutions, moving backward on a right backward outside edge.

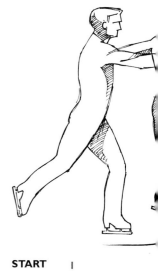

START   1

SINGLE SALCHOW JUMP

Although the Salchow is considered a "single" jump, the actual air turn is less than a full turn. This jump is very similar to the waltz jump and Axel family of jumps because the takeoff begins with a powerful drive off the left leg while the right leg's momentum leads the step into the air. On the Axel and double Salchow, after jumping off the left leg, there is a reverse airborne rotational position over the right side.

1. After completing a left forward outside three-turn or a right forward inside Mohawk, take a straight backward inside line, balancing over the left back-inside edge with the free (right) leg and arm extended and held powerfully behind the body to control rotational factors.

2. As the free (right) leg moves forward, increase the left knee bend in preparation for the takeoff and increase the pressure of the edge into the ice.

3. At the moment of takeoff, there is a powerful lift from the left leg as the right leg drives upward, as in the waltz jump.

4. As the body rises into the air, the legs stretch outward, creating a floating arc and the body rotates counterclockwise.

5. In preparation for landing, the right leg extends toward the ice with the left leg moving backward. Land solidly over the right foot with the left arm slightly forward and the right arm perpendicular to the skating side, as total body alignment is achieved on a backward outside edge.

5

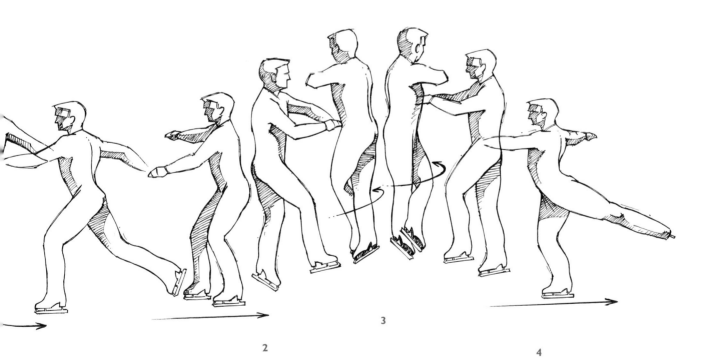

2

3

4

TRIPLE SALCHOW

The components are very similar to those of a double Salchow, but require greater jumping energy and quicker reflexes to achieve faster rotational speed and tighter body position in the air.

1. Repeat the first two steps of the double Salchow, but with stronger body control during preparation. The take-off is similar to the double Salchow, but there is a greater explosive jumping force off the left leg at the moment of takeoff, as the right leg makes a quick, short, angular step upward.

2. After stepping into the air, the weight of your body quickly transfers over the right side as the left foot crosses in front and the arms pull in to the chest. Three movements must take place simultaneously: the weight transferring, the feet crossing, and the arms pulling in. The body maintains its rotational axis over the right side for three revolutions in the air.

3. The left leg initiates the preparation for landing by lifting slightly and then passing close to the skating foot in a powerful backward motion, with the arms simultaneously extending outward. Maintain strong control of the right arm to control balance and rotation after impact.

4. As you land over the right foot, the skating knee bends to absorb the force of landing. Achieve a solid right backward outside edge with the free leg extended fully and turned out.

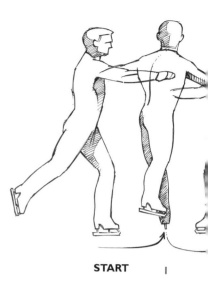

START I

SINGLE TOE LOOP JUMP

The toe loop is a jump that takes off with an assist from a toe tap. The air position for the single toe loop is the same as for the waltz jump.

1. After completing a right forward inside three-turn or a left forward outside three-turn, with a change of foot you will be on a slightly curved right backward out-side edge, balancing over the skating side with the arms powerfully held (left arm forward, right arm back) to con-trol rotational forces.

2. As the free (left) leg reach-es directly backward and in the direction of travel, the right knee bends in prepara-tion for takeoff.

3. Tap the left toe pick into the ice as the shoulders and hips begin a *slight* counter-clockwise rotational motion and the right foot draws backward toward the tapping toe. Takeoff occurs as the right leg draws past the left toe and the continuing momentum of the right leg and arms, combined with the power of the vaulting motion off the left leg, lifts you into the air.

4. As the body rises into the air, the legs stretch out-ward creating a floating arc. The body rotates counter-clockwise.

5. In preparation for the land-ing, the right leg extends toward the ice with the left leg moving backward, as you complete one turn in the air and land solidly over the right foot. Total body alignment over the right side is achieved on a backward outside edge.

START I 2

2   3   4

3   4   5

START   I   2

TRIPLE TOE LOOP

The components are very similar to the double toe loop, but require greater jumping energy, quicker reflexes to achieve faster rotational speed, and tighter body position in the air.

1. Repeat the first three steps of the toe loop, but with stronger body control during the preparation.

2. There is a greater explosive jumping force off the left leg at takeoff, as the right leg makes a quick, short, angular step upward.

3. After stepping into the air, the weight of your body transfers quickly over the right leg as the left foot crosses in front with a tighter, more compact rotational position than for the double toe loop, and the arms pull pow-erfully into the chest. This move requires three revolutions, with the body maintaining a balanced rotational axis over the right side.

4. The left leg initiates the preparation for landing by lifting slightly and then passing close to the skating foot in a powerful backward motion, with the arms simultaneously extend outward. Maintain strong control of the right arm to allow the body to control balance and rotation after impact.

5. As you land over the right foot, the skating knee bends to absorb the force of landing. Achieve a solid right backward outside edge with the free leg extended fully and turned out.

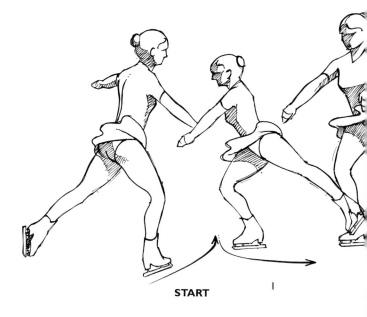

START   I

DOUBLE TOE LOOP

1. Repeat the first three steps of the single toe loop, with stronger body control, correct body alignment over the right skating hip, increased knee bend and a stronger reach before the toe taps into the ice.

2. After stepping into the air with a more powerful liftoff than the single toe loop, the weight of your body transfers over the right leg as the left foot crosses neatly in front of the right ankle and the arms draw close to the body. Continue rotation over the right leg.

3. In preparation for landing, the free foot uncrosses and passes closely to the back as the arms extend outward, allowing the body weight to balance over the right foot. Land on a backward outside edge.

3

2   3   4   5

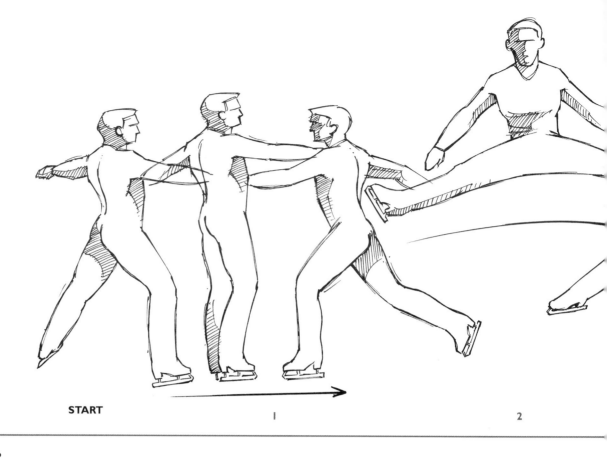

START   1   2

SINGLE LOOP JUMP

The loop jump is unique in that it takes off, rotates over, and lands on the same foot and edge. There is no weight transfer from the takeoff edge to the air position as in the Axel jump. The major difference between the loop jump and the toe loop jump is that the toe loop uses a toe tap for elevation, while a loop jump does not.

1. After either a three-turn or Mohawk, take a backward step onto the right foot and then glide backward on two feet, balancing over the skating side on a curving right backward outside edge. The arms will be held solidly (right arm and shoulder held behind, left arm placed in front) to control rotation, and the head faces the direction of travel.

2. In preparation for the take-off, the right knee bends as you increase the edge pressure against the ice. The arc of the takeoff edge tightens and the body weight remains directly over the skating side.

3. Lift up and off the ice with the right knee and ankle extending into a fully straightened position. The left leg lifts and stays in front of the rotating body and the arms assist the upward momentum.

4. Center the body weight in the air over the right side, with the arms in a rounded position in front of the body. The body rotates one full turn in this position.

5. In preparation for landing, the left leg moves backward and the arms extend outward, allowing the body weight to balance over the right foot as you land on a right backward outside edge.

START   1

SPLIT JUMP

Besides all of the multi-revolution jumps, skaters try to add some jumps into their programs that emphasize height and interesting air positions. Split jumps are one of the more spectacular of these.

RUSSIAN SPLIT JUMP

1. As you rotate counter clockwise, skate a right forward inside Mohawk. Reach back with the right leg to tap the toe into the ice while deeply bending the left knee in preparation for jumping.

2. With a vaulting action off the right toe pick, jump into the air using both legs in a coordinated effort to rise vertically. Lift and split both legs simultaneously into a Russian split position, with both knees locked, making one quarter of a turn to the top of the jump. Lean your body slightly forward and try to touch the toes of each boot with your hands. Keep your head up.

3. Then make another one quarter of a turn coming down to land forward on the left toe pick first, then immediately skating past the right toe pick on a right forward inside edge.

The differences between a Russian split jump and a standard split jump are the body, leg and arm positions in the air. In the standard split jump, at the top of the jump, the left leg and arm face straight forward, the right leg and arm face straight back and the body is in an upright position.

3

2   3

4

5

DOUBLE LOOP

1. Repeat the first two steps of the single loop, with stronger upper-body control and correct alignment over the right skating hip. Your weight balances on the front of the right blade as you increase the knee bend and foot and ankle pressure against the ice.

2. The right leg begins the takeoff with a more explosive push up into the air. The left leg lifts and stays in front of the rotating body as the arms assist the upward momentum.

3. In the air, the left ankle crosses neatly in front, with the arms held tighter to the body than in the single loop, as you continue rotation for two turns standing over the right side.

4. In preparation for the landing, the right leg extends toward the ice and the free foot uncrosses and passes closely to the back as the arms extend outward, allowing the body weight to balance over the right foot at landing after two revolutions, moving backward on a right backward outside edge.

START   I

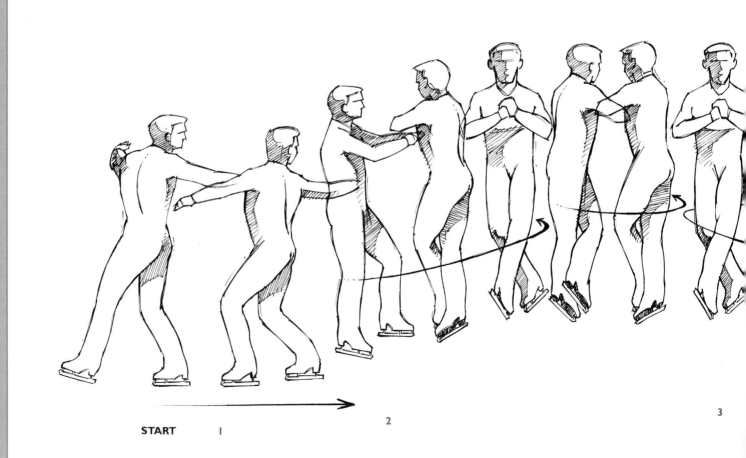

START   I   2   3

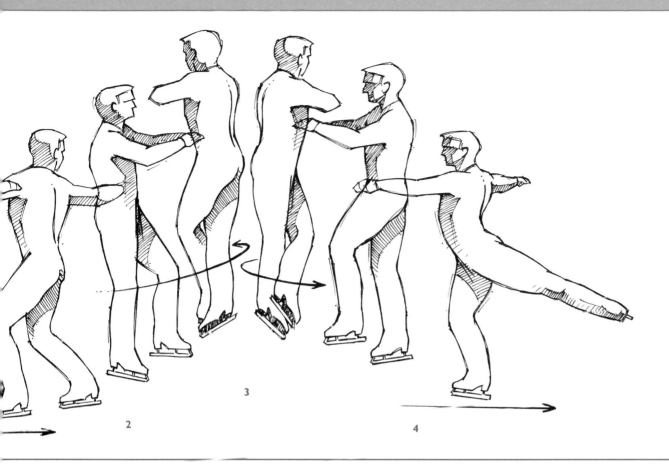

3

2

4

4

TRIPLE LOOP

The components of the triple loop are similar to those of the double loop, but require even greater jumping energy for increased jumping height, and quicker reflexes to achieve faster rotational speed via tighter body position in the air.

1. Repeat the first two steps of the double loop but with stronger body control during preparation.

2. There is a greater explosive jumping force off the right leg and foot at takeoff. Once airborne, maintain the body's axis over the right side while keeping the body as powerfully compact and straight as possible for three revolutions.

3. The left leg initiates the preparation for landing by lifting slightly and then passing very closely to the skating foot in a powerful backward motion, with the arms simultaneously extending outward. Strong checking of the right side of the body allows you to control balance and rotation after impact.

4. As you land over the right foot, the skating knee bends to absorb the force of landing. Achieve a solid right backward outside edge with the free leg extended fully and turned out.

THE FLIP JUMP AND THE LUTZ JUMP

The flip and the Lutz are similar in that both take off backward, vaulting off the right toe pick and landing backward on the right backward outside edge. The difference is that the flip takes off from a left backward inside edge after a turn from forward to backward and the Lutz takes off directly from the left backward outside edge. When a jump that is supposed to be a Lutz takes off from the wrong edge (inside), it will be thought of as a "Flutz" and will not be given full credit as a true Lutz.

FLIP JUMP

1. After completing a left outside three-turn or a right inside Mohawk, you will be skating on a left backward inside edge on a controlled straight backward line with the body weight lined up over the left skating side. The arms are checked with the right arm behind the body and the left arm in front to control rotation. The head faces the left hand.

2. The right free leg reaches and extends low and straight back as the left knee bends in preparation for takeoff.

3. With the right leg held straight, the toe taps into the ice as the left foot draws back toward the tapping toe.

4. Lift upward with a straightening action of the left leg and vaulting action off the right leg, as the arms assist the upward momentum.

5. Center the body weight in the air, standing over the right leg with the left free leg bent and held directly in front. Hold the arms in a rounded position in front of the body.

6. With the right leg extending toward the ice in preparation for landing, the left leg moves backward and the arms extend outward, allowing the body weight to balance over the right foot as you land on a right backward outside edge.

START |

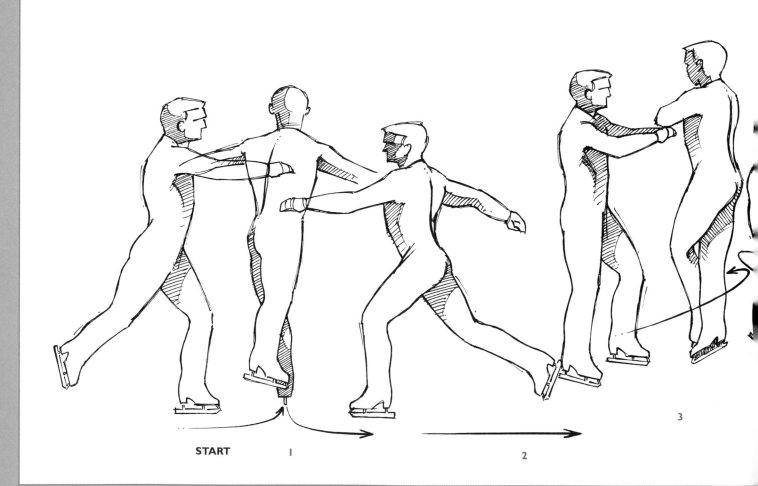

START | 2   3

2   3   4   5   6

4   5

DOUBLE FLIP

1. For the double flip, use the same pre-takeoff steps as for the single flip, but with stronger upper-body control, correct alignment over the left skating hip, and stronger vaulting action from the right leg.

2. Lift upward with a straightening action of the left leg and vaulting action off the right leg, as the arms assist a more powerful takeoff.

3. In the air, the ankles cross in a tighter position with the left foot crossed in front and the arms held tighter to the body as the skater continues rotation for two turns over the right leg.

4. With the right leg extending toward the ice, the left leg initiates the preparation for landing by lifting slightly and then passing close to the skating foot in a backward motion, with the arms simultaneously extending outward. Maintain strong control of the right side of the body to control balance and rotation after impact.

5. The right skating knee bends to absorb the force of landing as the skater achieves a solid right backward outside edge with the free leg extended fully and turned out.

TRIPLE FLIP

The components of the triple flip are very similar to those of the double flip, but the triple requires even greater jumping energy for increased jumping height, and quicker reflexes to achieve faster rotational speed due to more compact body position in the air.

1. Repeat the pre-takeoff steps for the double flip, but with stronger body and edge control during the preparation.

2. There is a greater explosive jumping force at takeoff. Once airborne, maintain your weight over the right side while keeping your body as tight and straight as possible for three revolutions.

3. With the right leg extending toward the ice, the left leg initiates the preparation for landing by lifting slightly and then passing close to the skating foot in a powerful backward motion, with the arms simultaneously extending outward. Maintain strong control of the right side of the body to control balance and rotation after impact.

4. As you land over the right foot, the skating knee bends to absorb the force of landing as you achieve a solid right backward outside edge with the free leg extended fully and turned out.

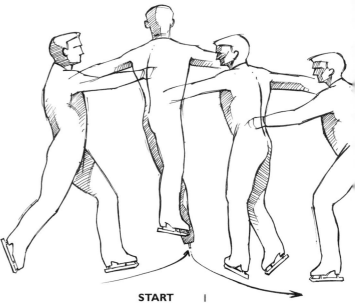

START I

START I   2   3   4

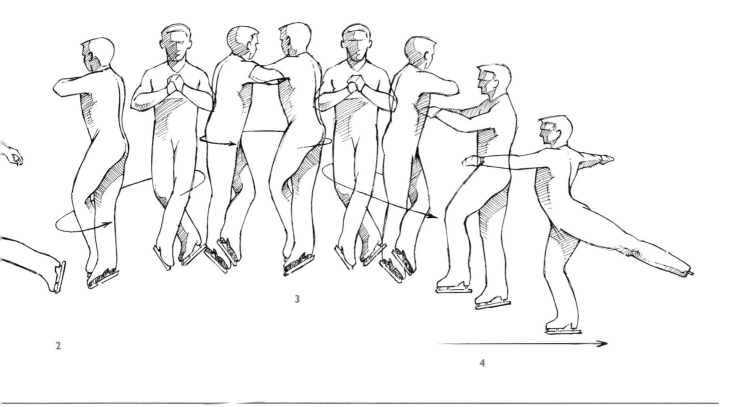

3

2

4

5

SINGLE LUTZ JUMP

The Lutz is a backward takeoff jump that uses an assist from a toe tap. The toe tap makes it a vaulting jump rather than an edge takeoff jump.

1. In preparation for takeoff, the skater usually takes a long controlled gliding pattern on a left backward outside edge, with the body weight balanced over the left side. During this glide your hips should be square and still to help keep the body from rotating as the arms prepare for takeoff. The head is facing the left hand.

2. With the hips held still and the body weight remaining over the left side to help maintain the left backward outside edge, the right free leg reaches and extends straight back as the left knee bends. The shoulders should remain level.

3. The right toe taps into the ice and the left foot draws back toward the tapping toe. The lift upward begins with a straightening action of the left leg and a vaulting action off the right leg as the arms assist the upward momentum. The body balances over the right skating side during the single rotation in the air.

4. To help center the body weight during the air turn, hold the arms in a rounded position in front of the body and the hands in front of the chest.

5. With the right leg extending toward the ice in preparation for landing, the left leg moves backward and the arms simultaneously extend outward, allowing the body weight to balance over the right foot at landing, moving backward on a right backward outside edge.

START   I   2   3   4

TRIPLE LUTZ

The components of the triple Lutz are very similar to those for the double Lutz, but the triple requires even greater jumping energy for increased jumping height, and quicker reflexes to achieve faster rotational speed due to more compact body positions in the air.

1. Repeat the pre-takeoff steps for the double Lutz but with stronger body and edge control during preparation.

2. There is a greater explosive jumping force at takeoff. Once airborne, maintain weight over the right side while keeping the body as tight and straight as possible for three revolutions.

3. With the right leg extending toward the ice, the left leg initiates the preparation for landing by lifting slightly and then passing close to the skating foot in a powerful backward motion, with the arms simultaneously extending outward. Maintain strong control of the right side of the body to control balance and rotation after impact.

4. As you land over the right foot, the skating knee bends to absorb the force of landing as you achieve a solid right backward outside edge with the free leg extended fully and turned out.

START   I

DOUBLE LUTZ

1. For the double Lutz, use the same pre-takeoff steps as for a single Lutz, with greater jumping energy, stronger upper-body control, correct alignment over the left skating hip, and a stronger right vaulting leg. The shoulders must remain level and you must maintain balance over the left side as you reach back with the right leg to tap.

2. The lift upward begins with a straightening action of the left leg and a vaulting action off the right leg, as the arms assist a more powerful takeoff.

3. In the air, the ankles cross in a tighter position with the left foot crossed in front. The arms are held tighter to the body as you continue rotation for two turns over the right leg.

4. With the right leg extending toward the ice, the left leg initiates the preparation for landing by lifting slightly, then passing closely to the skating foot in a backward motion. The arms simultaneously extend outward, keeping strong control of the right side of the body to control balance and rotation after impact.

5. The right skating knee bends to absorb the force of landing as you achieve a solid right backward outside edge with the free leg extended fully and turned out.

5

2

3

4

ROSALYNN SUMNERS

"Skating by myself"

Rosalynn Sumners loved training more than competing. Many of her favorite memories are from when she was skating alone, in a practice session. She remembers that during summer skating school, all the skaters would train in the morning from 5a.m. to 11a.m., then do ballet class and rush out to enjoy the summer day outside. But Sumners would come back in the afternoon when everyone else was gone for an extra practice session just to go over choreography.

ROSALYNN SUMNERS STRETCHES INTO A SPIRAL AT THE 1984 OLYMPIC WINTER GAMES.

"Some of my best times were in those late afternoons when I was out there skating by myself," she recalls. "To this day, I enjoy practicing even more than competing."

But Sumners has had some great competitive moments, too. The one she recalls most fondly is the first time she won the U.S. Championship, in 1982. Elaine Zayak had won the previous year, and Sumners knew it would be very difficult to beat her. And to make matters even more difficult, Sumners had a serious hip injury. All that she and her coach thought they could realistically hope for was to make the World team. They never believed she had a chance of winning the title that year.

Sumners was in fourth place after the short program. On the night of the free skate, she was the last to take the ice. Her injury had forced her to simplify her long program. "I filled my program with a bunch of double Axels because the injury made it so I could really only do one triple," she explains. At the time, she didn't know that all of the skaters before her had fallen several times.

"Every time I landed a jump, the crowd just went wild," she recalls. "Even though I was just doing double Axels, I think the crowd was thrilled that at least I was landing them.

"About thirty seconds before I finished my program the crowd stood up and started to applaud. It was the first standing ovation I'd ever had, which was such a thrill. And they just stayed on their feet for the whole ending of my program."

Sumners won the gold medal. She was shocked: "It was so amazing. I wasn't one of those kids who grew up dreaming of being Olympic champion. It wasn't until I started experiencing some success in lower-level competitions that I started to dream about any championship possibilities. And even then, my ultimate goal was to be national champion. To have it happen so soon and so unexpectedly was really special." ✳

CHARLIE TICKNER

"Concentrate on positive images"

Charlie Tickner's greatest moment took place at the U.S. Championships in 1977. To him, it was "a victorious ending that stemmed from a disastrous beginning."

In 1976 Tickner had been favored to make the Olympic team. "We were allowed two spots on the Olympic team," he recalls, "and I thought I had a shot at one of them. It really looked like it was going to happen. I was leading after the short program, and all I had to do to make the team was skate a good long program. But it didn't happen. I dropped to fourth overall. I didn't make the team—I wasn't even an alternate."

Tickner was twenty-two, an age that usually signaled the end of a competitive career in those days. Some people told him he should retire, but others told him that his competitive record hadn't been a true reflection of his capabilities.

Tickner recalls: "My coach asked me, 'Is this what you want to be remembered for—a poor performance and not making the Olympic team?' I went home and did some soul-searching. I didn't feel too old, so I decided to go back and try for one more year."

Back then, there weren't many competitions in a season, so skaters had very few opportunities to work out the kinks in their programs. Tickner didn't compete at all between the 1976 and 1977 U.S. Championships. He trained on the ice, focusing on program run-throughs to build up stamina.

"I wasn't learning new tricks at that point," he says. "It was just a matter of solidifying things that I was doing and trying to learn how to be more comfortable under pressure." Tickner used self-hypnosis and positive reinforcement to help him visualize getting through his programs. "I think we're pretty simple machines, and we can't focus on two things at one time. If you concentrate on positive images, then there's no room for the negative ones to take hold."

SHOWN HERE IN 1979, CHARLIE TICKNER CONTINUED TO SKATE COMPETITIVELY AFTER HIS INSPIRING VICTORY AT THE U.S. CHAMPIONSHIPS IN 1977.

At the 1977 U.S. Championships, Tickner was no longer a favorite to win. But, "Everything came together," he says, "and it was a really nice victory. It came out of what I considered to be my worst failure, and I feel that to succeed, first you have to know what it's like to fail."

Now a coach, Tickner encourages his students to have a life outside of skating.

"Nothing I did in all my years as a skater compares to the joy of the last fourteen years raising my sons. I witnessed the birth of all three of my sons—it doesn't get much better than that." ❋

GERMAN INGO STEUER DEMONSTRATES UPPER BODY STRENGTH AS HE LIFTS PARTNER MANDY WÖTZEL.

CHAPTER FIVE

FITNESS FOR SKATERS

*W*atching champion figure skaters on television, it's easy to focus on their gracefulness and to totally ignore the sheer athletic power that is behind them. Yet Elvis Stojko and Ilia Kulik, who have made quadruple jumps a standard aspect of their routines, exert as much energy in a four-minute program as America's fastest miler, Paul McMullen, expends in a 1,500-meter race. Both sports require speed and stamina at the same time, a combination that can easily hike heart rates up to 200 beats per minute, forcing the athletes to perform at the critical edge between oxygen supply and oxygen debt—one of the toughest tasks in any sport.

The demands of today's figure skating programs—multiple jumps and spins executed at intense speed—mean that all competitive skaters, from international competitions to the small local rinks, must do fitness training off the ice with the same dedication and effort they use when practicing their routines on the ice.

In the past, many skaters considered dance or ballet training the only necessary off-ice supplement to their on-ice practice, but today, strength and conditioning training, along with proper nutrition and rest, are widely recognized as essential to prevent injuries and to enhance skating performance. This is true for all skaters, from novices to Olympic champions; the level of fitness required simply increases with the level of competition.

Nutritional concerns are probably the most easily met—and most often ignored—factors in a successful fitness training program for skaters. Most of the top skaters know that they should balance their diet with twelve to fifteen percent protein (meat, beans, dairy products), twenty five to thirty percent fat, and fifty five to seventy five percent complex carbohydrates (grains, breads, fruits, and vegetables). How many of them adhere to this proven high-performance diet is anybody's guess. But one crucial aspect—fluid replacement—is a visible part of every championship skater's regular routine. Think back to the 1998 Olympic Ladies' free-skate competition. The gold medal was at stake. As skaters warmed up on the ice and stopped at the boards to get advice and encouragement from their coaches, intense concentration showed on their faces, but the first thing they did was grab water bottles and start sipping as they listened and prepared for their big moment. As a general rule, skaters should drink ten to fourteen ounces of water one or two hours before training, three or four ounces

MICHELLE KWAN DEEP IN CONCENTRATION BEFORE PERFORMIING AT THE U.S. CHAMPIONSHIPS IN 1998.

every fifteen minutes during training, and sixteen ounces or more (water or sports drinks) after training.

Aside from nutrition, an effective fitness training program—both on and off the ice—should include warm-up/cool-down, stretching, strength training, jump/plyometric (power) training, endurance conditioning, and periodization. While all of these components are important, they should be structured into an individualized training program and monitored regularly.

The purpose of off-ice training is to increase physical strength, flexibility, power, and endurance. This will not only result in a better performance, it will also prolong a skater's career by preventing debilitating injuries. The most common figure skating injury today—tendinitis—is caused by chronic overuse of knee and ankle joints and of the lower back and hips. This is primarily a result of the two to three hours of repetitive jumping that is standard in elite training regimens. Tendinitis can make joints susceptible to stress fractures as well. Pre-pubescent skaters (ages eight to thirteen) are at especially high risk for these injuries since their bones have not completely hardened, which means that off-ice fitness training is critically important for the youngest skaters. After age fourteen, skaters are usually more able to sustain the rigors of on-ice practice without such high risk of injury, but conditioning and strength work should still be an integral part of all skaters' overall training programs.

WARM-UP/COOL-DOWN AND STRETCHING

Now that figure skating has become such a popular televised sport, most fans have had the chance to see the top skaters in the warm-up area before a program, practicing their moves and getting the pre-competition jitters out of their systems. Yet many unseasoned skaters ignore those crucial pre-practice or pre-competition warm-ups and post-practice or post-competition cool-downs. Exuberant young skaters often hop right on the ice without any cardiovascular warm-up—such as jumping rope. Nor do they stretch the muscles that will be seriously stressed by all the jumping, spinning, and lifting. Not warming up greatly increases the risk of acute skating-related injuries: soft-tissue injuries (torn and bruised tendons and ligaments), and muscle strains and pulls. Knees, ankles, hips, and the lower back are particularly vulnerable, as are the surrounding muscle groups, especially hamstrings and calves.

And now that all skaters are jumping higher and faster and more often than ever before, it is also vital to remember one unavoidable truth: The more you jump, the more you fall. If you land wrong, you can seriously injure, even break, your wrists or your neck. Stretching beforehand helps prepare you for the acute stress of falls.

What is the best way to warm up or cool down? Since a warm-up is designed to prepare the heart and lungs as well as deep muscle and soft tissue, it should be done thirty to forty minutes before stepping onto the ice, leaving five minutes or so to put

WARMING UP IS A VITAL PART OF A SKATER'S PERFORMANCE. STRETCHING, BRIEF AEROBIC EXERCISE, AND SPECIFIC WARM-UPS DEPENDING ON THE ROUTINE ARE ALL INVOLVED IN A SKATER'S PREPARATION.

on skates. The goal is twofold: Get the cardiovascular system pumping and literally warm the muscles so they are more flexible.

GENERAL WARM-UP

1. Jump rope, jog in place, or do any form of aerobic exercise for five to eight minutes.

2. Do some total body flexibility stretching for ten to fifteen minutes. Start at the top of the body and work down: head circles, arm circles, trunk rotation, quadriceps pulls, straddle sit and reach, abdominal crunches, back extension, standing calf push, and Achilles tendon stretch. Skaters who are unfamiliar with these exercises may consult a variety of books on the subject, including Bob Anderson's *Stretching*.

SPECIFIC WARM-UP

A specific warm-up focuses on specific areas of the body by visualizing each aspect of a program and preparing for those exact movements. It merges mental and physical preparation.

Every movement about to be performed on the ice should be closely simulated off the ice beforehand. That way there will be no surprises to your body when it's on the ice, and every movement in a practice or performance will feel familiar.

SINGLES

1. Practice air-turns and rotational jumps off the ice.

2. Do low-intensity jumps in place off the ice.

3. Simulate any other choreography movements off the ice.

PAIRS

1. Do the same drills as the singles skaters, adding pair lifts and pair choreography movements.

2. Because pairs skating is so much more dynamic than any other discipline, stretching should include more work on the middle and upper body. Both members of the pair should spend extra time on their shoulders, wrists, and forearms, and men should pay special attention to their abdominals and lower back. The male partner of a figure skating pair undergoes the most stress of any athlete in the sport, both mental and physical. On top of the athletic, aesthetic, and competitive concerns every skater has, he's also lifting, carrying, and balancing his partner, who is at times entirely dependent upon him for her well-being. The pressure on him is great, and he should take whatever time he needs to make sure his body and mind are in sync.

STRENGTH TRAINING IS IMPORTANT FOR
SKATERS IN ALL DISCIPLINES, BUT ESPECIALLY
PAIRS SKATERS AND ICE DANCERS.
CANADIAN ICE DANCER VICTOR KRAATZ
HERE WORKS ON HIS UPPER BODY
STRENGTH.

ICE DANCING

1. Do some low-intensity dynamic lateral jumps or strides off the ice.

2. Practice footwork drills off the ice.

3. Simulate choreography movements off the ice.

4. Do the same stretching exercises recommended for pairs.

COOL-DOWN

Very few skaters seem to realize that a cool-down can make a noticeable difference in how well they are physically prepared for their next training session or competitive program.

A skater who recovers quickly and effectively has a competitive edge, especially when it comes to repetitive practices and warm-ups, or back-to-back programs, or events on consecutive days.

Skaters encounter an enormous amount of stress throughout a competition week; a single free skate with lots of jumps is extremely taxing on the body, and most skaters practice both their short and long programs seven or eight times every week. During such a punishing drill, intense neuromuscular stress is created through elevated heart rates and lactic acid accumulation; a skater who does not cool down and stretch afterward will eventually encounter problems of fatigue and soreness that may carry over to the next event.

During strenuous exercise, more blood is circulated to the muscles that are working hard—in this case, in the legs and arms—to deliver the needed oxygen. After a workout, the main objective of a cool-down is to allow blood flow in the muscles to ease off, to go back into the general circulation, instead of accumulating in the legs and arms, which causes that post-workout feeling of sluggishness and aching in the muscles. Light to moderately paced aerobic exercise will recirculate the blood, which helps clear the lactic acid that causes muscle tightening and knots.

Finally, total body flexibility stretching relaxes and lengthens muscle and soft tissue, reducing muscular soreness. Overall, the cooling-down process should take fifteen to twenty minutes.

FOR AN EFFECTIVE COOL-DOWN:

1. Reduce heart rate with light to moderately paced stroking on the ice, light to moderately paced jogging in place, or slideboard off the ice, for at least three to five minutes.

2. Do total body stretching as described in the general warm-up, holding each stretch for at least twenty seconds.

3. Drink at least two cups of water.

4. Replenish carbohydrates within thirty minutes after practice, taking in one to three grams of carbohydrate per kilogram of body weight. For a child, for example, this would be the equivalent of a banana and half a bagel; for a young woman, a bagel and a cup of yogurt or pasta; for a man, a bagel, a cup of pasta, and an ounce of raisins.

STRENGTH TRAINING

Off-ice strength training is crucial not only for injury prevention but also for high performance levels. The introduction of strength training should begin with the grassroots skating levels—preliminary, juvenile, and intermediate—and should continue throughout a competitive career. This type of training enhances movement skills on the ice and builds strength for stroking, holding spins, jumping, lifts, and holding positions.

The objective for an effective strength-training program is to strengthen the joint areas involved in skating (neuromuscular and soft-tissue strengthening as opposed to the isolated movement strengthening associated with bodybuilders). It also increases muscular and soft-tissue strength along with bone density and flexibility.

Even though some differences exist between skating disciplines, any strength training program should include some common areas: lower body, quadriceps and hamstrings, hip, lower leg or calf area, upper body, shoulders and upper back, and, finally, middle body and abdominals. At competitive levels of skating, even basic stroking involves not just the calves and the quadriceps but the middle body as well. Jumps demand the strengthening of the entire body. The quadriceps, lower legs, and hamstrings provide added support, as do the shoulders and the upper back. Spins call for isolated work on knee joints and the lower back.

A specific strength-training program for any discipline of figure skating requires an understanding of the biomechanical or movement patterns, common sites of injuries, and energy demands of that discipline. Strength training must also target the areas of muscular imbalances skaters develop from overusing quadriceps and hamstrings in jumping, for example, or overbuilding one side of the body from jumping to just one side. Ideally, the special needs generated by each discipline should be assessed by a strength and conditioning specialist.

A very important area that is often overlooked for all disciplines of skating is strengthening of the "core body." This includes the abdominals, obliques (sides of the abdominals), and lower back. Key areas for strength training in the three disciplines of skating include, for singles, the neck and middle body and abdominals; for pairs, wrists, forearms, and arms; and for ice dancers, inner thighs, arms, and wrists.

For all skaters, it is also very important to strengthen hamstrings and lower legs to prevent boot-related injuries such as tendinitis, which sometimes results from the limited range of motion the boots allow. Obviously, boots are a necessary part of the sport, so the only recourse for a skater who wants to avoid injury is to do some "preventive" strength training.

Pairs skaters need to work on almost all of the upper-body muscles, especially in the lower back/torso area. Strength training for ice dancers may include, in addition to the core exercises, isolated work for the lower back, abdominal/torso area, and upper and lower legs.

Increases in extensive muscle mass, or hypertrophy, should be avoided; too great a muscle mass can affect a skater's movements or the way he looks—and it may be

ELVIS STOJKO THRUSTS INTO ONE OF HIS POWERFUL JUMPS.

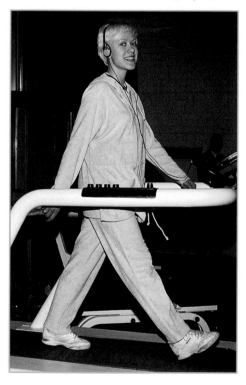

Aerobic training involves low-impact, long-duration activity that helps build endurance. Chen Lu (top) and Oksana Baiul (above) both include aerobic training in their overall conditioning programs.

difficult for a bulky skater to perform some of the fine-skill movements involved in the discipline, especially triple-jump rotations.

Jump/Plyometric Training

Success in almost any sport involves speed, strength, and power. Figure skating utilizes power in stroking, jumping, and lifts. All disciplines of skating benefit from supplemental power training, or jump/plyometric training, which means conditioning the neuromuscular system with speed-strength drills. These drills can enhance rotational jumps, stroking, and dynamic spins for singles skaters; jumps, lifts, throw jumps, and stroking for pairs; and stroking, footwork movements, and lifts for ice dancers.

The point of plyometric training is to train the muscle/soft tissue complex at the specific joint area to contract with the greatest force in the shortest amount of time to help increase jumping power. Jumping rope is a simple, low-intensity form of plyometrics, and in terms of figure skating, combination jumps and pairs or ice dance lifts are forms of plyometrics. The force and velocity of movement with which skaters perform throughout a competitive program contain various forms of speed and strength. A plyometrics program for skaters should incorporate exercises or drills for the ankles, knees, hips, torso, and shoulders.

> Jump/Plyometric drills:
> 1. Jump in place (e.g., ankle bounces).
> 2. Jump for height or distance (e.g., long jumps).
> 3. Do box jumps, using a plyometric box (a specially designed box that the athlete jumps on and off of).
> 4. Do torso/abdominal drills with weighted balls (e.g., weighted sit-ups).

Endurance Conditioning

Endurance conditioning is a necessity for any competitive skater. Many strong, powerful skaters perform exceptionally throughout most of their long program, only to fall apart at the end because they simply do not have enough energy left. The skater who can resist fatigue and finish a program with high energy and a dramatic or difficult climax is more than likely the one who will finish at the top.

All disciplines of skating require both speed and stamina, so an effective fitness program should involve both types of training: aerobic (low intensity, long duration) and anaerobic (moderate to high intensity, short duration). Aerobic training uses oxygen for energy, while anaerobic training uses carbohydrates (stored in muscles) and glucose (stored in blood).

The ultimate goal for the figure skater is to train at a level that equals or exceeds his or her competitive endurance capacity. Working only on skills such as jumps, spins, and spirals on the ice is not enough. Skaters must train at the same high-intensity level they will be using when they compete.

The best way for skaters to train at that level is to perform, on the ice, stroking and conditioning drills: continuous stroking, interval stroking, simulated program intervals, and program run-throughs. Off the ice, circuit training is good for conditioning, as are slideboard workouts, jumping rope, stationary bicycles, interval circuit drills, treadmills, bench-stepping, stairmasters, and so on. Running should be limited to soft track surfaces to avoid potential knee problems—avoid running on pavement.

PERIODIZATION

The key to successful endurance conditioning is to utilize cycles or differing time periods and intensities of both aerobic and anaerobic conditioning, and to combine both off the ice and on the ice conditioning drills. This concept of training is termed *periodization*.

Periodization takes into consideration the entire year's training and competitive schedule as well as the volume, intensity, type of exercises, frequency, and rest periods for all components of off-ice and on-ice training. It is extremely important to prevent the fatigue and staleness that can result from overtraining, and to reach peak physical performance.

Overtraining, which can occur both on and off the ice, can lead to injuries. Periodization modifies volume, intensity, and rest periods of training as needed to prevent overtraining or burnout. For example, after skaters reach a desired level of endurance from eight weeks of aerobic conditioning, they can switch to anaerobic training and still maintain their endurance. The important point is to combine both kinds of training without going too far in either direction. The exception to this for skaters comes just prior to and during their competitive season, when they strictly target anaerobic training.

The bottom line is: No matter how high skaters jump, how fast they spin, or how many medals and championships they win, there is life after skating. Competitive skaters have a lifetime to live after their last medal has been locked in the trophy case. So remember, in training as well as in competition, athletic performance is obviously important, but overall good health should always be the primary consideration. ✳

THE CONDITIONING PROGRAM OF MICHAEL WEISS HAS A SPECIAL EMPHASIS ON STRENGTH TRAINING.

ELAINE ZAYAK

"I have a lot of respect for the sport."

Elaine Zayak's greatest accomplishment as a skater was competing at the 1994 U.S. Championships. Zayak was the first former U.S. ladies' champion to regain her eligible status under the USFSA rule allowing reinstatement. Her last eligible competition had been ten years prior, in 1984. She had skated professionally for five years after that, then had retired from skating in 1989. But after attending the 1993 U.S. Championships, she changed her mind. "I realized how much I missed skating," she explains, "and the next week I decided it would be great to try and make a comeback."

Twenty pounds overweight when she started training, Zayak had her work cut out for her. She couldn't do her trademark triple jumps anymore.

"Getting back in shape was exciting, but also discouraging sometimes," she recalls. "For a while it seemed like I'd never be able to do a triple." Her good friend, Calla Urbanski, encouraged her. Though a few years older, Urbanski could still do triples with no problem. "Calla said to me, 'Elaine, you used to do seven triples in your program, are you telling me you can't get one triple back? If I can do it, you can.'"

Zayak was determined, though getting her triples back would require more effort than she had ever imagined. She had never done much off-ice training before. "I never had to," she says. But this time things were different. "It took me months to get my strength back," she remembers. "I worked with a trainer to re-learn the body movements for jumping, and I did a lot of cardiovascular work. Finally I was in such great physical condition that when I went back to trying triple jumps, it was easy."

Though she was entitled to compete in the U.S. Championships based on her previous record, Zayak chose to compete at the Regional and Sectional levels first. "I have a lot of respect for the sport," she explains, "and I wanted to work my way back to the Nationals. I didn't want it to seem like I had been given anything."

The lower-level competitions were nerve-wracking. "I was competing against kids who were fifteen years younger than me—and they were good."

When Zayak took the ice at the U.S. Championships, the crowd began to cheer even before her name was announced. "I couldn't hear the announcer say my name," she says. All that commotion was unnerving, and for a moment she didn't know if she could keep it together. But she skated two great programs and brought the audience to its feet both times.

Although she came in fourth, Zayak had done what she set out to do. "I wanted to prove to myself that I could get back in shape and skate as well as, or even better, than I had before, and I wanted to show other people that a 28-year-old woman can still compete." ❈

ELAINE ZAYAK DURING HER COMEBACK PERFORMANCE AT THE 1994 U.S. CHAMPIONSHIPS.

BRIAN BOITANO

"It was truly a case of mind over matter."

For Brian Boitano, the 1986 competitive season was vital because "it made the win in 1988 possible."

In practice two weeks before the 1986 U.S. Championships, Boitano severely stretched a tendon in his right ankle. "I could hardly even walk," he recalls. His doctor told him to rest, so for the next week and a half, he did nothing but compulsory figures. But that was far from easy: "Even just figures hurt tremendously," Boitano says.

But he did everything he could think of to help his ankle heal, and by the time he arrived at the U.S. Championships, he was feeling better.

"I hadn't done one jump in more than a week," Boitano remembers, "and to compete after not jumping for a week is unheard of." During his first practice session, he toed in for a triple Lutz and heard a "pop" and felt a searing pain—he had re-injured the tendon. He stayed off the ice until the competition began four days later.

"I stayed in the hotel room with my foot in a bucket of ice," he says. But all that "rest" skating figures paid off. Boitano won the compulsories. Still, he wasn't sure if he should try to jump.

"The morning of the short I asked my doctor whether I would make the injury worse by competing. He said no, so I did the short program." It was difficult and painful, but Boitano skated clean and held on to first place.

"I felt as if the hand of God had reached down and helped me out," he reflects. "Every time I vaulted off my right toe pick I felt a hot pain shoot through my ankle and up my leg. It was truly a case of mind

BRIAN BOITANO'S DIFFICULT SEASON IN 1986 SET THE STAGE FOR HIS OLYMPIC VICTORY.

over matter." But Boitano made it through the free skate as well, and won his second U.S. title.

After the U.S. Championships, he again tried to heal his ankle before the Worlds. Although it felt a little better by the time the competition started, he didn't skate his best in the short program, leaving him out of the top three going into the free skate.

"I got on the ice and said 'I can do this,'" Boitano explains. He was determined to put up with the pain. Between the injury and his placement after the short, Brian's chances of winning were slim. "But I was the only guy who skated clean," he remembers. Against all odds, Brian Boitano won the World title.

To Boitano, that 1986 season foreshadowed his Olympic victory in 1988. He believes that had he not won a World title before 1988, he probably would not have been seriously considered for an Olympic gold medal.

"It was a groundbreaking time for me," he says. "I showed myself that I was capable of overcoming pain and reaching a level of mental strength that I never knew I had." ✳

CHAPTER SIX

SKATING FASHION

*I*n the beginning was not the sequin. Perhaps that's hard to imagine now that skaters have been seen dressed as volcanoes and taxicabs and jungle animals, women have been known to accidentally fall out of their low-cut costumes in mid-program, and men wear sleeves more billowy than Sarah Bernhardt's. Costumes have always been an integral part of skating—and how skaters have been judged—but when the sport was first established, in the late 1800s, the primary importance of an outfit was not drama, flash, or aesthetics. It was survival. The ice was outdoors, and in order to avoid frostbite, skaters wore heavy, cumbersome garments—which may be why the triple Axel wasn't invented until much later.

Frigid weather notwithstanding, skating was a sport of prosperous ladies and gentlemen, who brought their stylish street fashion to the ice. Women wore close-fitting jackets that went to the hips and buttoned down the front. Skirts were ankle-length and full, often trimmed with fur and always worn with several petticoats for added warmth. A fur hat and muff were essential as well, as added compensation for the cold.

DESIGNER VERA WANG CREATED THE DRESS NANCY KERRIGAN WORE FOR HER FREE SKATE AT LILLEHAMMER IN 1994, ONE OF THE MOST BEAUTIFUL SKATING OUTFITS EVER SEEN IN COMPETITION.

By the time of the first international skating meeting in Vienna, in 1882, the dictates of skating fashion had begun in earnest. In 1883, *The Skaters Text Book* called for a balance between the styles of the day and the skater's needs: ". . . men and boys should leave off their overcoats and women's and girls' dresses should reach the ankle only; the limbs should be unencumbered for free use and corsets are very injurious during the hours of exercise." Considering that contraptions such as bustles were a big fashion item in those days, it's amazing that the Tenley Albrights of yesteryear could move around at all. In fact, with women modestly covered up, the best legs in sight at the skating venue were wrapped in wool tights and belonged to men.

GREAT BRITAIN'S KATE SHAW DISPLAYS GOOD FORM AT THE 1928 OLYMPIC WINTER GAMES.

1900s

As the popularity of skating increased again after the turn of the century, and the sport developed into a social event, skaters began to set their own fashion standards. Men wore sweaters and jackets with matching knickers and caps; women's dresses continued to be bulky but feathers and fur became increasingly popular in their chic, eye-catching bonnets.

In the early 1900s, when the U.S. Championships began and indoor ice rinks became more prevalent, women's costumes got a little more daring: Concerns about women being able to get about safely on the ice seemed to be less important than some other, more "aesthetic" issues. Hemlines now went up to the top of their boots and revealed, according to *Ice Skating* author T.D. Richardson, an occasional glimpse of a petticoat or, even better, black silk stockings. This new, more daring style included transparent chiffon blouses and, as always, showy plumed hats.

Some crusaders for liberating women from the confines of their corsets also seemed to have more on their minds than health. Richardson told of one society ingenue who shocked "half the smart world of Edwardian society" by skating in a black silk leotard and a "daringly short skirt." She was obviously wearing no corsets. "This caused the most tremendous sensation and considerable adverse criticism," Richardson noted. "But she looked so delightful, so graceful and so lissome that gradually a movement for freer clothing for skating began to take shape."

ULRICH SALCHOW (OPPOSITE, THIRD FROM LEFT) AND FRIENDS AROUND 1900. LEGGINGS REMAINED STANDARD ATTIRE FOR MEN UNTIL MID-CENTURY. STREET CLOTHES WERE THE CHOICE WHEN GERMAN DIPLOMAT JOACHIM VON RIBBENTROP (TOP, CENTER) VISITED BOSTON IN 1914. MADGE SYERS (ABOVE) DOES HER BEST IN A LONG SKIRT WHILE SKATING WITH HUSBAND EDGAR.

After World War I, fashion changed quickly—and skating fashion with it. In 1920, while her sisters were beginning to enjoy the social benefits of short flapper dresses, America's first national Ladies' champion, Theresa Weld Blanchard, grappled with the eternal fashion issue for an upcoming competition: "It was decided my dress would not do, so we dashed around looking for a dressmaker. . . . I insisted the result was far too immodest as it was only six inches below my knees, and I was sure my bloomers would show when I jumped."

Ten-time World Champion Sonja Henie, buried the long skirt forever. As an eleven-year-old competing in 1924, her outfits—made by her own Norwegian tailor and considered acceptable for a "child" skater—were scandalously short (knee-length) by ladies' standards and flowed freely, without petticoats, to accommodate Henie's athletic skating style of jumps and spins. As Henie grew up, though, she kept her short skirts. By 1928, flappers were the thoroughly modern norm, and skating hemlines had crept to just below the knee.

GERMANS MAXI HERBER AND ERNST
BAIER (ABOVE) GLIDE AHEAD IN
FINE ALPINE FORM.
ENGLISHWOMEN CECILIA
COLLEDGE (RIGHT) AND MEGAN
TAYLOR (OPPOSITE) WERE
PROFOUNDLY INFLUENCED
BY SONJA HENIE'S
SKATING STYLE, BUT
POSSIBLY LESS
SO BY HER
IMPECCABLE
SENSE OF FASH-
ION.

There was no escaping Henie's influence. She made sure then, as she did until the day she died, that everything matched. Even her practice outfits were color-coordinated, from tights to sequined caps. In 1931, Blanchard commented: "The European ladies first pick out their boots, black or beige, then get stockings to exactly match, and finally bloomers of the same color; this gives an almost unbroken line from the toe-point to the waist." When she turned professional in the mid-1930s, Henie took her style to Hollywood, where she became the movies' glamorous, spinning variation of Ginger Rogers.

Men's costumes during these years were "easy to describe and not original," wrote Blanchard. They wore the same costumes they would sport for the next fifty years: short, tailored black jackets and tights for competitions, and tights or skating trousers with sweaters for practice.

Both men and women carefully avoided overly elaborate outfits. Blanchard, an apparent arbiter of fashion at the time, dictated precisely what constituted an appropriate costume. Small hats, for example, were sometimes acceptable, but "Brims, unless very tiny, always seem out of place." Satin dresses could be worn, but only if the satin was "very heavy to give a rich look and not fly about too much." Despite all of her pronouncements, Blanchard complained that "style does not change much from year to year."

Women's costumes were much more colorful and adventurous than the men's. At the 1948 Winter Olympics, women wore every color and fabric imaginable for the free skate, from cherry satin and red velvet to white fur and pink chiffon. Dresses were getting tighter and shorter all the time; skirts were now above the knee.

Male skaters were also looking more to street fashion to update their style on the ice. By 1944, tapered slacks had replaced tights, and jackets, like women's skirts, had gotten shorter to allow more freedom of movement. But the men's drab palette remained the same: black and white. At the beginning of the 1950s, the basic tuxedo was the standard for men. It included the new Eisenhower jacket, with back fullness that allowed for easy body movement, a satin stripe on the trousers, a bow tie, a white shirt, and black boots. Then technological advances began to change what men wore when newly developed stretch fabric that molded to the body led to the two-piece "monkey suit." To avoid separation of the jacket and trousers, a one-piece suit was developed, with a fold at the waist that simulated the conventional two-piece cut.

CAROL HEISS (ABOVE) WAS KNOWN FOR HER SLIGHTLY FLIRTY COSTUMES; JACQUELINE DU BIEF OF FRANCE (ABOVE RIGHT) WAS FAMOUS FOR HER *REALLY* FLIRTY COSTUMES. IN THIS ONE, SHE RESEMBLED A BARBER POLE WHEN SHE RAISED HER ARMS IN MID-SPIN. BARBARA ANN SCOTT (RIGHT) FEATURED MORE INNOCENT, FUR-TRIMMED NUMBERS, WHILE DICK BUTTON (OPPOSITE) INTRODUCED THE EISENHOWER JACKET TO MEN'S SKATING WEAR.

As the 1950s progressed, women's love affair with color became even more daring. At the 1956 Olympics, Tenley Albright wore shocking pink and Carol Heiss wore bright aqua chiffon with a rhinestone necklace and a sequined cap. The following year, Heiss wore fire-engine red with rhinestones on her sleeves and cap, an outfit that easily could have moved from rinkside to cocktail lounge, if she had been old enough to have cocktails, which she was not.

1960s

At the beginning of the free-spirited 1960s, men skaters weren't exactly clad in hippie-style love beads and jeans, but they were making strides to update their on-ice image. At the 1964 U.S. Championships, 1962 champ Monty Hoyt broke out of the black-and-white mode by skating in a white jacket with red trousers. Two years later, John Misha Petkevich took the men's modest color rebellion a step further when he competed in a cinnamon jumpsuit with a turquoise turtleneck jersey.

Brightly colored chiffon embroidered with beads and sequins became the trademark of U.S. women skaters in the mid-1960s. Unlike Sonja Henie, most of these women couldn't afford designers to create their outfits; family members and local seamstresses used ordinary dress patterns and adapted them to suit the rigors and style of figure skating. Peggy Fleming won the 1968 Olympics in a flowing chartreuse outfit which, like all her costumes, had been designed and sewn by her mother.

Skating was not immune to the jarring juxtaposition of traditional propriety and rebellion that marked the decade. One of *Skating* magazine's "Look Well, Do Well" features offered some stern advice to those who would mix old and new: "I noticed some of the girls in the dance events wearing tiaras during the preliminary round in the morning. Seeing a girl wearing a tiara in the morning gives the impression that she has just arrived from a party. It would be better to resort to informal and formal dress rules, wearing tiaras in the evening only, substituting matching ribbons or bows for daytime wear. And avoid bouffant hairdos if your program is strenuous. One senior skater began her program beautifully coifed and by the time she was finished, every strand of hair stuck straight out. Need I say more?"

Heading into the next decade, one judge warned against too much decorative glitter in dance costumes: "Besides giving the impression of a Christmas tree, it detracts from the skater's performance." But more vibrant fashion days were just around the corner. And how.

"I can never remember a sloppily dressed skater being placed first by the judges. So when you prepare for your next competition, give a great deal of thought to your impeccably neat, attractive appearance on the ice. A good fit and utter simplicity are the greatest factors in a lovely costume."

Skating, 1964.

On the facing page, three-time U.S. Champion Tim Wood (top) shows off in a turtleneck, while Canadian Junior Champion Donald Knight (left) stays conservative. At bottom, two popular styles skaters could make at home. The Protopopovs (above) always had great taste, as did the young Dorothy Hamill (right), pictured here wearing the height of late 1960s homemade skating fashion.

The rebelliousness of the 1960s had established a looser era—in life and in competition—and the color, style, and experimentation in skating outfits reflected that change. Canadian Champion Toller Cranston opened creative doors with his unique skating style, and made stretchy jumpsuits—with a few sequins here and there—acceptable for men. For all the headlines grabbed by Dorothy Hamill's wedge hairdo, the costume she wore in the 1976 Olympics was conservative compared to what followed. Women's outfits soon plunged and scooped in places unheard of ten years earlier. There were cutouts, feathers, fur, and rhinestones, rhinestones, rhinestones.

Image became as important as jumps, spins, and footwork. Professional designers created eye-popping costumes to impress the judges and go with the music, down to the last stitch and bangle. But the glamour frenzy had drawbacks: Olympic silver medalist Linda Fratianne's bejeweled red outfit at the 1979 U.S. Championships prompted an audience member to issue a loud wolf whistle at the crucial moment before she began her program. Fratianne won that competition, but was told by officials that she looked "too much like a Las Vegas showgirl."

Designers in the 1970s became as important as coaches and choreographers. They collaborated with competitors to explore every extreme, from flowing graceful gowns to gaudy, bejeweled outfits suitable for the Folies-Bergère. Lycra and spandex became magic words. Combined with the new plastic sequins and beads that had all the sparkle and one-tenth the weight of their heavy glass predecessors, the stretchy synthetic fabrics let skaters jump higher, move more easily, and feel an unprecedented sense of pure physical lightness that went hand-in-hand with technical breakthroughs: more revolutions in jumps, trickier and more innovative positions in spins.

DOROTHY HAMILL (ABOVE, CENTER) AT THE 1976 OLYMPICS WAS NOT THE ONLY SKATER WITH A TASTE FOR SOMETHING SIMPLE AND SHORT. TOLLER CRANSTON (OPPOSITE) WAS AS RADICAL IN HIS CHOICE OF COSTUME AS HE WAS IN HIS CHOICE OF SKATING MOVES. LINDA FRATIANNE (ABOVE RIGHT) WON THE 1979 U.S. CHAMPIONSHIP DESPITE A FEELING BY SOME THAT SHE HAD GONE "LAS VEGAS." U.S. ICE DANCERS COLLEEN O'CONNOR AND JIM MILLNS (RIGHT) EPITOMIZE THE SLICK STYLES OF THE 1970S.

1980s

The showiness continued into the 1980s, but one exception to the Glitz Brigade was Scott Hamilton's costume for the 1984 Olympics. Believing that sequined male skaters looked more like peacocks than competitors, Hamilton opted for a patriotic red, white, and blue speed-skating style outfit. He won the gold, but few followed his fashion lead. Crisp military outfits were also popular.

After a revealing 1988 season that featured bare-chested male skaters, French-cut ladies' costumes, bare midriffs, unitards, and see-through fabrics, the ISU issued in 1989 costume guidelines: "Costumes for Men cannot be theatrical in nature or sleeveless, must have a neckline which does not expose the chest and be without excessive decoration, such as beads, sequins and the like. . . . Costumes for Ladies cannot be theatrical in nature. They must have skirts and pants covering the hips and posterior. A bare midriff is not acceptable. Costumes must be without excessive decoration, such as beads, sequins, feathers and the like." Failure to comply could result in a penalty of a 0.2 deduction in the presentation score. But the guidelines were often ignored, or applied selectively. The wording—no "excessive" sequins—left loopholes big enough to do flying camels through.

SCOTT HAMILTON (ABOVE) AND BRIAN BOITANO (ABOVE RIGHT) CHOSE SIMPLE BUT WELL-CONSIDERED OUTFITS FOR THEIR FREE SKATES. EXPOSING THE CHEST WAS RESTRICTED NOT LONG AFTER PETR BARNA'S APPEARANCE AT THE 1988 OLYMPICS (FAR RIGHT). ELIZABETH MANLEY (RIGHT) OF CANADA REVEALED MUCH OF HER BACK, WHILE KATARINA WITT (OPPOSITE) IN 1984 REGALLY WORE A FANCIFUL TYPE OF PEASANT GARB.

1990s

In 1992, all three Olympic Men's medalists wore funeral black. The top male competitors had abandoned the glitter, but in its place they ushered in the era of the Billowing White Sleeve, donning enough weskits, vests, and flowing fabric to outfit a gaggle of Edwardian poets. As for the women, the costumes included everything from faux wedding dresses to sequin-encrusted and intricate, barely-there extravaganzas. Necklines and backlines continued to plunge. Skirts were shortened in some cases to mere wisps of fabric.

Costumes had become an important extension of the music and a key to presentation in programs that increasingly had a character and a theme. The ladies were not just skaters, they were gypsies, Russian czarinas, Greek goddesses, harem girls, chorus girls, Spanish temptresses, geishas, or birds of paradise. Ice dancers dressed as racing cars, robots, and jungle animals.

Fashion took a graceful step forward in 1994 when Nancy Kerrigan hired New York designer Vera Wang—known for her elegant bridal dresses—to create her

Philippe Candeloro of France (opposite and above left) is well known for his innovative costumes. Michael Weiss (above) takes a more romantic approach, as do Alexei Yagudin (far left) and Rudy Galindo (left).

Olympic costumes. Kerrigan skated in a simple white stretch-lace dress for practice sessions and a black velvet outfit with illusion sleeves for exhibitions. The crowning glory, though, was her Breakthrough Dress, a combination of champagne stretch-satin—adorned with more than five thousand sequins—and shimmery illusion sleeves. Deceptively simple, the dress belied the one hundred hours it took to make. Today that blend of simple lines and illusion fabric can be seen in just about every competition.

The designer influence on skating seems to be here to stay. After Donna Karan created outfits for both Todd Eldredge and ice dancers Elizabeth Punsalan and Jerod Swallow at the 1998 Olympics, her company—DKNY— became the USFSA's official outfitter for that season.

MICHELLE KWAN AS SALOME (ABOVE). CHEN LU'S COSTUME HIGHLIGHTS HER NATURAL BEAUTY. (BELOW). NANCY KERRIGAN (OPPOSITE) SHOWS OFF A WANG CREATION, AND TONIA KWIATKOWSKI (LEFT) EXUDES A SPARKLING GLAMOUR.

In olden days a glimpse of stocking was something shocking, on the frozen pond or on the street. But today in skating, as in life, anything goes. Skaters have gone from bustles to bugle beads, gloves to glitter, plus fours to quads done in a stretch jumpsuit updating yesteryear's long johns. Fashion, whether the outfit is a symphony of spaghetti-strap and velvet minimalism or an extravaganza embroidered within an inch of its teeny life in rhinestones and sequins, is very subjective. ✳

GETTING OUTFITTED

Almost anything can be worn for recreational skating or practice figure skating sessions. Most skaters make comfort a priority so they can focus on the skills they are trying to learn, and a big part of comfort is warmth. Indoors or outdoors, the best bet is to wear layers. Once muscles are warmed up, layers can be removed.

Many female skaters wear tights as their first layer of clothing. Men may wear sweats, loose pants, or one or more layers of leggings with a thin sock. On top of the tights, women could wear sweats, leggings, a one-piece skating skirt or dress with built-in panty, or a special pair of skating sweats that zip on both sides for easy removal.

Indoors, wear two layers on top—a turtleneck practice dress and a zip-up sweater for women, or a cotton turtleneck and a pull-over sweatshirt for men. Outdoors, wear three or four layers—an undershirt, a cotton turtleneck, a pull-over sweater, and a zip-on jacket. Many skaters like to wear lightweight knit gloves both indoors and outdoors, and some beginners wear protective wrist and knee guards.

Most of these things can be found at a department store or sporting goods store. Skating dresses or skirts, whether for practice or competition, and skating sweatpants (with zippers down the sides so they can be removed without taking off the skates) can be found at many rink pro shops or through mail-order catalogs. Pro shops may have a limited selection of low-level competition dresses, ranging from $80 to $150, and they can also special order dresses with specified fabrics, cuts, and designs. These dresses might cost from $100 to $250, or more if a lot of decorative beading is requested.

Here are some suggestions for skating outfits in various price ranges, from least to most expensive:

BUDGET: Pantyhose ($3), sweatpants ($15), cotton T-shirt ($5-$15), sweatshirt ($20-$30), gloves ($3), and, for extra warmth outdoors, cotton undershirt ($7-$10) and zip-up heavy sweat jacket ($30-$50).

MID-RANGE: Dance tights ($10), cotton/lycra leggings ($25-$40) or skating skirt with panty ($25-$40), cotton turtleneck ($15-$30), zip-up skating sweater ($40-$60), gloves ($3), and, for extra warmth outdoors, silk undershirt ($15-$25) and any waist-length zip-up outdoor jacket ($50-$80).

ILIA KULIK HAS SAID THAT THIS OUTFIT (OPPOSITE) IS AN HOMAGE TO ART DECO. SCOTT DAVIS'S SIMPLE APPROACH SHOWS THAT SOMETIMES THE BEST COSTUME IS NO COSTUME AT ALL.

HIGH-END: Microfiber skating tights ($20), velvet leggings ($35-$60) with supplex turtleneck ($30) or practice dress ($50-$150), zip-up fleece skating pants ($100-$125) with matching zip-up fleece jacket ($80-$100), and, for outdoors, silk undershirt ($15-$20) and lightweight Polar fleece zip-up jacket ($100-$200).

LINDA FRATIANNE

A Victory over Fear and Self-doubt

One of Linda Fratianne's fondest memories is from the 1979 World Championships in Vienna, Austria. She had won the World title for the first time two years before, but in 1978 she finished second behind Anett Poetzsch of East Germany. That year—between her loss of the title in 1978 and the competition in Vienna—was the most difficult of her competitive career.

At the 1979 Worlds, Fratianne trailed Poetzsch after the compulsory figures, but then pulled up to first place after the short program. But Poetzsch had already gotten high marks in the free skate when Fratianne took the ice for her long program. The pressure was enormous, but she managed to get past it. She focused on her program and skated her best.

When her marks came up, she saw her name in first place on the leader board. She was so excited, she remembers looking up into the stands at her mother and her coach, Frank Carroll, and with tears in her eyes, yelling, "Mom! Frank! I won!"

THOUGH SHE WAS BEST KNOWN FOR HER JUMPING ABILITIES, LINDA FRATIANNE WAS ALSO EXTREMELY GRACEFUL ON THE ICE, AS SHOWN IN THIS LAYBACK.

There were still a few competitors who hadn't skated, and even though they were not likely to pose a serious threat, Carroll—described by Fratianne as her idol to this day—said, "Well, you have a couple of skaters to go."

Linda Fratianne's victory in Vienna meant more than just another gold medal; it was a victory over fear and self-doubt. ✳

KITTY AND PETER CARRUTHERS

"I was afraid to go to sleep."

Although their personal triumph at the Sarajevo Olympics in 1984 certainly stands out for Peter Carruthers, he recognizes an earlier moment as pivotal in helping him work toward that victory. Four years earlier, the Carruthers competed at the 1980 Olympic Games in Lake Placid, and Peter particularly remembers watching the U.S. hockey team win the gold medal. Just as with pairs figure skating, many considered the Soviet ice hockey team to be unbeatable. Few expected the U.S. team to be able to defeat the Soviets, and when they did, it inspired Peter. "It was exciting to see them realize their dream. It made me realize that with some hard work, maybe in another four years we would be able to get closer to realizing our own dream."

The Carruthers beat the odds themselves four years later at the Sarajevo Olympics when they skated the performances of their lives and won the silver medal. They both express how important it was to them that they experienced it all together, and that their whole family was there for them in the stands when they won.

Kitty remembers both of her Olympic experiences as being special, for different reasons. "Lake Placid was really special—competing in our first Olympics in our home country, being part of the opening ceremonies, sharing the excitement of the U.S. hockey team. . . . That was pretty big stuff for us. And our team was like a little family. Sarajevo was great for a lot of the same reasons, but the icing on the cake was skating the best that we could have possibly skated and winning a medal. And ours was the first medal won for the U.S. in that Games, which was a great feeling. I remember that night I was afraid to go to sleep. I was afraid I would wake up the next day and find out it had all just been an incredibly vivid, great dream." ✳

KITTY AND PETER CARRUTHERS WERE SURPRISE WINNERS OF SILVER MEDALS AT THE 1984 OLYMPICS IN SARAJEVO.

KRISTI YAMAGUCHI EARNED HER GOLD MEDAL WITH AN EVOCATIVE ROUTINE AT THE 1992 OLYMPIC WINTER GAMES.

CHAPTER SEVEN

CREATING A ROUTINE

*I*t's hard to believe that just a short time ago, the free-skating program occupied a relatively small part in the sport of figure skating. School figures dominated the sport, and the champion was the skater who could trace the best figure-eight patterns over and over again on a tiny patch of ice. The skater who captivated the audience with grace, style, and athletic prowess in the free-skating program often didn't even make it to the podium at the end of the competition. But today, all of that has changed. These days the program is everything and the champion is the skater who can put together all of the required elements with the greatest artistic flair within a few short minutes of music.

Whether you are a skater working on your own program or a fan who wants to know how the stars come up with their dazzling routines, this chapter should answer your questions. Creating a program is one of the most fun and creative things about being a skater. A good program reflects the skater's personality, from the whimsical and humorous side, to the romantic side, to the deep, insightful side. Whatever direction the program takes, it is important to love the music—whether it's Mozart, the Beatles, Gershwin, or Metallica—because the skater will be listening to it hundreds of times as she choreographs, rehearses, and performs a program. The music must continue to inspire her every step of the way.

AMERICAN SCOTT DAVIS BRINGS PERSONAL-ITY AND ENTHUSIASM TO HIS PERFORMANCE.

WHY, WHEN, AND WHAT?

The process of creating an effective program can be pursued in a variety of ways. But before the music is selected and the creating begins, there are questions every skater must consider:

1. Why are you doing this program? Will it be used for a competition, a test, an exhibition, or a personal challenge?

2. When is the program needed? How much time do you have to create and perfect it?

3. What skating moves or elements must you include and which ones do you choose?

Once these questions have been answered, you can select your music and begin to choreograph the program.

Elite skaters usually include a choreographer as part of their team, and what is covered in this chapter falls into that person's job description. But it's not just the big-name skaters who use choreographers these days. Because coaches find they need to concentrate more and more on the increasing technical demands placed on their skaters, choreographers have to be brought in to contribute the creative, expressive element needed in any competitive skater's program. At the lower levels, skaters meet with a choreographer and bring with them their music, a video of themselves skating, and a list of their strengths and their specific elements. At the higher levels, the choreographer takes a much more active role, working closely with the coach and skater to decide what will go into the program—from the music and costume to the placement of elements.

WHY? Once the purpose of the program is clear, it's time to define what should be included. For a competition or test, there are mandatory elements and a specific length of time. But the skater may have a more personal goal. Skaters create programs for reasons ranging from just having a challenging and fun cardiovascular workout to romantic birthday presents and get-well gifts (taped and sometimes sent across the country). When the program is to be used in this way, or in a show or exhibition, there is virtually no limit to what the skater can do musically or choreographically.

WHEN? Once you determine how much time you have to prepare the program, you'll know how demanding you can make it. The more time you have, the better off you'll be. Elite competitors generally begin working on new programs four to nine months in advance of the competitive season. The elements required for each season are normally decided upon by the ISU at their summer congress the year prior (for example, the moves required in the 1998–99 season were chosen at the 1997 summer congress). The skater's "team" begins planning the program around April, after the competitive season has ended. A singles or pairs program doesn't take long to lay out, but having it in rough shape by the start of summer gives the skater the chance to work through

BRIAN ORSER'S MEMORABLE FREE-SKATING PROGRAM AT THE 1988 OLYMPIC WINTER GAMES EARNED HIM THE SILVER MEDAL.

and refine it, as well as get feedback from judges and others whose opinions can make a difference. Ice dance choreography is more intricate and time-consuming because the choreographer doesn't spend time on consecutive crossovers for jumps, jump preparations, and spins. Some elite skaters will try programs out at lower-level competitions during the summer and early fall; others go straight into the preseason competitions that start in late August and September. Short and long programs are often created at the same time, one of each per season, unless a program proves extremely successful and it makes sense to keep it intact for another year or simply modify it for a new year.

If you have lots of time, you'll benefit from creating a program that is "a few sizes too large" for you. The jumps, spins, footwork, and movement should be within reach, but not yet doable with comfort or performance quality. That way, as you work on it, you'll be pushing your own envelope in all these areas each day. The challenge should make the day-to-day workout much more exciting.

For example, in the short program you may need to perform a jump combination consisting of at least one double. Let's say last year you did a double toe loop/double toe loop combination. This year you'll want to work toward doing a harder combination, like a double Lutz/double toe loop.

If your time frame for getting the program done is a short one, stick to moves that you know you can perform well under pressure now. Making the new choreography your own will be enough of a challenge without having to worry about new technical elements.

If, as you get closer to competition day, you're still consistently unsteady or falling on the new combination, with a slight adjustment on the entry, you can always go back to the jump you know you can land cleanly. While you want to challenge yourself during training to be a better skater, when it comes time to compete, you want to perform with confidence and style. So if you have to replace an inconsistent move at the eleventh hour, do it—and you will have the speed and confidence that comes with knowing you can skate a clean program. It's true that the judges will know the combination is easier, but it's better to perform an easier combination with speed and style than to perform a harder one more slowly and with great trepidation. Also, your artistic marks will benefit from a clean and confident performance.

When elite skaters create their new programs, they keep a backup plan for some of the harder jumps and combinations. For example, if they have a triple Axel/triple toe loop planned early in the program, but they leave out the triple toe loop, they may be able to add it on in combination with another jump later in the program. Or if they are struggling with an injury, they may be able to replace jumps that cause pain with jumps that put less strain on the injury.

MICHAEL WEISS OFTEN LEAVES ROOM IN HIS PROGRAMS FOR AN ATTEMPT AT A QUADRUPLE JUMP.

WHAT? Once you know your deadline, make a list of what elements you'll need and want to have in the program. Almost all competitions require specific moves based on your level. For example, under the USFSA system, an intermediate ladies' skater has specific requirements for jumps, spins, footwork, and edge work that are different from a senior man or an adult bronze-level skater. Under other competitive systems, such as the Ice Skating Institute (ISI), requirements for an intermediate ladies' skater can be different.

Rules to be considered before selecting music are the required length of the program and whether or not vocals are allowed. For example, in a USFSA competition, the senior ladies' free-skate program must be four minutes long. There is some leeway, in that the program may be ten seconds shorter or longer and still be acceptable. And USFSA tests and competitions do not allow vocals in the music; with a narrow exception for the senior-level original dance program, the skater may use only instrumental music. So before you choose your music, consult with your coach and rulebook to determine all the requirements you will have to meet. Within the requirements, the skater has many choices as to which elements to use to gain the best competitive advantage. The free skate has no required elements, but it should include as much technical content as can be executed in an artistically pleasing manner. For exhibition pieces, the music will dictate the moves.

GETTING STARTED — SELECTING THE MUSIC

Selecting the music is probably the most important decision toward making a memorable program. Almost everyone at any given level will be performing similar elements—though with a few interesting variations and some stronger in technique than others. So the one thing that can make a program memorable to an audience regardless of a skater's relative technical strength, is how deeply he or she connects with and conveys the emotion of the music. Therefore, no matter what the ultimate purpose of the program is, a sure way to gain an advantage is to choose a piece of music you really love.

SELECTING MUSIC FOR A COMPETITIVE PROGRAM OR TEST

Again, the music usually cannot have lyrics and must be a specific length—based on the skater's competition level. Smart skaters choose music that highlights their strengths and minimizes their weaknesses, something with climactic moments for the jumps, fast-paced segments for footwork sequences, and slow segments for spiral sequences and deep edge work. Most skaters or coaches edit the music to alternate the pace and allow for some rest between the more demanding sections of the program.

Age, body type, and personality should also affect the music selected. If you are tall, long, and lithe, you'll want music that highlights your long line, like Debussy's "Prelude to the Afternoon of a Faun." By the same token, if you have a powerful, athletic frame, and can handle the explosive demands of the music, Leonard Bernstein's "On the Waterfront" could be extremely effective. No matter what your body type, if you have a problem with a certain style of expression, like long graceful spirals, or quick, choppy footwork, then stay away from music that cries out for that style of movement.

When you skate a program, you are essentially assuming a character for those few minutes, and you'll want to take on a character that the judges and audience will find believable. Everyone knows that Scott Hamilton is a fun-loving guy with a terrific sense of humor. You're not likely to see him skate to a Wagner opera—unless he's making fun of it. And as playful as Katarina Witt can be, it is highly unlikely that she would skate to "Thumbelina," or that Tara Lipinski would do Kurt Browning's version of the Commodores' "Brick House." To do so would be to play a character outside of their believable range; it wouldn't make sense and the audience would be left scratching their heads. When Michelle Kwan first competed at the senior ladies' level, at the age of thirteen, she could not have pulled off a program portraying the character of Salome. But three years later, she had developed the maturity and expressiveness to do it so well that it earned her U.S. and World titles.

Some people are fortunate to be versatile enough to pull off classical and contemporary, as well as offbeat styles of music. Kristi Yamaguchi is a perfect example: She can skate a slow, classical piece like "Romeo and Juliet" and follow it up with a sexy, funky contemporary piece like "Your Favorite Dish."

Another factor that may influence the music selection is knowing who else will be appearing in the competition. While you'll need to pick music that will distinguish you from your competitors in the eyes of the audience and judges, don't do something just to be different—unless you know you can pull it off. If you can't do hip-hop, don't try. If you skate to something that doesn't move you, the audience will see that and won't enjoy it as much. And, if you skate to something that doesn't fit you, the audience will feel uneasy.

EDITING YOUR MUSIC

In competitive programs, it is extremely rare to use a piece of music without having to edit it. There are so many things that need to be accomplished in the program, no single two and a half to four and a half minute piece of music can accomplish it all, with the possible exception of a Broadway overture or a medley that covers many different songs in one continuous instrumental piece. Whatever you choose, you should have a clear vision of what you want the finished piece to sound like before you meet with the music editor.

DEBI THOMAS AT THE 1988 CALGARY OLYMPICS, AS SHE SKATES THE ENERGETIC PERFORMANCE FOR WHICH SHE WON THE BRONZE MEDAL.

When it comes to editing different pieces of music together, find pieces that complement each other. Your audience won't enjoy hearing Dave Grusin's beautiful slow piano music from "On Golden Pond" mixed with a strident, brassy John Philip Sousa march. You might choose to stick with one orchestral work, but use different movements. That way you are more likely to have an internally consistent program. Kristi Yamaguchi did this with her Olympic gold medal–winning program in 1992 to Lecuoma's "Malaguena," and Paul Wylie did it that same year with the music from the movie soundtrack to "Henry V."

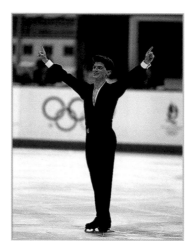

PAUL WYLIE (ABOVE) USED THE STIR-RING MUSIC FROM THE MOVIE "HENRY V" AT THE 1992 OLYMPIC WINTER GAMES. OKSANA BAIUL (RIGHT) PERFORMED A VERY TRADI-TIONAL, BALLETIC PROGRAM FOR HER FREE SKATE AT THE 1994 GAMES IN LILLEHAMMER.

CHOREOGRAPHING THE PROGRAM

Once the goal, elements, and music have been established, it's time to start putting it all together on the ice. Decide where in the program you would like to put certain elements and com-municate that to the choreographer. The way I like to work when I am choreographing a pro-gram is first to lay out the placement of all the main elements in the program. The skater must be happy with the placement of the technical elements, especially if it's a competition or test program. The most difficult jump should be early in the program—perhaps within the first forty-five to sixty seconds—when the skater is fresh, not at the end when the skater is extremely tired. Also, the placement of each element should be well rounded. Don't put two out of three spins in the same place, or all the jumps in the first half of a program.

When laying out the program, I always establish where the judges will sit in relation to the skater's starting position. Then I can plan the patterns to give the judges the best angle from which to see each move. When creating your own layout, allow yourself enough time to reach the place on the ice (for your element) at the right place in the music. Each phrase of the music should highlight the element it goes with. But it's always more important to hit the move than to be "on the music." As you choreograph the preparation or entry into each element, make sure that you have enough speed and time to take that special moment you may need to set up your jump.

Now it's a matter of connecting the "dots"—that is, putting the elements as they occur on the specific musical indications. But as you do so, allow yourself the freedom to change the game plan if it will fit the music. For example, you may decide to step into a spiral sequence where you'd planned the layback spin. The most important thing is to be as true to the music as possible while including all the nec-essary elements.

Mapping a Routine

Although a well-performed program appears to be almost unplanned, in fact every moment has been plotted out, timed, and practiced according to this kind of choreographic blueprint. This diagram maps out a sample short program, with each jump, spin, and step sequence in place. The choreographer has prepared this with the required moves and the music to be used in mind, spacing out the elements physically across the ice and for maximum impact in concert with the music. The skater then learns this seemingly random swirl of lines and begins to bring it to life on the ice. Here, photos of Tara Lipinski illustrate some of the moves.

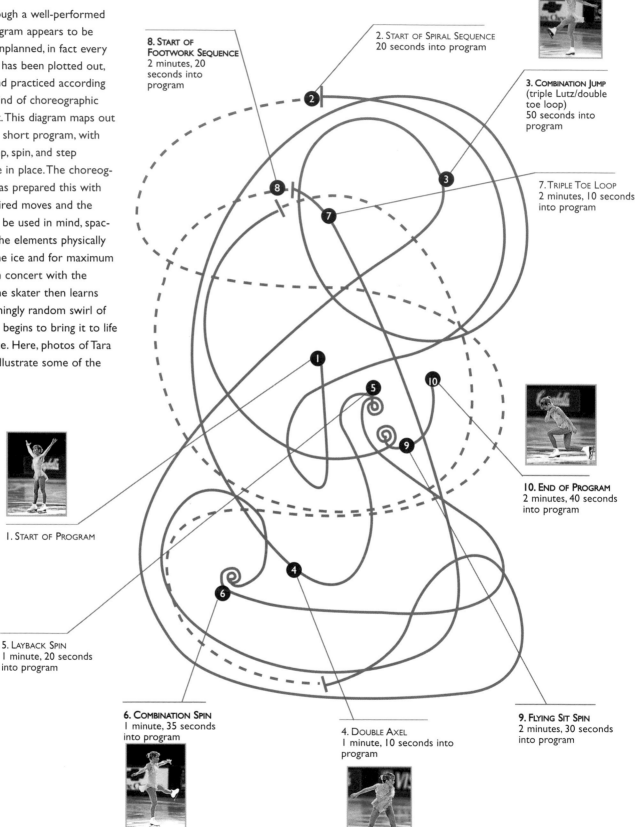

8. Start of Footwork Sequence
2 minutes, 20 seconds into program

2. Start of Spiral Sequence
20 seconds into program

3. Combination Jump
(triple Lutz/double toe loop)
50 seconds into program

7. Triple Toe Loop
2 minutes, 10 seconds into program

10. End of Program
2 minutes, 40 seconds into program

1. Start of Program

5. Layback Spin
1 minute, 20 seconds into program

6. Combination Spin
1 minute, 35 seconds into program

4. Double Axel
1 minute, 10 seconds into program

9. Flying Sit Spin
2 minutes, 30 seconds into program

When laying out your program, cover as much ice as possible and keep the pattern on the ice interesting. Don't skate in little circles in the center of the ice, or follow the same pattern over and over. And make sure you're not doing all of your best moves in the same spot.

It is important to feel free to try different things. The first new move you try may be interesting, but the third or fourth variation you try may be great. Be inventive. See if you can come up with a new way to enter a jump, or a new arm position. Brian Boitano came up with doing a spread eagle right before his triple Lutz, holding one arm high over his head during the jump. He named the move the 'Tano Lutz. Paul Wylie does a straight spiral right into his triple flip jump; the spiral sets him up well technically (nice and straight), and it also happens to be breathtakingly beautiful. The combination also surprises the audience members because they don't expect to see the triple flip jump right after a spiral.

BE AN ACTOR

Many choreographers and skaters like to create a "story" to inspire the movement. The most effective performers on ice are those who express themselves through their moves and convey the emotional life of the story and the character. Even if no one in the audience ever gets the story or who the character is, it gives the skater a specific point of view, an emotion to express through his or her moves.

Capture the audience's attention at the beginning of the program with something compelling or charming. Establish your character within the first fifteen seconds of music. This opening movement can be done in a small area or on a pattern, weaving or going straight down the ice. Once you get to the other end, change the pattern to begin your preparation for your first element—a jump, spin, edge move, or footwork. Always keep your pattern moving and flowing.

AS WELL KNOWN AS HE WAS FOR HIS JUMPING, BRIAN BOITANO WAS ALSO AN INNOVATOR. HERE, HE LEANS INTO A SPREAD EAGLE IN PREPARATION FOR HIS TRIPLE LUTZ JUMP.

I always tell my sweet, shy students that their character on the ice may not be anything like them. Perhaps the character they're portraying is the very boastful Peter Pan, or a bird soaring over forests and through the Grand Canyon. Off the ice they can be sweet and shy, but once that music begins, they must become the character. They soon discover that it's wonderful fun to play-act as someone else. Regardless of the character you're portraying, shy body language—stiff arms low and close to the body, rounded shoulders, and poor posture—just won't fill the bill.

I remember performing a piece to Stravinsky's "Tango, Tango" with 1976 Olympic Champion John Curry. It was first created for his Broadway show *Ice Dancing*. Peter Martins, who choreographed it for us, was a principal dancer with the New York City Ballet (and is now its resident director/choreographer). He created a fresh and unique piece totally unlike anything a skater would have thought up. But despite all of us trying as hard as we could, the piece wasn't working. Then the show's director, acclaimed Tony award–winning Broadway director Ruth Mitchell,

sat us down in the theater the afternoon before we opened and said, "It's not believable or interesting because you're just going through the motions. You're not feeling that burning 'Latin' passion that should be erupting beneath the surface of the steps of a tango."

I thought, "Well, I'm a California blonde with Irish roots, John is an Englishman and we were choreographed by a Dane, but, hey, if it's steamy Latin passion they want, I'll give it my best shot." Ruth said she'd rather we overdo it and let her pull us back. Since the sky was the limit, I really let myself go! My melodramatic "Tango Lady" was great fun in juxtaposition to John's serious, intense, steamy Valentino. Ruth was right. It worked. The critics and audiences loved it. The characters grew every time we performed the piece (which turned out to be a lot, all around the world).

The lesson here is: It's not always what you do, but how you do it that counts.

Consider the style and mood of your character when you're creating steps or arm movements. Rent a video or read some books that could give you some glimpses into the character. If you're skating to a piece of classical ballet music, try to rent the video of a performance of it. You'll gain lots of insight as to costuming as well as how to use your arms, feet, and head. If your music is a 1930s or 1940s Cole Porter or Irving Berlin kind of piece, rent a Fred Astaire/Ginger Rogers movie and soak up their sophisticated elegance. The theater and dance world are infinite resources of inspiration for skaters. When my pairs partner Ken Shelley and I were doing Gershwin's "Slaughter on 10th Avenue," we rented *An American in Paris* to watch Cyd Charisse and Gene Kelly's steamy dancing. Even if you don't come away with a single step, you'll understand more about the essence of your character and it will have an impact on your creativity.

TEMPO AND PHRASING

Sometimes, when working with fast-tempo music, a skater will want each beat to have a step or arm or head movement; at other times she'll want to use only every second beat or every fourth beat. Ultimately, she must choose the tempo and rhythm that works best for her skating. The music is your leader, but the skater shouldn't let it force her into a tempo that makes her skating look sloppy, unsteady, or out of control.

In skating, "phrasing" is the placement of the movements in relation to the music. A lot of skaters use very slow music but fill each phrase with three times as many movements as there are beats or chords. An example would be Jenni Meno and Todd Sand in their 1998 Olympic program to "Pomp and Circumstance." When I first learned they were using it, I thought the movements would be very slow and held. Then I saw it. This section of their program is full of movement that is more complex and fast-paced than the slow, even, and deliberate chords of "Pomp and Circumstance." But still they managed to keep the integrity of the music with their elegance, technical prowess, and the deliberate phrasing.

MAKE THOSE CHALLENGES WORK FOR YOU

Once I was choreographing a short program for David Liu, a brilliantly artistic skater who was representing Chinese Taipei in the Olympics. David had been trained in classical ballet at the School of American Ballet, the training ground for dancers for the New York City Ballet under George Balanchine, so from the start I knew I was working with a great and well-trained talent. For his 1992 Olympic short program, David had chosen music from the movie *The Mission*. This piece inspired him personally and artistically, and he was committed to it. My challenge was that the music was almost all slow, and doing footwork sequences to slow music generally doesn't garner very high marks from judges. The only fast portion was the forty-five second opening in which we put a fast circular footwork sequence and a double Axel. While it was a joy to choreograph to the lush slow orchestrations, I had to include another footwork sequence. So to give it a much greater degree of difficulty, I made David do it all on one foot.

At first David thought he couldn't do it, but once we did basic power pulls on one foot—outside, inside, outside, inside, both forward and backward—he saw that the knee action kept the flow going without putting the other foot down. Then we added a variety of turns, hops, and twizzles. In no time, he had a fascinating straight-line footwork sequence on one foot from one end of the rink to the other.

JoJo Starbuck and Ken Shelley won three U.S. Pairs Championships, and finished third at the 1971 and 1972 World Championships.

It greatly impressed the audience and judges, and helped both his technical and artistic marks.

IF YOU HAVE A CHOREOGRAPHER

Different choreographers work in different ways. Some of them map out a program on paper in great detail, while others have a general idea of what they want to do, then engage in an improvisational give-and-take with the skater to work out the specifics of what looks best with the skater's body. Your choreographer may ask you to try things that you've never done before, things that may feel silly or uncomfortable. But keep in mind that your choreographer wants you to look good. If you look silly, it won't make the choreographer look good, so trust that the choreographer is on your team.

Believe it or not, there are some basic steps that even elite skaters can't do with much finesse. It's like clothes: A great step is no good if it doesn't look good on you. (I once worked with an extremely accomplished and artistic Olympic champion who had trouble with a relatively simple Bob Fosse–style step that we were using for a finale.) Both you and the choreographer have to be attuned to which moves look best on you.

REHEARSING THE PROGRAM

Ice rinks come in all different sizes, and you need to find out the size of the ice on which you will be performing your program. If you're practicing on big ice, yet you know the ice you'll be performing on is smaller, you'll need to rehearse your program using cones (either real or imaginary) to simulate the size of the performance ice. Nothing can throw you off during a performance worse than almost running into the boards because you're used to bigger ice.

If the thought of skating through the whole program is overwhelming, don't worry. Every skater feels that way at first. To build the stamina to get through the program, just move ahead one step at a time. Skate through the program without the difficult elements, performing only the steps, stroking, and easier moves. But skate through it with as much speed and style as possible. Once you can do that, begin to add the harder elements, one or two at a time. Do the whole program with the first few difficult elements, and then add more each day until you can get through the whole program. Once you've done that, add three fast laps of stroking after the program. Then, when you can do that, add a jump or two or three after the laps.

You can't really overprepare for a performance. The nerves, pressure, and spotlights usually take away from a skater's personal best, and there will always be an unpredictable last-minute issue. So the more you have prepared, the more you will be ready to deal with any unexpected problem.

Always, with every run-through of your program, push yourself to enhance your style, posture, and flow. If you do, you'll be getting through that program quicker than you think, and your general skating will improve as well.

AND FINALLY

I've known Peggy Fleming since I was a kid learning to skate in California. As long as I can remember, whenever I've asked her about her plans, or her programs, or anything, she always started her reply with, "Well, I really wanted to have fun with this, so. . . ." I think that's great advice for everything in life. Don't get too intense over your skating goals; if you do, you'll lose the joy of your skating. While it can be consuming and it's lots of work, don't ever forget to have fun and smile! Those are the most important ingredients for creating a program. ✳

IN EXHIBITIONS, COMPETITIVE SKATERS SUCH AS ILIA KULIK HAVE THE CHANCE TO EXPRESS THEMSELVES IN SOME LESS TRADITIONAL WAYS USING MUSIC, OUTFITS, AND EVEN CERTAIN MOVES THAT ARE NOT SEEN IN STANDARD PROGRAMS.

NANCY KERRIGAN

"For those two performances, it all just came together."

TO NANCY KERRIGAN, THE TWO BEST PERFORMANCES OF HER LIFE WERE AT THE 1994 OLYMPIC WINTER GAMES IN LILLEHAMMER, WHERE SHE WON THE SILVER MEDAL.

If I had to narrow it down," Nancy Kerrigan says, "I would have to say my last two amateur performances, at the Olympics in Lillehammer." Kerrigan makes a clear distinction between her 1994 Olympic experience as a whole—which was dominated by the media frenzy around her and Tonya Harding—and her moments alone performing on the ice.

"The overall experience was very stressful, completely different from the 1992 Olympics," Kerrigan says. "In Albertville I had a lot of fun and felt I was part of the team, whereas in 1994 I felt alienated. Even going to the cafeteria in the Village, people would stare at me like I was some kind of freak."

The stress of Kerrigan's off-ice experience in Lillehammer made her time on the ice that much more pleasurable. "On the ice I felt free and comfortable and relaxed." There were no bodyguards or press on the ice, and she could just enjoy herself.

Although she'd had more fun in Albertville, Kerrigan had not been satisfied with the way she skated there. "I did okay, and well enough to get a medal, but I didn't do what I had been training to do." Her goal in 1994, even before she was clubbed on the knee at the U.S. Championships, was to better withstand the pressure of competition. She had sometimes struggled with remaining focused throughout both the short and free-skate programs, but in 1994 she was determined to change that.

"I have no idea how I was able to do it," Kerrigan says. "Something just clicked and I was in a zone for the seven weeks between nationals and the Olympics. It was automatic. I focused on healing and on training, and I worked much harder than I ever had in my life." Kerrigan practiced her programs until she could perform them twice in a row with no mistakes or omissions. "It gave me the confidence that one time through would be relatively easy."

The hard work paid off. She gave the two best performances of her life, back to back.

"The feeling in the arena each time I stepped on the ice was overwhelming. I think people were proud that I could even show up and be there after being injured. I believe you're capable of more than you ever think you are, and it's only when you're faced with a situation that really tests you that you realize what you can do. You always try to do your best—some days it works and some days it doesn't. For those two performances, it all just came together." ✳

ELIZABETH PUNSALAN AND JEROD SWALLOW

"We were proud of ourselves."

Both Elizabeth Punsalan and Jerod Swallow remember the 1994 U.S. Championships—the first time they qualified for the Olympic team—as one of the highlights of their career.

They had won the U.S. title in 1991, but in 1992 they came in third, and didn't make the 1992 Olympic team. Going into the 1994 championships, they knew that only one dance team would be allowed to go to the Olympics, and they didn't want to be disappointed again. The pressure was intense.

Punsalan remembers that as "a special time" in their lives. "We had just gotten married the previous September," she explains, "and to have the nationals in our home town where all our family and friends could be there was wonderful."

"It was quite a celebration," Swallow says. "Everyone we could have possibly wanted to be there for us was right there. It seemed as if the entire arena was either from our neighborhood or from where we had grown up. Each corner we went around, we heard or saw someone that we recognized."

Swallow believes the familiar atmosphere allowed them to perform their best. He and Punsalan won the title and the coveted spot on the Olympic team.

"It was a dramatic week," Punsalan remembers, "and it was so important to me that my father was still alive to see us make the team."

Her birthday fell that same week, and during the exhibition performance after the competition, the announcer made a big deal about it. The entire crowd of twenty thousand sang "Happy Birthday" to her.

PUNSALAN AND SWALLOW WERE AMERICA'S LEADING ICE DANCING TEAM THROUGH MOST OF THE 1990S.

To Swallow, the 1998 Olympics were also very important. "It wasn't just the competition, but being with the other athletes and experiencing their highs and lows and getting to know them," he says. "If I had to choose one performance as a highlight, it would probably be our free dance there. It was a brand-new program, it was the first time we had debuted it before an audience, and to perform so well under those circumstances was extremely elating.... I think the main thing about Nagano is that we were proud of ourselves and satisfied with what we had done, regardless of our placement. That's a great feeling when all the expectations of medals are thrown away, and you can just be satisfied with your skating." ❋

MICHELLE KWAN AT THE 1998 U.S. CHAMPIONSHIPS IN PHILADELPHIA.

CHAPTER EIGHT

COMPETITION

The final two steps to a championship's podium are the end of a long and challenging road. While for millions of people on lakes and rinks and ponds across the country, learning how to skate with confidence and style is satisfaction enough, there are others who go beyond the simple pleasures of skating to test themselves, to try their skills and abilities against others. For them, skating is more than a pastime or a recreation; it is a competitive sport.

One of the reasons for the founding of the USFSA was to create a system of standards and competitions for skating in the United States. In theory, anyone can climb to the top of the skating world if they have the talent, determination, time, and persistence. Elite skaters aren't picked in a draft or recruited by major league teams; they are people who have used their abilities to rise through the competitive structure created in the 1920s and 1930s by the USFSA, a structure open to all qualified members. Of course, not every skater who wants to compete aims for the Olympics. And the USFSA provides competitions at every level as well as different kinds of competitions. This chapter lays out what types of skating competitions there are and, later, goes into depth about the history of each discipline and what takes place for each during a competition.

To qualify for USFSA competitions, a skater must be an amateur and must belong to the USFSA—most belong to a skating club affiliated with the USFSA. There are approximately 500 affiliated skating clubs in the United States (listed in the Skating Clubs section in back), and even the most famous gold medal–winning skater belongs to a club with members ranging from children just learning crossovers to senior citizens who remember seeing Sonja Henie. The USFSA skating clubs offer lessons with basic learn-to-skate programs such as Skate with U.S., and it is at their club where most member skaters take the tests that move them up through the eight levels of skating expertise.

Currently, the eight levels are Pre-Preliminary, Preliminary, Pre-Juvenile, Juvenile, Intermediate, Novice, Junior, and Senior. (There is no Pre-Juvenile level for Pairs.) Getting to the highest levels of free-skating competition involves passing through these eight levels. As young skaters such as Tara Lipinski and Michelle Kwan have shown, there's no set time for how long it takes a skater to pass up the ladder;

THE MARIBEL VINSON OWEN TROPHY, AWARDED TO THE U.S. SENIOR LADIES' FIGURE SKATING CHAMPION.

REGIONS OF THE U.S. FIGURE SKATING ASSOCIATION

The USFSA divides up the United States into three sections, which are in turn broken down into nine regions.

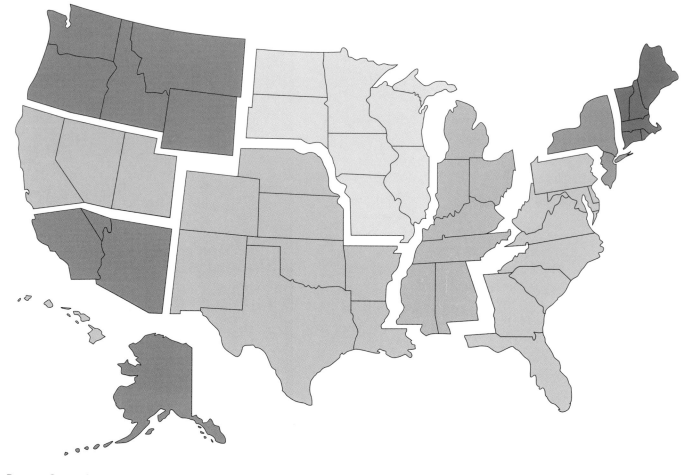

PACIFIC COAST SECTION:

CENTRAL PACIFIC REGION: California (including Visalia and all cities north thereof), Hawaii, Nevada (excluding Las Vegas, Nevada), Utah, and, for Precision only, Colorado teams

NORTHWEST PACIFIC REGION: Alaska, Idaho, Montana, Oregon, Washington, Wyoming (excluding Casper, Wyoming)

SOUTHWEST PACIFIC REGION: Arizona, California (including all cities south of Visalia, California), and Las Vegas, Nevada

MIDWESTERN SECTION:

EASTERN GREAT LAKES REGION: Alabama, Indiana, Kentucky, Lower Peninsula of Michigan, Mississippi, Ohio, Tennessee (excluding Chattanooga, Tennessee)

SOUTHWESTERN REGION: Arkansas, Colorado, Kansas (including the greater Kansas City area and St. Joseph, Missouri), Louisiana, Nebraska, New Mexico, Oklahoma, Texas, and Casper, Wyoming, except that, for Precision only, Colorado teams are excluded

UPPER GREAT LAKES REGION: Illinois, Iowa, Upper Peninsula of Michigan, Minnesota, Missouri (excluding the greater Kansas City area and St. Joseph, Missouri), North Dakota, South Dakota, Wisconsin

EASTERN SECTION:

NEW ENGLAND REGION: Connecticut, Maine, Massachusetts, New Hampshire, Rhode Island, Vermont

NORTH ATLANTIC REGION: New Jersey, New York, and Erie, Pennsylvania

SOUTH ATLANTIC REGION: Delaware, District of Columbia, Florida, Georgia, Maryland, North Carolina, Pennsylvania (excluding Erie, Pennsylvania), South Carolina, Virginia, West Virginia, Chattanooga, Tennessee

her talent and determination will decide where she is placed. Each level has two tests: Moves in the Field and Free Skating. The Moves in the Field test requires skaters to perform certain moves and skating skills appropriate for the level. For example, the Pre-Preliminary test requires displays of forward perimeter stroking, basic consecutive edges, and waltz edges; the Preliminary level tests types of three-turns, spirals, and crossovers; all the way up to the sustained edge step and power double inside and outside rockers at the Senior level. Once a skater has passed the Moves test at a level, he or she is allowed to take the Free Skating test for that level. Ice dancers face a thirteen-step test structure, with a compulsory dance test and a free dance test at each level. More than sixty thousand tests are given each year by USFSA figure skating clubs as skaters across the country try to test up to the next level. For skaters twenty-five and over, there is an Adult test structure for Free Skating and Dance, and a Masters test structure for Dance for those over fifty.

THE TOP FOUR LADIES' FINISHERS AT THE 1996 U.S. CHAMPIONSHIPS. FROM LEFT, TONIA KWIATKOWSKI (SECOND PLACE), MICHELLE KWAN (FIRST PLACE), TARA LIPINSKI (THIRD PLACE), SYDNE VOGEL (FOURTH PLACE).

Skaters have a lot of choices as to how they want to pursue their sport; they can be as serious as they want to be. A skater moving up through the levels doesn't have to compete—gaining a desired level of proficiency is the goal of most skaters. But those who do want to compete have two kinds of competitions to choose from: qualifying and nonqualifying.

Nonqualifying competitions include club competitions, open competitions, and competition levels below Juvenile. These competitions are not part of the annual series of competitions that lead to the U.S. Championships—and possibly beyond to the international level. A skater's performance in any of these has no bearing on his or her rise through the USFSA competition structure. Some elite skaters perform in these competitions to try out new routines, while up-and-coming skaters often compete so as to be seen by judges and to gain experience.

Qualifying competitions lead to the annual U.S. Championships. The USFSA breaks the United States into nine regions, and each region hosts a championship, usually in October or November. Regionals are one of the most exciting and entertaining aspects of figure skating in the United States. These competitions are open to all qualified member skaters in each region, so the number of entrants can be high and the skills varied. Often, qualifying rounds are needed to separate those who will compete for the titles. Everyone has a chance, though, to show what they can do. The regionals are skating at its most democratic.

The top finishers at the nine regionals earn spots at the three sectionals in December or early January, and the top four finishers in each discipline there advance to the U.S. Championships, held in late January or early February. The U.S. Figure

Skating Championships rotate every year between the three sections of the country. The field of entrants starts with the twelve sectional qualifiers in the four disciplines—Men's, Ladies', Pairs, and Dance—and at three levels of competition—Novice, Junior, and Championship levels.

In some cases, the USFSA adds to those entry lists for a variety of reasons. Top finishers from the previous year receive automatic "byes" and do not have to participate at regionals or sectionals, and other individuals or teams who have fared well at the U.S. Championships the previous year and represent the United States at the international events that could be held at the same time as the sectionals may ask for and receive "byes" into the U.S. Championships. Injury "byes" are also possible for established skaters. In this way, the fates can be balanced so that the very best Men's, Ladies', Pairs, and Dance skaters will have every chance to take part and help determine worthy U.S. champions. One bad performance, one slip, won't destroy an entire year's work.

Many skaters and their entourages, including coaches and family, begin arriving at the U.S. Championships site on the weekend prior to the events. That gives everyone ample time to become acclimated and comfortable in the surroundings, and it provides each competitor or team a sufficient number of practices. The practice groups are drawn at random far in advance, so all competitors know who will be in what session. Also, the different groups rotate their skating order for performing their routine with music at each practice, to be as fair as possible.

Sometimes different rinks can have different shapes, particularly in the corners, and the workouts give skaters the chance to make sure their programs "fit" the surface, and allow them time to get acclimated to the conditions. Another reason for participating in those practices is to check the music—sometimes it can play faster or slower than at home, and that can have a major effect on a tightly packed choreographed program. Most skaters consider looking consistently solid at practice a top priority.

By Monday night, the figures and novice events are done, and the juniors and seniors are ready to take their turn. From Tuesday through Saturday, short and free-skating programs in Men's and Pairs, compulsory original and free dances for Ice Dancing, and the Ladies' short program, build to the Ladies' free skate on Saturday night. At the end of each discipline's competition, a winner is crowned.

At the Championship level, the winners in each discipline also win a place on the team representing the United States at the World Championships. The other places on the team are selected by a committee that considers a number of factors, including a skater's performance at the U.S. Championships along with the rest of the skater's other performances that year and whether they've represented the United States in the past. ✳

AMERICAN MICHAEL WEISS DISPLAYS THE POWER NECESSARY IN MEN'S SKATING TODAY.

MEN'S

From the earliest English skating clubs, which required top-hatted dandies to leap over chairs and scribe complicated figures into the ice, to today's small group of quadruple jumpers, men's skating has pushed the limits of what is possible on ice. But if innovation has been a constant, so has competition. Though no one can pinpoint exactly when the first competitive men's figure skating meet took place, it can reasonably be placed somewhere in the mid-nineteenth century, when skating anchored itself in the popular culture of the United States and Europe.

Jackson Haines, creator of the International style, is credited with winning the first "Championship of America" in 1863. After Haines's death in 1875, the city of Vienna hosted what is widely believed to be the first world competition. Leopold Frey, a student of Haines's, won the event and received as his prize a silver trophy bearing the likeness of his skating mentor.

Seven years later, Norwegian Axel Paulsen displayed a jump that revolutionized figure skating. Paulsen, an accomplished speed skater, skated forward into a jump, made one and a half turns in the air, and landed skating backwards. Nothing like this had ever been seen before, and so here, in the creation of the "Axel" jump, was the beginning of the athleticism that predominates in men's skating today, at the close of the twentieth century.

With the establishment of the ISU in 1891, the first World Championships were held, in St. Petersburg, Russia, in 1896, featuring only figures. Gilbert Fuchs of Germany won that year, but Sweden's Ulrich Salchow, the following year's silver medalist, would make a greater impact on the sport than even Paulsen. Salchow not only won three silvers and an unmatched ten golds at the Worlds, he also was awarded the first Olympic gold medal for Men's figure skating and invented the jump that still bears his name. No one came close to equaling Salchow's competitive record, and the combination of his technical skill and creative imagination helped the emerging sport build standards and establish validity.

Salchow finally handed over the World title in 1912 to Fritz Kachler, launching an Austrian dynasty that lasted almost a quarter of a century. From 1912 to 1938, Austrian men won the World Championship sixteen out of twenty times. The only non-Austrian to break through their ranks was Gillis Grafstrom, a Swede who won three consecutive Olympic gold medals between 1920 and 1928, the Olympic silver medal in 1932, and three World titles (1922, 1924, and 1929).

Given that the first U.S. Championship in the International style wasn't held until 1914, American men had a good deal of ground to cover just to catch up with

AXEL PAULSEN OF NORWAY IN 1885. INVENTOR OF THE AXEL JUMP, PAULSEN WAS ALSO A SKILLED SPEED SKATER, WHICH EXPLAINS HIS POSE AND HIS LONG SKATES.

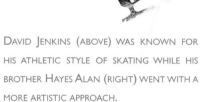

the rest of the world. Despite the considerable skills of early champions Nathaniel Niles and Sherwin Badger, it took until 1930, when seven-time American champion Roger Turner won a silver, for an American man to win a medal at the Worlds. Turner again won silver in 1931, and those two medals were the sum of American men's pre–World War II medals at the World Championships and Olympics.

World War II changed everything. Although some of the weakness of European teams was understandably due to nearly ten years of Nazi deprecations, the change in post-war skating was more accurately a positive expression of the skills of one man—Dick Button—and the style of skating he brought to the sport. New Jersey native Button did not placidly glide about the ice—he burst across it. His jumps were explosive—high and long and full of the American power that was making itself felt all over the world. Button awoke modern skating to the potentials within its moves; two consecutive Axels in a routine had previously been considered a triumph, but Dick Button began doing double and triple jumps, redefining what skating could look like and what it should demand of the athlete. Though it would be decades before the sixty/forty judging ratio between figures and the free skate would be abandoned, Button's remarkable style and skill brought the ratio into question. From 1946 to 1952, he won seven U.S. Championships, five consecutive World titles, and two Olympic gold medals.

Between 1947 and 1960, American men continued Button's mastery of the sport, winning twenty-six out of forty-two possible medals at the Worlds and seven out of twelve medals at the Olympics. Brothers Hayes Alan and David Jenkins each won an Olympic gold, while Ronald Robertson made history without enormous leaps—his art was spinning. The speed of Robertson's spins—reportedly at a rate of between seven and ten revolutions per second—remains unsurpassed.

But power and technique were certainly not the only factors in the Americans' success. Dick Button's image had done as much to establish men's skating in the modern age as his skating style. Putting aside the leggings of pre–World War II skaters, Button wore the trousers and military-style jacket which had become familiar to most Americans—many of whom were former servicemen—and lent men's skating a heartier, more patriotic air.

The energy and style of the American men spread to the rest of

DAVID JENKINS (ABOVE) WAS KNOWN FOR HIS ATHLETIC STYLE OF SKATING WHILE HIS BROTHER HAYES ALAN (RIGHT) WENT WITH A MORE ARTISTIC APPROACH.

the men's division, as well as to the ladies' and pairs. At the 1962 World Championships in Prague, Canadian Donald Jackson, skating in the same athletic style as the U.S. men, became the first person to perform a triple Lutz jump in competition.

The Americans had become accustomed to being on top of the figure skating world, but a horrible tragedy interrupted their success. In 1961, the entire U.S. team and many of its coaches were killed in a plane crash on the way to the World Championships. The national skating program was seemingly decimated, but a new crop of American skaters would soon produce fresh victories. Just three years after the plane crash, fourteen-year-old Scott Ethan Allen won the bronze at the 1964 Olympics and took silver the following year at the Worlds. Gary Visconti followed Allen's accomplishment with bronze at the 1966 and 1967 Worlds. Then Tim Wood stepped forward for a silver at both the 1968 Olympics and Worlds, and went on to win two consecutive World titles in 1969 and 1970, the first American man to do so since David Jenkins in 1959.

One American man who advanced men's skating in the mid-1960s was John Misha Petkevich. With electrifying aerial performances, Petkevich began a movement away from the traditional models of men's skating. He was an unparalleled free skater, but his figures were not at the same level. And since he was never able to compensate for his low marks there, he never won a medal in a World or Olympic competition—though he did win gold at the 1971 U.S. Championships. Still, his influence was deep; while some felt he went over the top in his presentation, many welcomed his departure from the stiff-backed style of the era. Ultimately, the rules and what was "acceptable" began to change; In the mid-1970s, competitive requirements were altered to put more emphasis on free skating. The new rules also brought more jumping—American Terry Kubicka went so far as to perform a back flip in the 1976 Olympics, a move that was quickly banned from competition—and some of the day's dominant skaters, such as East German Jan Hoffman, Soviet Vladimir Kovalev, and American Charles Tickner, used jumping to great effect. The shift also introduced a return to a more dance-centered approach. Toller Cranston of Canada and Robin Cousins of Great Britain took popular and modern dance as their inspiration, while Great Britain's John Curry went back to Nijinsky and classical ballet, sometimes mystifying judges as he ventured into new artistic grounds.

Scott Hamilton's victory at the 1981 World Championships in Hartford, Connecticut, heralded an era in which excellence in men's skating would be judged against a single standard. Good-natured and eloquent, Hamilton matched his matu-

BEFORE THE JENKINS BROTHERS CAME ALONG, DICK BUTTON (ABOVE) HAD PAVED THE WAY IN THE LATE 1940S AND EARLY 1950S WITH HIS OWN BRAND OF POWER SKATING. HE COULD JUMP AS HIGH AS THE BOARDS ALONG THE ICE.

MEN'S PROGRAM: WHAT YOU'LL SEE

The requirements of both singles disciplines are quite similar, but given the importance of jumping right now, men's skating offers a more athletic sport.

JUMPS. All jumps, except for the outlawed back flip, will be seen in the Men's competition. Edge jumps, so named because the skater is propelled off blade edges, include Axels, Salchows, loops; toe jumps, which involve pushing off the toe of the blade, include toe loops, flips, and Lutzes (for full descriptions, see "How to Skate"). Triple jumps at this point are required but limited in number to avoid programs consisting only of them. At the elite international and national championship levels today, a quad will often be attempted. In jumping, judges watch for proper takeoffs and air position, no underrotation, no hand touching down after, or change of foot before, and correct landings. Falls are the most obvious unfortunate occurrence that can happen, but the greater the technical difficulty of the jump, the less the skater's marks will suffer for a fall as long as all the required moves have been completed.

SPINS. Although Jackson Haines himself

invented the sit spin and Dick Button gave us the flying camel, spins, while required, do not define men's skating in the manner jumps do. Only Ronald Robertson, the American spinning specialist from the mid-1950s, has ever made a name solely on spins. There are only three basic spins—upright, camel, and sit. Any other spin is a variation of one of these three. Variations on the upright spin include back spins and blur spins, first performed by Austrian Karl Schafer in the 1920s, and the headless spin, a variation on the blur spin in which the skater's

head is dropped back for dramatic effect. Camels can be recognized by the arabesque position during the spin. The sit spin is just what one would expect: The skater appears to be sitting, with bent legs and torso down. Both jumps and spins can turn clockwise or counterclockwise, though most skaters tend to do both in the same direction. Flying spins require the skater to enter the spin with a jump, and skaters have the option of performing a sit or camel, depending on the spin. Along with clean, straight body lines, judges watch the skater's ability to maintain speed and rotation—the number of revolutions and the speed at which they achieve them—and centering.

FOOTWORK. Jumps and spins alone would hardly constitute a well-balanced program. The connecting series of steps (counters, rockers, brackets, three-turns, Choctaws, and Mohawks) are needed to create the possibility of interest in a routine. These are the elements that provide

JUMPS ARE AN ESSENTIAL ELEMENT OF MEN'S SKATING. ELVIS STOJKO (ABOVE LEFT) AND JOHN CURRY (ABOVE) PERFORM THEM HERE WITH INTENSITY AND ARTISTRY. AMERICAN SCOTT DAVIS (LEFT) IN A SIT SPIN, AND SCOTT HAMILTON (BELOW) SHOW THE POWER AND SPEED POSSIBLE WITH CREATIVE FOOTWORK.

expression, drama, and the skater's personality. These are the moves that take the skater over the ice, and form the foundation for the "style, rhythm, grace, and sureness" judges look for in a championship skater, such as American great Scott Hamilton, a master of footwork. The better the skater, the higher the expectations for complex and varied footwork.

rity off the ice with well-rounded performances on it. As comfortable skating figures as he was executing a perfect Axel or playing to a crowd, Scott Hamilton brought a genuine personality to men's skating that fit well with every aspect of the sport. And each of the champions who followed him—Americans Brian Boitano and Todd Eldredge; Canadians Kurt Browning, Brian Orser, and Elvis Stojko; Russia's Viktor Petrenko—learned that lesson. While they all had their own style, some leaning toward athleticism, others toward dance, each created an integrated package, highlighting their strengths without becoming specialists.

One of the greatest evenings in men's skating took place at the Calgary Olympics in 1988, when Brian Orser and Brian Boitano faced off in the "Battle of the Brians." These two maverick skaters, dressed in similar military outfits, met head-to-head in two of the finest long programs ever seen in the Men's discipline. Millions of television viewers around the world watched Boitano edge Orser with a near-perfect performance that for once made men's skating as glamorous and as dramatic as the ladies'.

What the new century will bring is anyone's guess. Stylistically, the romanticism of Russian skaters Ilia Kulik and Alexei Urmanov seems a counterweight to the rock-and-roll approach of Elvis Stojko and France's Philippe Candeloro. Todd Eldredge's classical consistency has raised him to the top tier of all-time American men's skaters, while Michael Weiss tries to bring some showy, athletic, Michael Jordan–like moves to the ice. What they all have in common is the quadruple jump. Since 1988, when Kurt Browning landed a quadruple toe loop at the World Championships, the quad has become the goal of every men's skater, though to date only Stojko and Kulik have been able to perform the jump with consistency. What is clear is that men's skating is once again pushing the limits of what can be done on ice. Don't be surprised when not too far off in the future someone lands all the quads, from Salchow to Lutz—and the quint won't be too far behind. ✳

THE MEETING BETWEEN AMERICAN BRIAN BOITANO (ABOVE) AND BRIAN ORSER OF CANADA AT THE 1988 CALGARY OLYMPICS WAS A HIGH POINT IN MEN'S COMPETITION.

TERRY KUBICKA OF THE UNITED STATES LANDED A BACK FLIP AT THE 1976 OLYMPIC WINTER GAMES. THE MOVE WAS IMMEDIATELY BANNED FROM COMPETITION, THOUGH SKATERS DO CONTINUE TO PERFORM IT IN EXHIBITIONS.

COMPETITION

The Men's competition, like the Ladies', is divided into a short program and a free-skating program. Given that it counts for 66.7 percent of the skater's final score, free skating is where the championship is usually decided, but the short program is a crucial test of concentration. The technical ability of a great skater is consistent throughout both of his programs or, even more telling, not apparent; the best skaters make it look easy, merging athletic skills with artistry.

SHORT PROGRAM

Skating order in the short program is decided by blind draw. Each year a different group of eight elements is required. In 1998–99 they are:

- Double Axel
- Triple jump immediately preceded by connecting steps and/or other similar free-skating movements
- Jump combination: a double and a triple jump, or two triple jumps
- Flying spin
- Camel spin or sit spin with one change of foot
- Spin combination with only one change of foot and at least two changes of position
- Two step sequences of a different nature (straight line, circular, or serpentine)

These moves must be performed within two minutes and forty seconds, but they can be done in any order and to music (without vocals) of the skater's choice. Two marks are given by each judge: one for required elements and one for presentation. These count as 33.3 percent of the final score. More difficult jumps may result in higher scores in the first mark because of the difficulty, but a fall in the short program can be deadly to a skater's chances. A saying well known among skaters goes, "The short program can't win a competition for you, but it can lose a competition."

After each performance, the judges add up the two marks for each skater and rank him relative to the other skaters. These rankings are called ordinals. At the end of the night, the skater with the majority of first-place ordinals wins the event. Where each skater placed is then multiplied by 0.5 to arrive at his "factored placement." This number will later be combined with the skater's factored placement in the free skate to determine the overall champion. Finishing first in the short program doesn't guarantee a championship, but it may put the skater in a position where he will be hard to beat; depending on how competitive the second- and third-place skaters are, the title will often be his to win or lose.

FREE SKATE

The championship is decided with the free-skating program. The order of skating is decided by standings after the short program, but skating order within each group is determined by a random draw. Unlike the short program, which has required elements, skaters can choose the elements in the free-skate program. There are, however, balanced program guidelines:

- Jumps must include at least one jump combination or sequence, but no more than three.
- Only two different triples can be repeated, and then only if one is in combination and the other is either in a combination or in a sequence of jumps. (This means that the top skaters will be trying to land a triple Salchow, a triple toe loop, a triple loop, a triple flip, a triple Lutz, and a triple Axel, as well as two more in a combination—a total of eight triples.)
- Four different spins must be performed, with one in a combination and one with a flying entry.
- Two step sequences—one circular and one Move in the Field that uses the whole ice surface.

The men's routine duration is four minutes and thirty seconds, and it is done to

FIVE-TIME U.S. CHAMPION TODD ELDREDGE (ABOVE) AND RUSSIAN ILIA KULIK (OPPOSITE), 1998 OLYMPIC GOLD MEDALIST.

the skater's choice of music (again, without vocals).

Beyond the required moves, difficulty is considered, along with artistry, creativity, innovation, and the technical skill with which moves are performed. The judges give two marks, one for technical merit and one for presentation. As in the short program, the skaters are ranked by each judge according to the score they give them, with the winner decided by the majority of first-place finishes. The free-skate placements are multiplied by 1.0, and then added to the factored placements from the short program. The skater with the lowest overall factored placement wins.

Ties in the free-skate are decided by higher presentation scores. An example of the importance of presentation came in the 1992 Olympic Winter Games, when American Paul Wylie skated first in the final group. He skated well, watched his marks, then put on his street clothes as he waited for the rest of the group to skate. At the end of the night he won the silver medal by one-tenth of a point on one presentation score from one judge—a margin akin to 0.02 of a second in a speed-skating race.

LADIES' SKATERS TODAY SUCH AS NICOLE BOBEK CAN USE THEIR BODIES TO CREATE WORKS OF ART.

LADIES'

Figure skating, so it was said at the turn of the century, was of great benefit to women primarily because it compelled them to loosen their corsets and breathe deeply, mending lungs that had surely been scarred by sooty urban air. But the sport helped to emancipate women in far more profound ways than undoing their girdles, and the twentieth century would prove that the benefit was mutual—figure skating as we know it today owes its popularity and strength to the work of women both on and off the ice.

Ladies' figure skating expresses the sport's unique position between athletics and performance; it is truly art in competition. Women have been vital to the directions figure skating has taken throughout its history, and, in turn, the sport has propelled women to positions of power they have rarely seen in other sports. Some would argue that there might not have been a Babe Didrikson, a Martina Navratilova, or a Jackie Joyner-Kersee without Madge Syers, who earned an asterisk in the record books by winning a silver medal competing against men at the 1902 World Championships (there was no division for women).

It is not surprising that Syers won the medal in London or that she herself was English; the British educational system included athletic development for women as early as the 1880s, when Swedish gymnastics was introduced in their schools. English women were already engaged in athletic activities, such as horseback riding and bicycling, with men, and were fully accepted as recreational participants in the sport of figure skating—on the same ice. Nets did not have to be lowered, dimensions did not have to be changed, equipment did not have to be altered to accommodate special needs. All a woman needed was a pair of skates, just like any man. In these early days of special figures and artistry—jumps and more athletic skating styles were considered improper in ladies' skating well into the twentieth century—a woman could perform to the same level if not beyond some of what a man could do, despite the long, heavy skirt she was surely wearing.

And Madge Syers, by all accounts, performed at least as well as any man at the 1902 World Championships, except perhaps Ulrich Salchow, the legendary Swede who won the gold medal that year. Syers had signed up for the championships when she noted that no rule specifically prevented a woman from entering, and the ISU, to its credit, recognized the loophole and allowed her to compete. Immediately after Syers won the silver medal, however, the ISU banned women from competition

UNDER THE CONSTRAINTS OF PERIOD MODESTY, MADGE SYERS PERFORMED TO THE LEVEL OF THE FINEST MEN'S SKATERS.

against men. A separate discipline was finally established in 1906. Syers won the first two Ladies' World Championships in 1906 and 1907, as well as the first Olympic gold medal for Ladies' figure skating in 1908 and the first Olympic bronze in Pairs with her husband, Edgar, that same year.

The twenty years between Madge Syers's Olympic gold and Sonja Henie's belonged to Hungarian women Lily Kronberger and Opika von Horvath, and Austrian Herma Plank-Szabo. Kronberger won four straight World titles from 1908 to 1911, and von Horvath took the next three, until World War I broke out and put a temporary halt to international competition; then Plank-Szabo won five straight titles from 1922 to 1926.

The ladies' skating of this time was even closer to the ground than the men's— American Theresa Weld Blanchard landed a Salchow jump in the 1920 U.S. Championships, but the judges did not approve, and ladies' skating remained intimately if not officially bound to dance. Choreography was related to specific positions and the use of expressive movements rather than the sense of a structured order of skating moves. Charlotte Oelschlagel, a noncompetitive skater who helped popularize the International style in the United States, performed pieces choreographed by the Russian dancer Anna Pavlova, and Lily Kronberger used a live band to accompany her at the World Championships in 1911, the first time music was used in direct relation to a skating program. These early ladies' skaters had begun to create the modern notion of figure skating as a sport of competitive beauty.

The great American women skaters of this era were Theresa Weld Blanchard and Beatrix Loughran. From 1914

BEATRIX LOUGHRAN (ABOVE) WAS ONE OF THE FIRST AMERICAN WOMEN TO BREAK INTO THE TOP LEVEL OF INTERNATIONAL SKATING. THERESA WELD BLANCHARD (PICTURED AT RIGHT, WITH LOUGHRAN IN THE MID-1920S) WON THE FIRST OLYMPIC SKATING MEDAL BY AN AMERICAN WITH A BRONZE IN 1920. BOTH ALSO EXCELLED AT PAIRS SKATING.

IN 1956, TENLEY ALBRIGHT OF MASSACHUSETTS (BELOW RIGHT) WON THE FIRST OLYMPIC GOLD MEDAL BY AN AMERICAN WOMAN, AS WELL AS THE FIRST WORLD CHAMPIONSHIP.

to 1927, the two won the U.S. Ladies' title nine out of ten times, while Blanchard won nine Pair titles with her partner, Nathaniel Niles. Blanchard was the first American skater to win an Olympic medal, a bronze in 1920, and Loughran followed with a silver in 1924, a bronze in 1928, and a silver in Pairs with Sherwin Badger in 1932.

The eleven-year-old Norwegian girl who finished last in the 1924 Olympics would soon change the nature of not just ladies' skating but skating itself. When Sonja Henie returned to the Olympics in 1928, she won the gold medal and went on to capture the next two as well (1932 and 1936), along with ten straight World Championships. No one has ever dominated the sport as Sonja Henie did, and through her immense popularity, even before her successful movie career, she affected what people did on the ice, what they wore while they did it, and how much they got paid. Her jumps and dancelike choreography, while barely on the meter by today's standards, liberated women skaters, as did her short skirts. When Henie went professional after ten years of ruling the sport, she turned the notion of local ice carnivals into spectacular touring ice shows, and she soon became one of MGM's most popular movie stars. One of the toughest—and richest—businesswomen in the world, Henie created a professional outlet for a sport that had been essentially an amateur pursuit.

Englishwomen Cecilia Colledge and Megan Taylor stepped into competitive skating when Henie left, but their years on top were cut short by World War II, after which their precise, technical style—including the first women's double jump, by Colledge—was surpassed by Canadian Barbara Ann Scott. Scott was the first North American to win a World Championship as well as an Olympic gold medal and a European Championship. She was able to land double jumps and other athletic maneuvers that defined skating in the years of Dick Button and the American style, but Scott's greatest appeal was her charming personality on the ice.

Sonja Henie of Norway (above) won her first of three Olympic gold medals in 1928, when she was only sixteen. Canadian Barbara Ann Scott (left), famous for her crowd-pleasing charm, became in 1948 the first North American woman to win an Olympic gold medal. Pictured here with Dick Button in 1947.

North American women continued their dominance through 1960, with Tenley Albright and Carol Heiss of the United States both winning Olympic gold and seven out of eight World titles between 1953 and 1960. Since 1952, American women have won at least one medal in Ladies' figure skating at every Olympic competition except 1964—six of those medals being gold.

The sport was no longer simply a balance of compulsory figures and the artistry of the freestyle. Due mostly to the influence of Button and other Americans, jumping and athleticism were now established elements of the sport. During the early 1950s, women such as Jeannette Altwegg and Jacqueline du Bief won World Championships largely on their jumping abilities. In addition to their competitive value, jumps were crowd-pleasers, and could lead to professional careers as well. The fact that compulsory figures still counted for 60 percent of a skater's final score kept women such as Sjoukje Dijkstra, who won three World Championships in the early 1960s based on the strength of her figures, in the top competitive tier, but women skaters continued to jump, even though the scoring ratio lagged behind the trend. In 1968, the ratio was shifted to 50 percent figures and 50 percent free skate to reflect the change in the sport, but Canadian Petra Burka continued to force the issue by landing the first ladies' triple in 1965. The balance would be altered even more as television, which had made Carol Heiss an overnight sensation as she won the Ladies' gold medal in front of millions of viewers at the 1960 Olympics in Squaw Valley, California, became an even greater factor in the development of the sport.

The 1968 Winter Olympics introduced the biggest star in ladies' skating since

Sonja Henie. Peggy Fleming's gold-medal performance at Grenoble was not her best that year, but relayed live on satellite throughout the world, it made her a sensation literally overnight. Fleming starred in seven television specials after that, becoming not just an American icon but a global spokesperson for the sport. Her youthful glamour and natural elegance launched another wave of American interest in figure skating, especially on the women's side, and anchored it as a television event.

Peggy Fleming was universally popular, but the contrast between American Janet Lynn and Austrian Beatrix Schuba in the early 1970s brought the issue of artistry versus figures versus jumping back to the fore, this time in a very visible fashion. Lynn, beloved for the purity and joyful expressiveness of her skating, won only the bronze in the 1972 Winter Olympic Games because of her poor showing in the untelevised compulsories. Schuba, by far the best skater of figures, won the gold after an undistinguished televised free skate, leaving television viewers to question how the sport was scored. The controversy led the ISU in 1973 to reduce the

PEGGY FLEMING PRACTICING FOR THE 1968 OLYMPIC WINTER GAMES. SHE WENT INTO THE OLYMPICS AS THE FAVORITE TO WIN THE GOLD MEDAL, AND BECAME AN INTERNATIONAL STAR AFTER HER VICTORY.

value of the compulsory figures, but the result was not more artistry. The value of figures and the free skate went to 40 percent each, and the short program, worth 20 percent of the final score, was introduced.

With more value loaded on free skating, the jumpers took the advantage and continued to push forward into the 1980s, with Americans Linda Fratianne and Elaine Zayak, and Denise Biellmann of Switzerland, consistently increasing the numbers and types of triple jumps used in competition. In 1976, the free skate became 50 percent and the figures 30 percent. Compulsory figures were eventually phased out in 1990, making the balance between jumping and artistry, a tension that affects ladies' skating even now. For every expressive Katarina Witt, there is a jumping phenomenon like Midori Ito, and the emergence of skaters such as Tara Lipinski and Michelle Kwan, who are able to land triples with artistry, will surely keep this issue at the forefront of ladies' skating.

Peggy Fleming's triumph in 1968 had established a new role in American culture: the figure skating queen. After Fleming came Janet Lynn, whose $1.5 million contract with the Ice Follies following her retirement from competition made her the highest-paid female athlete of her time, and in 1976 there was Dorothy Hamill, Olympic gold medal winner at Innsbruck. Every four years, it seemed, America crowned a new queen, elevating the popularity of ladies' skating, and creating a wealth of great American women skaters—Debi Thomas, Tiffany Chin, Jill Trenary, and Olympic gold medalist Kristi Yamaguchi.

Interest in ladies' skating reached an unprecedented height at the 1994 Olympic Games, when U.S. Champion Nancy Kerrigan went up against Ukrainian Oksana Baiul for the gold medal. An earlier attempt to injure Kerrigan, allegedly involving fellow American skater Tonya Harding, made the meeting arguably the biggest sports story of the year and drew the largest television audience ever for an Olympic event. The background faded, though, once the competition began. Baiul's victory, by one of the thinnest margins ever, was a dramatic high point in ladies' skating.

American skaters Michelle Kwan and Tara Lipinski are at the leading edge of today's great ladies' skaters, a group which includes Irina Slutskaya of Russia, China's Chen Lu, and Surya Bonaly of France. Given the height of their jumps and the popularity of the sport, it's certain that ladies' figure skating is definitely headed upward. ✳

A YOUNG MICHELLE KWAN ARCHES INTO A LAYBACK SPIN. KWAN'S GRACEFUL, FLUID STYLE HAS BEST DEFINED HER SKATING CAREER.

LADIES' PROGRAM: WHAT YOU'LL SEE

JUMPS. You will see lots of jumps. Great jumping has become a natural aspect of ladies' figure skating. Championship-level ladies' free-skating programs will now include six or seven triples, sometimes including the most difficult, the triple Axel—three and a half turns (1,260 degrees). It was one extra triple that Oksana Baiul threw in at the end of her Olympic long program that let her defeat Nancy Kerrigan in 1994. Such things drive skaters to load in as many jumps as they can, assuming, as Baiul did, that if all else is equal, one more triple can make the difference, especially since missing an unrequired jump is not heavily penalized.

You will also see falls. As common as triple jumps have become, they have not gotten any easier to do. Triples are risky; they're the figure skating equivalent of swinging for the fences; you hit a lot of home runs that way, but you strike out a lot, too. Some also believe, though it is impossible to prove, that the absence of compulsory figures has allowed a generation of skaters to come along who do not have the command of edges and technical expertise figures made necessary.

SPINS. Whereas men's spins tend to emphasize speed or jump entries, spins give women skaters a chance to display balletic grace and sometimes a gymnastic flexibility. The layback spin, a type of upright spin in which the skater drops her head and shoulders and arches her back, can create an extremely beautiful form, while the spin invented by Denise Biellmann of Switzerland, which involves grabbing the skate of the free leg while it is extended overhead, may not be as pleasing aesthetically, yet remains impressive for the physical challenge it represents. Camels and sit spins are the two other types of spins, and ladies' skaters have also crafted these into showcase combination spins, with a well-known example the Hamill Camel first performed by American Dorothy Hamill, which moves from a back camel (as an arabesque) into a back sit spin. There are a wide variety of spins, all depending on entry, position, and direction, but it's the differences in leg, arm, and torso placement that create the artistry of the move.

DENISE BIELLMANN OF SWITZERLAND (ABOVE LEFT) INVENTED THIS SPIN, WHICH HAS SINCE BECOME A STANDARD MOVE IN THE REPERTOIRE OF MANY WOMEN SKATERS, INCLUDING NICOLE BOBEK (ABOVE RIGHT). ELAINE ZAYAK (BELOW) IN A TRADEMARK JUMP. ZAYAK WAS AMONG THE FIRST WOMEN SKATERS TO CONSISTENTLY LAND TRIPLE JUMPS.

FOOTWORK AND MOVES IN THE FIELD. Rule changes in recent years have added more footwork to help balance the jumping now so prevalent in ladies' skating. Spirals, in which the skater glides on one skate with the free leg extended behind her, Ina Bauers, and step combinations display the skater's deftness, flexibility, and precision.

COMPETITION

Ladies' competition is, like men's, divided into a short program and a free skating program and, once again, the short program accounts for 33.3 percent of the skater's final score and the free skate 66.7 percent. With school figures completely eliminated now and required elements in the short program only a third of the final mark, the spotlight is very much on free skating, but the technical expectations placed on skaters within the free skate are higher now than ever; triples are a must. The winning skater must be able not only to perform the championship-level skills expected of her, but also be able to innovate and use her abilities to create artistically satisfying programs.

SHORT PROGRAM
Skating order for the short program is determined by blind draw. Each year a different group of eight elements is required. In 1998–99 they are:
- Double Axel
- Double or triple jump
- A jump combination: double jump and a triple jump, or two triple jumps
- Flying spin
- Layback or sideways leaning spin
- Spin combination with only one change of foot and at least two changes of position
- One spiral step sequence and one step sequence of a different nature

The moves required in the short program can be done in any order and to whatever non-vocal music the skater chooses, but they must be performed within two minutes and forty seconds. The pressures of jumping weigh just as heavily on the women as they do on the men; more difficult jumps may lead to higher scores, but they're dangerous—missing a required element is a mandatory deduction, as is making a second attempt at one. Even though the short program eval-

uates technical merit, artistry can't be ignored while presenting a total program.

Just as for the men, each skater receives two marks from each judge: one for required elements and one for presentation. Each judge is continually ranking the skaters at the end of each performance based on the scores they give them. These rankings are called the ordinals. At the end of all the short programs, the skater with the majority of first-place votes wins the short program; the skater with the most second-place votes takes second; and so on. The skater's placement is then multiplied by 0.5 to come to each skater's "factored placement," which will come into play again at the end of the free skate.

THE FREE SKATE
The final scores for each skater are not cumulative but based on their finish—first, second, third, and so on—in each of the two events, so a skater cannot build an insurmountable lead in the short program. This means that the Ladies' championship is decided with the free-skating program, often held as the final event of the entire competition. The skaters are grouped in fours and fives, based on the standings after the short program. Skating orders within the groups are determined by draw. As each group of skaters takes to the ice, the tension continues to build to the appearance of the final group, which has the leaders and, almost

TARA LIPINSKI (CENTER) WITH MICHELLE KWAN (LEFT) AND CHEN LU (RIGHT) AT THE 1998 OLYMPIC WINTER GAMES. (OPPOSITE) LIPINSKI. (BELOW) FLOWER GIRLS PICK UP BOUQUETS THROWN ON THE ICE.

always, the winner.

There are no requirements for the free-skating program, but a well-rounded free skate should include certain things: Jumps must include at least one jump combination or sequence, but no more than three. Only two different triples can be repeated in combinations or jump sequences and, if repeated, one must be as a combination jump and the other may be either as a combination or in a sequence of jumps. Four different spins must be performed, with one in a combination and one flying. Ladies must also do one step sequence that uses the entire ice surface and also one sequence of spirals and/or free-skating movements, such as arabesques and spread eagles, that uses the entire ice surface. The routine can be no longer than four minutes, with ten seconds leeway in either direction, and the skater uses music of her own choosing.

Beyond the suggested moves, the judges consider difficulty, along with artistry, creativity, innovation, and the proper technical competence with which moves are performed. The judges again give two marks, one for technical merit and one for presentation. As in the short program, the judges give the scores and rank the skaters after each performance based on those scores. The winner of the free skate is decided by the majority of first-place votes. The skater's placement in the free skate is then multiplied by 1.0 for the factored placement for the event. Both factored placements are then added and the skater with the lowest overall factored placement wins the Ladies' title.

Ekaterina Gordeeva and Sergei Grinkov embodied the irresistible beauty of pairs.

PAIRS

The earliest woodcuts we have of ice skating, dating back to seventeenth-century Holland, show couples gliding together arm-in-arm across the ice, and the scene is repeated over and over again throughout history. From London's Regent's Park to Central Park in New York City, to the canals of Holland, whenever figure skating has been in style, its unique position in many societies and times as the only sport that men and women could do together has led countless generations to exploit its courtship possibilities. The sport's genteel air, and the natural harmony it can evoke between two skaters moving in unison, make skating in a pair almost inescapably romantic.

As a competitive discipline, Pairs is a bit younger than Ladies' or Men's singles. The first exhibition of pair skating was in 1888 and the first competition was held in 1891, but it was not included in the World Championships or the Olympics until 1908. The new way of viewing women in competition, which Madge Syers's surprise entry in the 1902 World Championships forced onto the skating world, certainly helped speed the increasing acceptance of pair skating as a discipline, as did the advent of aesthetic modernism in the early years of the twentieth century. Though it would be many years before pairs skating would begin to fully realize its artistic possibilities, the appearance of dancers such as Pavlova and Nijinsky took the simple pas de deux to a new, more sensual, place, and opened minds to other expressive, overtly romantic forms of art.

The pas de deux may have been the inspiration for pairs skating, but only the more rudimentary forms of balletic art were incorporated during the discipline's first years. For the most part, pairs skating prior to World War I consisted of a couple performing singles moves while holding hands; the lifts and death spirals that seem the very essence of the discipline today were half a century away. While this very earthbound style of tandem skating necessitated a certain kind of talent, it did not break new choreographic ground; still, skating fans were clearly taken with the new form—or at least with the possibilities it presented. Unison, the most important aspect of pairs skating even now, was in place by this point and contributed to the discipline's growing appeal. The pre–World War I years were dominated by three couples: Anna Hubler and Heinrich Burger of Germany, Phyllis and James Johnson of Great Britian, and the Finnish couple Ludowika Eilers (later Jakobsson) and Walter Jakobsson. These pairs won six out of seven World Championships between 1908 and 1914, while Hubler and Burger took the gold at the 1908 Olympics and the Johnsons took the silver. (Women's skating groundbreaker Madge Syers and her husband, Edgar, won the

HENDRICK GOLTZIUS (DUTCH, 1558-1617). AFTER "ELEGANT COUPLE ON SKATES," BY JAN SAENREDAM. CIRCA 1600. COPPER ENGRAVING. (WORLD FIGURE SKATING MUSEUM AND HALL OF FAME)

bronze.) In the United States, Theresa Weld Blanchard and Nathaniel Niles won the American title every year from 1918 to 1927, exceeding even Blanchard's mastery of the U.S. Ladies' singles, which she won six times, plus their strength in both the Waltz and the Fourteen Step in ice dancing. A noncompetitive skater, Charlotte Oelschlagel, performed the first death spiral with her future husband, Curt Neumann, during these years.

When the World Championships began again in 1922, the Austrians and Hungarians dominated the pairs scene. After a silver and gold in 1922 and 1923, respectively, by the Jakobssons, Austrians and Hungarians won twenty-four out of thirty-six total World Championship medals from 1924 to 1935 using a uniformly sharp style based on symmetry and unison. The two exceptions were the French couple Andrée and Pierre Brunet and Americans Beatrix Loughran and Sherwin Badger, though both teams are exceptions only in as much as they weren't Central European. The Brunets' style went the tight, refined, and low-to-the-ground style of the Austrians one better, and the team won each of the four times they competed in the World Championships and won two Olympic gold medals. Loughran and Badger were also stylistically similar to the Austrians, and with a silver medal in Pairs at the 1932 Olympics to go with her silver in 1924 and bronze in 1928 for singles, Beatrix Loughran became the only American woman to win figure skating medals in three separate Olympic games. Austrian Herma Plank-Szabo also excelled as both a pairs skater and in ladies' singles; at the same time that she was winning World Championships in 1925 and 1927 with her partner Ludwig Wrede, she took, from 1922 to 1926, the World Ladies' singles title.

Germans Maxi Herber and Ernst Baier held the spotlight prior to World War II, with four consecutive World titles between 1936 and 1939, along with the Olympic gold in 1936, but the war brought an end to European dominance in Pairs. The athletic American style, introduced in the years just after World War II, crossed into pairs skating as well, but athleticism here did not mean just jumping. Instead, this was the time when the lifts, throws, and other dramatically physical moves that we associate today with pairs skating entered routines, mainly from North American skaters. Canadians Suzanne Morrow and Wallace Diestelmeyer made double jumps a regular element of their routines, while Frances Dafoe and Norris Bowden performed the first throw jumps, catch lifts, and twist lifts. Karol and Peter Kennedy in 1950 became the first Americans to win a World Championship in Pairs, and the second to medal in the Olympics when they won a silver in 1952, while Canadian teams such as Dafoe and Bowden, Barbara Wagner and Robert Paul, and Maria and Otto Jelinek, who had defected from Communist Czechoslovakia, won seven of nine World Championships between 1954 and 1962.

The World Championship silver medal won by Soviets Ludmilla and Oleg Protopopov in 1962 marked a new era in pair skating. With graceful, flowing movement and an elegance of line comparable to the finest dance pairings, the Protopopovs pushed pairs to a level that it had

ANDRÉE AND PIERRE BRUNET OF FRANCE WERE THE WORLD'S LEADING PAIRS TEAM DURING THE 1920S, WINNING FOUR WORLD TITLES.

MARINA ELTSOVA AND ANDREI
BUSHKOV OF RUSSIA ARE DISTIN-
GUISHED BY THEIR GREAT SPEED AND
EMOTIVE ABILITIES.

yet to see. Their highly romantic style, reminiscent of the grand Russian ballet tradition, seemed a reaction to the kinetic but sometimes impersonal North American way of pairs skating. The Protopopovs used choreography in the true sense of the word, creating a pas de deux on ice, and it is this tradition that continues to be the basis of pairs skating. Since 1964, skaters from former Soviet territories have won the World Championship in Pairs twenty-seven times out of thirty-three, and all nine Olympic gold medals awarded in those years.

While the Protopopovs may have remade pairs, two Russian women—Irina Rodnina and Ekaterina Gordeeva—have lived, both on and off the ice, the romantic drama that pairs skating is supposed to only represent. Irina Rodnina had won four World Championships and an Olympic gold medal with Alexsei Ulanov in the early seventies, but then Ulanov announced that he was in love with a woman in another Soviet skating pair. So distracted was he by his new love that he dropped Rodnina on her head during the World Championships in Calgary in 1972. The two won the title anyway, but Ulanov broke away to skate with the woman he loved and had by then married. Rodnina was left to find a new partner, but she did not suffer from the change. She picked Alexandr Zaitsev, and three years and three World Championships later he became, for a time, her husband. Rodnina and Zaitsev won a total of six World Championships and two Olympic gold medals, making Irina Rodnina one of the most successful figure skaters of all time. Despite the drama of her story, Rodnina's style, no matter who her partner, was more about power skating than pure art.

The story of Ekaterina Gordeeva and Sergei Grinkov did not end as happily. Their deeply expressive routines seemed to be merely extensions of an ideal marriage; their on-ice embraces no different from those they shared at home. That the emotions displayed in their routines were genuine gave a new luster to pairs skating; something true and wonderful happened when they were on the ice. Then, in late 1995, Grinkov died of a massive heart attack. Though Gordeeva has gone on to a successful professional career as a solo skater, one of the world's favorite pairs—both on and off the ice—was tragically broken.

The success of American pairs such as Cynthia and Ronald Kauffman, JoJo Starbuck and Ken Shelley, Tai Babilonia and Randy Gardner, Caitlin (Kitty) and Peter Carruthers, Jill Watson and Peter Oppegard, Jenni Meno and Todd Sand, and Kyoko Ina and Jason Dungjen over the last thirty years has kept pairs skating an active pursuit of many young American skaters. ✳

PAIRS PROGRAM: WHAT YOU'LL SEE

As anyone who has ever watched pairs skating knows, many acrobatic, dance-inspired moves distinguish it from singles skating.

LIFTS: Judges look for many things to differentiate good lifts from bad ones. First, the skaters should continue moving on the ice during the lift, not stop. Second, the man should not use his toe picks or scrape the ice. Third, both skaters must achieve full extension early into the move and keep it throughout. Fourth, while in the air, the woman's position should be strong, in control, and attractive. Finally, the woman should be brought down at full speed, in control, and should land upon the ice softly. There are dozens of lifts, varying in where the woman is held (armpit, waist, hand), how she is lifted, how far the man extends his arms, and in what position the woman is held.

Twist lifts are lifts that involve the man releasing the woman to rotate in the air and then catching her in the course of the move. All the requirements of a good

lift apply to twist lifts, but the skaters also have other concerns. The lifts should not slow before the woman plants her toe pick to elevate. Second, the man should reach full extension as the woman is over his head. Third, the twist should take place after the man's arms are extended and after her split in a split twist. Fourth, she should be caught at the waist while she is still overhead and her landing should be soft. Finally, both skaters must end the lift on one foot.

SPIRALS: The death spiral is a very dramatic, distinctive element in pairs skating in which the man pivots while holding the woman's hand and she leans back fully extended, parallel to the ice. The move varies with the edges used, but all death spirals must include the man holding a strong pivot; neither skater using toe picks, scraping, or sliding on the boot; the woman staying low and parallel to the ice, with her back as straight as possible; and the woman coming up easily and quickly at the end of the move.

THROWS: A throw jump is just that: The man throws the woman as she jumps. The throw should produce a longer and higher jump than she would be able to perform on her own. The entire move should be done at a good speed and the landing must be strong and in control.

UNISON: Unison is the final element that makes pairs skating unique and, to many, special. Before any of these moves were invented, unison was already fundamental to pairs skating, and when performed well, an accomplished pair makes unison seem effortless. Their jumps and spins are all in close proximity and even the rotations on solo spins are synchronized. Mirror skating, in which each member of the pair moves in opposite directions and mirrors what the other is doing, and shadow skating, where the two skaters perform the same manuevers simultaneously, are very clear examples of unison.

COMPETITION

Like singles skating, pairs competition has two programs: the short program and the free-skate program.

SHORT PROGRAM

As with the Men's and Ladies' competitions, the skating order for the short program is set by a blind draw several days in advance; in this way the best teams may have to compete very early instead of together in the final group, as they will for the long program. The short program requires each pair to perform, in no particular order, eight required elements that change from year to year. In 1998–99, the elements for championship-level pairs are:

- Any lasso lift takeoff
- Twist lift (double)
- Solo jump (double or triple)
- Solo spin with only one change of foot and at least one change of position
- Pair spin combination with at least one change of foot and at least one change of position
- Death spiral backward inside edge
- One spiral step sequence and one straight line, circular, or serpentine step sequence

The best pairs will not only be solid in all their requirements, but they will also demonstrate a polish and command that separate them from the others. The short program lasts two minutes and forty seconds and is performed to non-vocal music of the skaters' own choosing. Each judge gives two scores, one for the required elements and one for presentation; together these account for 33.3 percent of the pair's final score. As in singles, the judges rank the skaters after each performance based on the scores, with first place determined by which pair was first on the majority of scorecards. Placements are then multiplied by 0.5 to come up with the factored placement for each pair.

FREE SKATE

The pairs finish with their free-skating program. As in other disciplines, the field is split into groups based on short-program standings, with teams drawing to set the order within each group. The free-skating, or long, program counts for 66.7 percent of the final score and is judged, like singles skating, on technical merit and presentation.

There are few limits on the free skate at the championship level. It is four minutes and thirty seconds long and is again performed to the skaters' choice of non-vocal music. Here is where viewers will see the majority of dramatic lifts, throws, and spins, and any innovations the skaters may want to introduce. Top pairs challenge themselves in the free-skating program by attempting tough moves, which usually makes the outcome more obvious than in other disciplines because teams can distinguish themselves with difficult side-by-side triples, throw-triples, and more acrobatic lifts.

A good free-skating program must include:

- Three different lifts, but not more than five, and one of them (but not more than two) must be a twist lift with the man fully extending his arms
- At least one, but at most two, throw jumps
- One solo jump
- One jump sequence
- One pair spin combination
- One pair spin
- One solo spin
- Two different types of death spirals
- One step sequence that fully utilizes the ice surface
- One sequence of spirals and/or free-skating movements that fully utilizes the ice surface

With two-thirds of the final score earned here, standings can change radically, though obviously the winners of the short program have a distinct advantage. The judges again add up both scores for each pair, rank them, and name the winner of the free skate based on who has the majority of first-place finishes. The factored placements are calculated by multiplying placements by 1.0. Adding these numbers to the factored placements in the short program decides the champion. Any overall ties are broken by the presentation scores in the free skate.

Kyoko Ina and Jason Dungjen (left), Kitty and Peter Carruthers (above) and Jenni Meno and Todd Sand (right), three outstanding American pairs.

THE DRAMA OF ICE DANCING, AS SHOWN BY RUSSIANS MAIA USOVA AND ALEXANDER ZHULIN

ICE DANCING

Although ice dancing is a more recent addition to the figure skating disciplines, its roots in fact go back to Jackson Haines and the very beginnings of the sport. Prior to the influence of ballet and modern dancers such as Pavlova and Nijinsky around the turn of the century, dance in the context of figure skating is related to social, or ballroom, dancing. Pairs skating, also in its early years then, was already considered a more artistic form of the sport, while a couple skating in a manner that resembled ballroom dancing, to music that was played in ballrooms, was just something done for fun. As this vernacular form of ice dancing spread to even casual skaters, the seeds of a formal ice dancing discipline were planted with the creation, in 1889, of the first pattern, the Ten Step, in Vienna by Franz Scholler. Home of Jackson Haines and the International style, Vienna was also home of the waltz, the most famous ballroom dance of all, and so it was almost inevitable that in this city all three would be combined to create the first form of ice dancing.

RUSSIANS PASHA GRISHUK AND EVGENY PLATOV ARE THE REIGNING POWERS OF ICE DANCING, HAVING WON TWO OLYMPIC GOLD MEDALS AND FIVE WORLD CHAMPIONSHIIPS.

Ice dancing was soon brought to England, where it found a place among Edwardian society and figure skating circles. While championships were not held at the international level, individual countries held their own championships beginning in the 1910s. Until 1935, the United States awarded titles each year in two dances, usually the Waltz and either the Fourteen Step or an original dance (in 1920 it was the Ten Step). Often the same people who made their marks in other disciplines also competed in ice dancing: Theresa Weld Blanchard and Nathaniel Niles won three Waltz titles, two Fourteen Step titles, and an original dance title to go with five silver medals and three bronze; Beatrix Loughran won the 1922 Waltz with Edward Howland, Sherwin Badger won a silver medal and two bronze, and Irving Brokaw, one of the men responsible for bringing the International style to the United States, won his only U.S. Championship in 1920 when he took gold in the Ten Step with Gertrude Cheever Porter. Other, lesser-known names, though, made ice dancing their specialty. Sydney Goode and James Greene won three Fourteen Step championships and three silvers in Waltz from 1923 to 1926; Rosalie Dunn and Joseph Savage won four titles together from 1926 to 1928, while Savage went on to win three more with a new partner, Edith Secord, from 1929 to 1932. These early skaters created a rich tradition of American ice dancing that continues today.

Back in England, though, ice dancing was about to be transformed into a serious discipline. Both ballroom dancing and roller skating enjoyed boom periods during the 1930s, and the interest soon seeped over to the ice, where more complex moves developed by ballroom dancers and roller skaters were applied. Dancers and

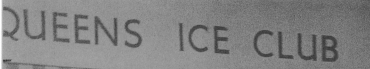

ENGLAND'S COURTNEY JONES WITH HIS SECOND PARTNER, DOREEN DENNY. JONES HELPED SOLIDIFY ICE DANCING IN BRITAIN DECADES AFTER IT FLOURISHED THERE IN THE 1930S. JONES WON FOUR WORLD CHAMPIONSHIPS; TWO WITH HIS FIRST PARTNER JUNE MARKHAM, AND TWO WITH DENNY.

roller skating coaches put on skates and ice dancing began to move into the English spotlight. During these years, such teams as Eva Keats and Eric van der Weyden, Daphne Wallis and Reginald Wilkie, Trudy Harris and Paul Kreckow, and Lesley Turner and Robert Dench created in London ice skating rinks the majority of ice dancing patterns still used today. The nation staged its first championship in 1937 and the first international championship, though not yet sanctioned by the ISU, was held thirteen years later and won by an American couple. Two years later, the ISU sanctioned the first World Championship, which was won by the British couple Jean Westwood and Lawrence Demmy, who went on to win the next three.

Early ice dancing raised some issues for skating officials that have remained with the sport: namely, what exactly differentiates ice dancing from pairs. During the 1930s and 1940s, when lifts and throws had not yet entered into the repertoire of pairs skaters, ice dancing and pairs split along the ballroom versus ballet lines, and the practicalities of how the dances were performed mainly served to differentiate the two. Given its lineage in social dancing, English ice dancing, especially that of five-time World Champion Courtney Jones and his partners, involved face-to-face positions transposed to the ice rather than the unison moves of shadow skating and mirror skating seen even in the early days of pairs, so even while there were few restrictions at first on what ice dancers could do, the foundation of its ballroom dancing paradigm was always there. By the time ice dancing came under ISU oversight in the 1950s, pairs had begun to incorporate American style athletic moves. This finally gave ice dancing the primary distinction from pairs that remains today—no throws, overhead lifts, or rotational jumps. Through the years, the rules for ice dancing have been altered to reflect changes in the discipline and to help maintain its unique identity; to a great extent, the rules have reinforced the primacy of precise footwork, close skating, and set-pattern dances that maintain the sport's kinship to ballroom dance. The relationship to the music is also much more direct in ice dancing than it is in pairs or singles, with the rhythm of the selected piece dictating its interpretation.

Czechoslovakia's Eva Romanova and Pavel Roman won four World titles in the early 1960s; then England's Diane Towler and Bernard Ford took the championship

ICE DANCING SET PATTERNS

PASHA GRISHUK AND EVGENY PLATOV PERFORM THE CHA CHA CONGELADO.

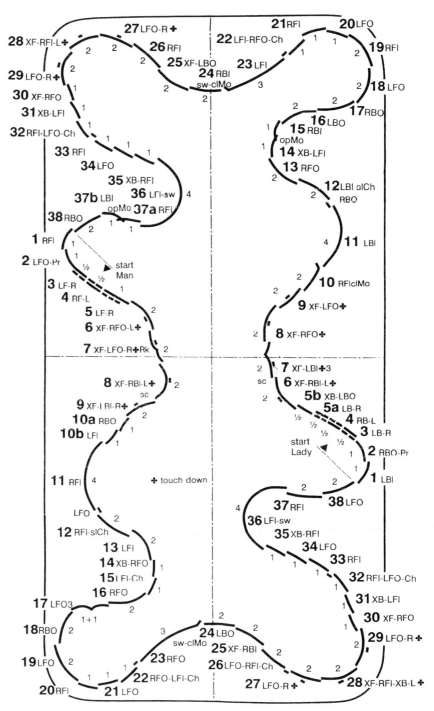

Since Franz Schöller invented the Fourteen Step in 1889, thirty more dances have evolved to form the canons of ice dancing. These dances, used in the compulsory dance section of the competition, have strict requirements and are anything but free skates. At right is the pattern for the Cha Cha Congelado, created by Bernard Ford, Kelly Johnson, Laurie Palmer, and Steven Belanger and first performed in 1989. As can be seen, every step of the routine is choreographed for each partner, though it is up to the couple to bring passion and movement to the dance. The set patterns may seem slightly formal in such a fast, fluid sport as figure skating, but they provide a vivid link to the sport's history.

Abbreviations

R	Right foot	I	Inside edge	slCH	Slide Chasse
L	Left foot	XF	Crossed step in front	Mo	Mohawk
F	Forward	XB	Crossed step behind	op	Open
B	Backward	Pr	Progressive (run)	cl	Closed
O	Outside edge	Ch	Chasse	sw	Swing

JAYNE TORVILL AND CHRISTOPHER DEAN OF ENGLAND CREATED SOME OF THE MOST MEMORABLE ROUTINES IN ICE DANCING HISTORY, INCLUDING THEIR "BOLERO" PROGRAM PICTURED HERE. THE TEAM ESTIMATES THEY'VE PERFORMED IT NEARLY 2,000 TIMES. THE SOVIET COUPLE PAKHOMOVA AND GORSHKOV (OPPOSITE, TOP) BROUGHT A FIERY PASSION TO ICE DANCING, AND BEGAN THE SOVIET/RUSSIAN DOMINATION OF THE DISCIPLINE.

back to Britain with four straight of their own from 1966 to 1969. American teams such as Andree Anderson and Donald Jacoby, Lorna Dyer and John Carrell, Carol Peters and Daniel Ryan, and in the 1970s Judy Schwomeyer and James Sladky and Colleen O'Connor and Jim Millns won their share of silver and bronze medals (including the only U.S. Olympic medal in ice dancing, a bronze in 1976 for O'Connor and Millns), but the 1970 victory of Liudmilla Pakhomova and Aleksandr Gorshkov in the World Championships ushered the Soviets into the center of ice dancing. English ice dancing until then did not differ all that much from the old English style of free skating: straight up and down, especially in the upper body. Pakhomova and Gorshkov broke the plane, curling around each other and dancing more like a couple in love than partners at a tea dance. They also communicated more with the audience, using holds that broke away from the face-to-face style. From 1970 on, ice dancing became primarily a Soviet, and then Russian, preserve. Between 1970 and 1997, Soviet or Russian teams won twenty-two out of twenty-eight World Championships in Ice Dancing, and with the introduction of Ice Dancing as an Olympic sport in 1976, six out of seven gold medals. The three most successful American teams during that time have been Judy Blumberg and

Michael Seibert, who were three-time bronze finishers in the World Championships from 1983 to 1985, Renee Roca and Gorsha Sur, and five-time U.S. Champions Elizabeth Punsalan and Jerod Swallow.

The one great break in the Soviet domination of the sport came in the early 1980s, with Jayne Torvill and Christopher Dean. While a few may question whether or not this English team was the greatest ice dancing couple ever, they were undeniably the most popular. Exuberance and intelligence flowed through their routines, and like all great champions, they tested the limits of their sport and changed it forever. In the course of winning four World Championships from 1981 to 1984 and an Olympic gold at Sarajevo in 1984, Torvill and Dean blurred lines, forced issues, tried the untried. That lifts and jumps were severely limited and frowned upon by the judges was enough to make most teams avoid them, yet Torvill and Dean devised jumps and lifts that obeyed the letter of the law even as they

ICE DANCING: WHAT YOU'LL SEE

Music is the foundation for ice dancing. While other disciplines use music merely to showcase the action, ice dancing is itself the expression of the music. Rhythm, timing, and interpretation of music make up the core of the judging.

There are very specific limits on what kind of music may be used, depending on the kind of program. In general, music must be danceable. Vocal music is not usually used unless the voice itself is the instrument and there are no lyrics, though it was allowed when jive was the musical style selected for the 1997-98 original dance. Classical music or music from the theater must be rearranged to be danceable. In the compulsory dance section of the competition, the music is pre-selected, but in the original dance and the free dance, skaters can choose their own music,

ISABELLE AND PAUL DUCHESNAY OF FRANCE IN THE FAMOUS "JUNGLE FEVER" ROUTINE.

knowing that their choice will be considered by the judges as part of their performance. Using illegal music can cost a team a deduction.

The kinds of music heard for an ice dancing competition vary, but obviously it's all dance music—waltz, polka, rumba, samba, blues, and now even rock and roll.

LIFTS AND JUMPS

Ice dancing is also defined by what you won't see much of, namely full-extension lifts and jumps. Both are strictly limited to distinguish this discipline from pairs. One skate of each ice dancer must be on the ice at all times, except when performing one of the few circumscribed lifts or jumps. But being too earthbound isn't allowed either; lying on the ice, excessive sliding, or kneeling on both knees is forbidden.

PATTERNS

Another unique aspect of ice dancing is the pattern of steps used in the compulsory dances. Created over the years by some of the great ice dancers, the patterns are extremely complex routines, mapped out step-by-step both in diagram and in notation. Skaters must master these not just because they form a part of the competition, but because these dances are the basis of the sport.

FOOTWORK AND CLOSENESS

The team's footwork must be complicated, difficult, fast, and close—so close, in fact, that ice dancers wear special skates with blades shortened in back to avoid contact. Edges must be deep and only limited separations between skaters are allowed, usually only to change holds and for just one measure of music. Face-to-face positions are considered best, mostly because they're the most difficult. Ballroom dancing is about movement and footwork, about two dancers moving as one unit, as opposed to ballet and other types of formal dance that use two individuals to create tableaux. The same difference applies between ice dancing and pairs.

COMPETITION

Competition in ice dancing is the most complex of all skating competitions. With the end of school figures in singles, ice dancing is now the only discipline judged in three parts: two compulsory dances, each worth 10 percent of the final score; an original dance that counts as 30 percent; and a free dance that makes up 50 percent. The ice dancing competition requires more on-ice time than any other discipline; the routines are complex and fast-moving.

COMPULSORY DANCES

The first phase is two compulsory dances drawn from a group of four, which are chosen at the beginning of the season from a larger group of thirty-one dances, which all teams are able to perform. The dances follow strict patterns and steps around the ice, in time with music prepared and presented (usually in different versions but with the same time length) by the governing association of the competition, such as the USFSA or the ISU. The judges are concerned with timing, meaning that the dancers must be in rhythm with the music; expression, in that the movements of the skaters must express the nature of the specific dance; accurate and precise footwork; adherence to the preset dance patterns; an upright but not stiff style, with unison and an ease of movement; and use of the whole ice surface.

For each dance, the team receives one mark for technique and one mark for timing/expression. Each of the compulsory dances is worth 10 percent of a team's final score. The judges give scores and rank the teams after each program, deciding on a winner for each of the two dances. Each team's placement in each dance is then multiplied by 0.2 to find the factored placement; the numbers arrived at are added together, and the leader in the competition is the team with the lowest overall factored placement to that point.

ORIGINAL DANCE

After the compulsories, a random draw determines the skating order for the next aspect of the competition, the original dance. Here, a basic dance is picked— such as the blues, waltz, or tango—before the beginning of the competitive season, along with a defined tempo range. Each team chooses two minutes of its own music and creates its own version of the required dance. Whether or not vocal music with lyrics is allowed depends on the musical style of the dance. The original dance should have the character of a ballroom dance. Face-to-face positions— more difficult than side-by-side or hand-to-hand—are encouraged; two dance lifts are allowed, but one must be at the beginning or end of the program times; the dancers cannot separate except to change their hold. Complex and original footwork must be used, skaters can't push or pull each other by the skate, and they can stop twice within the program, as long as the stops are made to execute moves appropriate to the music.

The judges want to see creativity; originality; clean, sure skating with flow; use of the entire ice; and interpretation of the music—all of which are reflected in the composition mark. The second half of the mark, presentation, evaluates the timing, choreography, expression, style, carriage, and unison in relation to the music. Once again, skaters are ranked and a winner for the event determined. This time, the placements in the original dance are multiplied by 0.6 to find the factored placements, and these are added to those from the compulsory dances. By now, it's possible for a team to have stretched out to a big lead, but still only half of the total score has been determined. The championship can never be finally decided until the last event—the free dance.

FREE DANCE

Usually after a rest day, the teams return for the free dance. As in the original dance, the skating order is set by a draw, with the field broken up into an appropriate number of smaller warm-up groups if there are more than ten couples. The free dance gives teams much more freedom, within the limitations of ice dancing, to display their creativity and personality. The limitations of ice dancing, though, are quite complicated. In brief, the free dance is four minutes long; must not resemble a pairs free skate; must be difficult enough to highlight the athletic aspects of the sport; must show good technique, and must combine new and existing dance moves to convey the teams' conception of the performance. The music must be danceable; classical or theatrical music can be used only if it has been arranged as a dance. Small lifts and jumps can be used, but the lifter can't raise his hands higher than his head and jumps can only be one revolution. Except for these moves, one skate must always be on the ice. Spins can't go beyond five revolutions. Five separations for footwork and five stops are allowed, but lying on the ice, pulling, pushing, or holding each other's boots are not. Costumes must not be too showy; men must wear trousers and sleeves; ladies, skirts; and no props are allowed.

The judges give a technical mark and a presentation mark. The former takes into account the variety and difficulty of the moves and steps, the quality of the skating, and whether or not any pair skating has crept in. The latter mark considers the music, timing, rhythm, interpretation, style, unison, and harmony of the team. As always, the judges give their scores and rank the skaters accordingly. To arrive at factored placements for the free dance, positions are multiplied by 1.0; these are then added to the sum of the earlier factored placements. The champions are the team with the lowest overall factored placement.

surely went against the spirit. They used classical music, memorably in their landmark "Bolero" routine, which earned them the gold at Sarajevo, pushing them closer to pairs. The public loved them. Thousands attended their practices and after they turned professional, they performed to sold-out arenas around the globe, even in countries with no ice skating tradition.

Something new had been let out of the bottle. Even the great Russian teams of Natalia Bestemianova and Andrei Bukin, and Marina Klimova and Sergei Ponomarenko, combined winners of the next six World Championships, were skating routines that made Pakhomova and Gorshkov look restrained. Isabelle and Paul Duchesnay, a brother and sister team from Canada who eventually represented France, performed routines in the late 1980s and early 1990s that verged on performance art. Putting aside traditional holds and the quasi-romantic air that once hovered over the discipline, the Duchesnays selected unusual, sometimes conceptual, music; wore colorful, surprising outfits; and did moves that were risky, fascinating to watch, and bore no resemblance to old-fashioned ice dancing. Though judges often did not know exactly how to evaluate them, the Duchesnays did win the World Championship in 1991, the only non-Soviet or Eastern Bloc couple, other than Torvill and Dean, to win since 1970.

As in all sports, as soon as something is shown to be possible, or legal, everyone else must keep up, and the early 1990s saw a race for who could be the most extravagant. In reaction to the innovations of Torvill and Dean, and even more to the innovations of those who followed, the ISU passed new rules in 1994 to once again delineate the differences between ice dancing and pairs. Strictures on jumps, lifts, and sliding were tightened, and ballet music was banned—Torvill and Dean's gold medal–winning "Bolero" routine would not have been allowed under the new rules. Russians Evgeny Platov and Oksana (now Pasha) Grishuk, winners of four consecutive World titles since 1994 and two Olympic gold medals, and most other ice dancers now skate with a more precise, less conceptual vision of what, a century ago, was just something fun to do on the ice. ✳

MARINA KLIMOVA AND SERGEI PONOMARENKO OF THE SOVIET UNION WON THREE WORLD CHAMPIONSHIPS, AN OLYMPIC GOLD MEDAL AT ALBERTVILLE IN 1992 AND A SILVER AT CALGARY IN 1988 BY CONTINUING THE EXTRAVAGANT TRADITION BEGUN BY PAKHOMOVA AND GORSHKOV IN THE 1970S.

THE HAYDENETTES OF LEXINGTON, MASSACHUSETTS

PRECISION SKATING

While the better-known figure skating disciplines attract the media attention, precision skating—probably the least familiar of the five disciplines recognized by the ISU—is the fastest growing. More than 242 precision skating teams competed in U.S. sectionals in 1997, and approximately two thousand skaters participated in the 1998 U.S. Precision Team Championships. And though it is the youngest of the disciplines—still working toward a berth in the Olympic Winter Games—precision skating has existed in some form since early in the twentieth century.

If singles and pairs share a kinship with formal dance, and ice dancing takes ballroom for its inspiration, precision skating draws off a chorus- and dance-line tradition. Before the creation of the competitive discipline of Precision Skating in Ann Arbor, Michigan, in 1954, precision skating could be found in both professional and amateur ice shows, but only as an entertainment. The formation of the first precision team that year, the Hockettes, by Dr. Richard Porter, created a structure for the idea of choreographed group skating. Because it did not feature individual stars, Dr. Porter used it as a way to encourage skaters of different expertise levels to work together and continue toward proficiency goals besides those of the other disciplines.

By the 1970s, precision skating had spread to Canada and had begun to take firm root there. One of the things that makes precision skating unique is that it is largely a North American creation. Whereas the delay in accepting the International style until just prior to World War I put early North American singles and pairs skaters a few strides behind their European counterparts, the impetus behind the growth and acceptance of precision skating has come from the New World. Teams competed in the 1970s within the USFSA structure at the regional and sectional levels, and in 1976 Ann Arbor hosted the first precision-only championship. The popularity of precision continued to expand through the 1980s, into Japan, Australia, the Scandinavian countries, and across Europe, while Canada held the first national championship competition in precision in 1983.

The appointment in 1994 of an ISU technical committee for precision skating constituted the discipline's official recognition by figure skating's international governing body. It was the culmination of an effort that had begun in the late 1970s. The first attempts at codifying the rules of precision skating were made in 1977, and twelve years later a meeting of North American precision skating leaders in Toronto pushed this process along, with an eye to official recognition by the ISU. That same year, 1989, Molndal, Sweden, hosted the first international precision skating competition, and the first competitions under ISU regulations were held in 1990 in Boston, and in 1992 in Östersund, Sweden. The first ISU World Precision Team Championships were awarded to Minneapolis for the year 2000. A sport must first have a recognized world champion to be considered for inclusion as an Olympic

TEAM ELAN OF DETROIT DEMONSTRATES A
BLOCK FORMATION DURING AN EXHIBITION.

sport, so this competition will be the discipline's first step toward that goal.

Thirty-six countries currently have precision skating teams, including South Africa, Australia, Italy, France, and Russia. Sweden and Canada have the strongest teams at present, while in the United States, the Haydenettes of Lexington, Massachusetts, have been the national powerhouse, winning eight out of the fourteen U.S. Championships awarded since 1984. Detroit's Team Elan, with one gold, four silvers, and one bronze since 1992, and the Miami University Team, with one silver and three bronze since 1994, are also very competitive. ✳

PRECISION: WHAT YOU'LL SEE

Imagine the Radio City Music Hall Rockettes on ice. Each precision skating team has twelve to twenty-four skaters, all skating in unison to music of the team's choosing. Precision skating routines incorporate five formations, all connected with footwork that should effect smooth transitions that blend the moves without telegraphing them. The five formations are: circle, block, intersection, line, and wheel.

CIRCLE: Skaters are linked and rotate in a circular motion using step combinations. Circles can go either forward or backward, but the goal is to keep the circle perfectly round.

BLOCK: Skaters line up one behind the other in more than two straight lines to form a block. The block moves over the entire ice surface.

INTERSECTION: One half of the skating team moves through the other half of the team.

LINE: All skaters on the team are side by side, in a single or double line.

WHEEL: Skaters form lines that connect to and rotate around a central point.

All the moves must be done harmoniously to the music. Only half-jumps are allowed. No one skater can be highlighted; this is team skating, and unison is vital. Heads, arms, and footwork must all move together, but with no counting or marching. Lifts and back spirals are not allowed,

and any other moves that could be considered dangerous with a large number of skaters on the ice are discouraged. But that doesn't mean that the sport is without risk; two back lines meshing together at a fast pace is definitely a challenging and perilous maneuver.

Precision skating is dance-oriented, so flow, speed, power, and edge quality are what judges look for, along with round circles, straight lines, complicated intersections, and controlled, well-constructed wheels and blocks.

One of the many attractions of precision skating is that it is a competitive discipline open to all levels of skaters, including those just starting out, offering a competitive outlet and a sense of teamwork.

COMPETITION

There are seven divisions in precision skating in the United States: Juvenile, Intermediate, Novice, Junior, Senior, Collegiate (all skaters must be full-time students), and Adult. There are no test requirements for the divisions; placement depends entirely on age, so it is possible, though unlikely, for a basic skater to belong to a senior team.

SHORT PROGRAM

As in singles and pairs, competition for Junior and Senior precision teams is broken into two sections, a short technical program and a long free skate. In the short program, the team must perform all five elements within two minutes and forty seconds, to music of the team's choosing; the music must have a constant beat and melody, and no vocals. Senior teams can do any number of circles, with at least one change of hold and one step sequence; any kind of single or double straight lines, but they must travel the full length of the ice surface and there must be one change of hold and one step sequence; a maximum of three wheels and three intersections; and a block using at least one hold change and two step sequences. Judges give a mark for required elements and presentation, which counts as 33.3 percent of the team's final score. As happens in the other disciplines, the judges rank the teams after each performance, and at the end, the team with the majority of first-place votes is the winner of the event. The placements, or ordinals, are then multiplied by 0.5 to arrive at the factored placement.

FREE SKATE

The long program is a free-skating event to the team's own music. For Seniors it's four and a half minutes, for Juniors four. Juniors and Seniors must have one change of tempo in their routine. A good free-skating program has a balance of all the elements, skated harmoniously, with expression and musical interpretation. There should be a wide variety of difficult elements, smooth transitions, good placement of maneuvers on the ice, and an overall synchronization of the team. Marks are given in the long program for technical merit and for presentation, which, combined, count for 66.7 percent of the team's final score. Again, the winner of the event is derived from the majority of first-place votes. Ordinals are again multiplied, but this time by 1.0. The two numbers are added together and the team with the lowest score wins.

THE HAYDENETTES ARE THE UNITED STATES' LEADING PRECISION TEAM, WINNING EIGHT U.S. CHAMPIONSHIPS SINCE 1988. SWEDEN AND CANADA ARE CURRENTLY THE POWERS IN PRECISION SKATING INTERNATIONALLY.

Tara Lipinski

"I believed in myself and in Saint Therese."

When you are just fifteen years old and you have already been on top of the world, it's easy to remember your greatest moment—so far. Tara Lipinski's top achievement as a competitive skater was winning the gold medal at the 1998 Olympic Winter Games in Nagano, Japan.

It seemed the whole world had already picked Michelle Kwan to win, so Lipinski felt that the only people who believed she could win the gold were those closest to her.

"My parents and my whole support system were there for me, and of course I believed in myself," she says, "but I felt that the press and most other people didn't think it was going to happen." That only made her more determined to show them that she could go, have a good time, and skate her best.

As expected, Lipinski was in second place going into the long program. "It was really nerve-wracking after the short program," she says, "because we had a whole day of no competing, just practice. I was kind of anxious and just wanted to get out there and do it. Waiting for the long was definitely the hardest part of the whole week."

To stay focused on what she had to do, Lipinski didn't read any of the press coverage of the Games, and she tried not to think about the negative expectations she had sensed from many people.

"I believed in myself and in Saint Therese," she said. At age fifteen, Saint Therese of Lisieux, a pretty girl of slight build, had entered the order of Carmelite nuns, against great opposition from those who believed she was too young. The young saint inspired Lipinski to forge ahead and do her best no matter what others might think.

"The best part was during my long program, because I realized that it didn't really matter what came out of it," Lipinski recalls. "I was under a lot of pressure, I was at the Olympics, and I was skating one of my best performances ever."

She especially remembers the moment of being in the "kiss and cry" area after her long program, seeing her name in first place, and appreciating that everything she had dreamed about was really happening. ✳

Tara Lipinski came from behind to capture the gold medal at Nagano.

JoJo Starbuck and Ken Shelley

"I knew we were experiencing it together."

JoJo Starbuck and Ken Shelley each prize moments from the 1968 competitive season. For Shelley, the magic started at the U.S. Championships in Philadelphia. They were just sixteen years old. It was the first time they had competed at the national championship as seniors. And it was an Olympic year.

"JoJo and I just wanted to get through our programs and skate clean," Shelley recalls. They were more than clean, they were terrific. They won a bronze medal as well as a spot on the World and Olympic teams. "I had dreamed of going to the Olympics," Shelley recalls, "but I never dreamed it would happen so fast."

That same year Ken also competed as a junior in Men's singles. He had tried the previous year, but hadn't qualified for the national championships. Most coaches would have advised him to focus on only one discipline, but Starbuck's coach, John Nicks, was different. "He always encouraged me to do both," Shelley says. "And I'm glad I did."

Ken Shelley not only qualified in 1968, he won the gold.

Starbuck's favorite moments are making the 1968 Olympic team and marching in the opening ceremonies in Grenoble, France.

"It was a dream come true," she remembers, "something that happened to other people but that we had only read about and seen on TV. I had only really become aware of the Olympics four years earlier when I watched Peggy Fleming, who skated at our rink, march in the opening ceremonies on TV. And now we were right there with her in France."

For Starbuck, the opening ceremonies were pure magic. "Here I am this kid from Downey, California, walking into a stadium in France with thousands of people all cheering and waving. What a thrill! It had been snowing all morning, but when the parade began and we entered the stadium, the clouds literally parted and the sun came shining through. As we lined up in the field, five jets flew in unison above our heads, skywriting colored Olympic rings.... It was beautiful.

"Then the French skating champion, Alain Calmat, ran from one end of the stadium to the other and up this long staircase to light the official Olympic torch—with a microphone taped to his chest. We could hear his heart beat. I remember feeling like my heart was beating just as loudly as his, and without a microphone.

"The whole experience was richer because I was sharing it with Ken and my mother," JoJo remembers. "When I was growing up, my mom sacrificed everything so I could skate. As I marched around the stadium, I knew she was somewhere out there in the stands watching, and I knew we were experiencing it together." ❋

JoJo Starbuck and Ken Shelley in Grenoble, France, practicing for the 1968 Olympic Winter Games.

FOUR-TIME MEN'S WORLD CHAMPION, GERMAN WILLY BOECKL, EXECUTES HIS SCHOOL FIGURES, CIRCA 1925.

CHAPTER NINE

JUDGING

$\mathcal{H}$er program finished, a skater sits in the "kiss and cry" area, panting to catch her breath, waiting for her scores to be posted. Within minutes, the judges punch their scores into a computer and send them to the referee, who posts them on the scoreboard high above the rink for all to see. Though they are in a way the whole point of the competition, many people don't know who these judges are, how they got there, what they're looking for, or how they arrive at those all-important scores.

The figure skating scoring system is somewhat unique. Unlike speed skating, where skaters race against the clock, or ski jumping, where the best skier is the one who jumps the farthest, in figure skating, the judge's job is to rank each skater in the competition in relation to every other skater. And when judges are asked to compare one skater with another, the scoring cannot help but rely in part on their opinions. So while it's possible to count revolutions in a jump or spin, or tell whether a triple Lutz was executed with technical precision, the effect of a skater's smile or a tilt of the head can't be objectively quanti-

BEFORE THE DAY OF BIG ELECTRONIC SCOREBOARDS, CARD CADDIES DISPLAYED THE MARKS AT COMPETITIONS.

fied. And while two skaters' triple Axels may look identical to the untrained eye, the judges can see subtle differences that allow them to form an opinion as to which skater is the best. In a sport where artistry plays such an integral role, it is up to the judges to form and announce those opinions.

Because different judges can—and often do—have different opinions about what they see, this system of judging sometimes leads to split decisions as to who should be ranked first. The Ladies' free-skating program at the 1994 Olympic Winter Games in Lillehammer is a classic example. Nancy Kerrigan and Oksana Baiul each skated very well. The results of that competition have been hotly debated ever since, but what mattered on that night was that five judges thought that Oksana Baiul was the best, and four judges thought that Nancy Kerrigan was the best.

BECOMING A JUDGE

It takes a long time and a lot of hard work to become a figure skating judge. There is no typical profile; some of them are former competitive skaters, and some have never skated before. Having a skating background will cut down the amount of time and effort that is required to learn to be a good judge, but that doesn't mean a relative newcomer to the sport cannot become a terrific judge. Some of them are work-at-home parents, and some are doctors, lawyers, or corporate CEOs. What they all do have in common is a love for figure skating, and a willingness to devote countless hours of their free time volunteering to serve the sport. All prospective judges must study the rules, attend judges' schools, and spend dozens or even hundreds of hours practicing as a trial judge before they ever get to do the real thing.

MIDORI ITO OF JAPAN WAITS FOR HER SCORES IN THE "KISS AND CRY" AREA AFTER PERFORMING AT THE 1988 OLYMPICS IN CALGARY.

New judges start at the lowest level of test judging and work their way up to the highest judging appointment, which is as an ISU World/Olympic competition-level judge. It can take longer to become an Olympic-level judge than it takes to become a doctor. And save for a one-time test during the 1997-98 competition season, judges are not paid. Still, for the $500 the judges received at the 1998 U.S. Championships, they were required to judge three events, watch all of the competitors practice for those events, and attend the judges' meetings after each program of each event. To endure the time and effort of becoming and being a judge, it must be a labor of love.

A prospective judge must first become a "trial judge"—in essence, a practice judge. The candidate must be at least sixteen years old and a member of the USFSA. The first step of all candidates is to request permission from the test chair of their club to trial-judge a low-level proficiency test. The trial judge's scores are not counted toward the results of the test, but they are reviewed by the officials and kept on file as a record of the candidate's judging performance.

To be eligible to be appointed as an official test judge, a candidate must be eighteen years of age and have trial-judged a specified number of test sessions. Within those sessions, they must have judged a minimum number of tests in different levels and have a record of at least 70-75 percent agreement with the outcome of the test, depending on the particular test at issue. In addition, before a candidate will be promoted to test judge, he or she must attend a judges' school and take the annual judges' exam.

Satisfying all of these requirements can take quite a long time. So for candidates who have themselves passed a number of skating tests at a certain level there is an "accelerated" program, and for skaters who have competed at the Junior or Senior national level, a "select" program. These candidates have fewer requirements for trial judging before they become eligible for an appointment.

Once the typical candidate gets an appointment as a test judge, he or she must serve as a judge at the lowest level for a minimum of one year and judge a minimum number of tests and skating levels before they are qualified for an appointment to the next judging level. These requirements are also somewhat relaxed for candidates in the accelerated program, and a select candidate is permitted to begin at a much higher level of test judging. The higher the judging level, the fewer judges needed within the structure of competitive skating. For example, there are currently only twelve ISU World/Olympic level judges in the United States, so a candidate for that level may wait years for an appointment, and may, in fact, never get the chance.

WHAT THE JUDGES DO

Competition judges must score the skaters based on how they skated that day, not on how a skater has done in previous competitions, or how enjoyable a skater is to watch in an exhibition.

A judge's primary job is to rank the skaters relative to one another and to avoid ties whenever possible. Judges must watch practice and come up with what they call a "base mark" for each skater. This mark is the judge's determination of how the skaters could potentially rank relative to one another based on the technical difficulty of the program each skater has planned. Of course, during the actual competition, a skater may do something easier or harder than what they were practicing. In that case, the judges increase or decrease the base mark depending on what happens in the competition. This base mark is what the judges deduct points from in the short program if the skater leaves out or makes a mistake on a required element. (The details of how the scores are ultimately calculated will be discussed later in this chapter.)

For example, one skater may have planned a triple flip/double toe loop combination in her short program, while another skater may intend to perform a triple Lutz/double toe loop combination. The second skater's combination is technically harder, so the judges will assign her a base mark relative to the first skater—let's say a 5.2 for the first skater versus a 5.6 for the second. But what if during the competition the first skater instead does a triple Lutz/double toe loop combination and touches her hand down on the landing, while the second skater does a

JUDGES AT THE U.S. FIGURE SKATING CHAMPIONSHIPS IN PHILADELPHIA. SCORING A SKATING ROUTINE DEMANDS INTENSE CONCENTRATION AND THE ABILITY TO THINK AND EVALUATE COMPLEX MOVES IN AN INSTANT.

clean triple Lutz/double toe loop combination as planned? The first skater's base mark will start higher than the 5.2 she had going into the competition, but she will have points deducted for the hand touching down. So for technical merit, the first skater may end up with a score of 5.4 and the second a 5.6.

If there are twenty-four skaters in a competition, each judge will assign twenty-four different sets of scores on a scale of 6.0. If the judges were to watch a competition cold, with no prior knowledge of the potential ranking of the competitors, then they could fail to leave themselves room on the scoring scale for the best skaters. One skater early in the lineup may skate a beautiful program and get a score of 5.8/5.9. But what if there are ten skaters to go and six of them skate better than that skater? There are only four marks that are better than the first skater's marks. The judge would not have left enough room to accurately rank the field of skaters.

During the competition, each judge has a score sheet on which notes are kept for each skater. The judges must try to keep their eyes on the skater at all times, so they learn to make notations in very small boxes without looking down. Having watched the practices may help, because the judges will know when there is a moment of rest or stopping point in the program. These brief moments give the judges a chance to glance down at their score sheets to make notations.

This is not always a foolproof system, however; skaters sometimes add elements that were not in their originally planned program. Surya Bonaly and Christopher Bowman have each improvised their free skates without warning in major competitions. In the 1994 Olympics, Oksana Baiul added an extra jump at the end of her free skate. If a judge had assumed the program was over after the last planned jump and looked away, he or she would have missed the extra jump.

Sometimes it can be difficult for a judge to see subtle mistakes, like whether a skater has touched the toe of the free foot down on the landing of a jump. But they are not allowed to consult with each other, and they do not yet have the benefit of instant replay, although some countries are beginning to experiment with that. It may be only a matter of time before instant replay is a commonly used tool, but until then, if a judge is unsure whether there has been a touch down or other similar mistake, the skater must be given the benefit of the doubt.

Once a national- or international-level competition is over, all of the judges must meet with the referee and the officials of the governing body sanctioning the competition to discuss the results of the scoring. After the short program, the primary focus of discussion revolves around what kind of deductions each judge took off of each skater's required element score. After the free skate, the judges discuss

Judging Score sheet

Officials in all sports must make split-second decisions, but no sport comes close to figure skating in the intensity and precision of the judges' job. Baseball and football have breaks between every play; basketball, hockey, and soccer, for all their movement, have relatively long stretches where a referee can take stock of what's happening. But a figure skating judge must pay constant, close attention to everything a skater does for either two or four minutes, depending on the program.

In order to keep track of each skater's performance, judges use score sheets. There is no correct or recommended way to keep a scoresheet; a few longtime experts are reputed not even to use them because they can accurately judge the field without notes. Developing a quick and legible shorthand system that can be deciphered to create scores after each routine is one of the skills that judges in training work on. In each competition that they practice-judge, they'll tinker with it until they feel comfortable and confident. The score sheet at right, from a sectional competition, shows the range of what a judge must watch for and how she must record what she sees.

SINGLE FREE SKATING

No	Competitor	Double Jumps	Triple Jumps	Jump Combinations and Jump Sequences	Spins and Spin Combinations	Steps, Spirals and Movements	Total Deductions	1st Mark	2nd Mark	Total Mark	Ordinals
1 gold	sp/mu change ++	Dlo A ½ ½	TFL TSC TTL	DTL TTL DLu DLo Dlo DTL	6 ct C bs 6ct 6+ 6+	Fw+ spt EB Fw		5.3	5.5	10.8	2
2 blue+ silver	music ✓ smile+ mch+	DA DSC SE	TTL ✓ w/landing Flu Flo P	DTL DLo DA DTL IFo	64+ Slbs+ Lu?? cSlb bs10+	BSP Fwe slow turns		4.8	5.1	9.9	4
3 black silver	m/s c/t+l BF	DA Dlu	TTL TSC Tlo TFL	Tku DTL D DTL	clbb cbscbs 8+/8+ 8/8 Lb 10+ tas FB	FS/PF/ Fw		5.5	5.7	11.2	1
4 red	ort music +spr #	DtA Dlu wc DTL	TTL TSCt Tlof	TTL DTL DA DtK	8fc+ 6 Lb+ cSlb fastv	Steps Fw-slow PF-BF+ EB	keep top 6+	4.9	5.1	10.0	3
5 light blue	-strong easy c/stot -mvt spt-+	DA 3 out Dlo DTL	TTL Isc TSC	DtL DTL	fc fc++ 6 6+ cbc ++P cSlb FsB	SP F sp SEtm Fw 2A	speeds spins lower positions #	4.7	4.9	9.6	7
6 black flowers	mc/ pc smile o-	DA DA Dlu DTL DSC	TTL Tku	TLG DTL D DTL	Lb Lb ot Lbt 6+ 6t/6t 5 6+	Fw Fw PSPFw+		4.9	4.9	9.8	5
7 black	cha +t Drr mctsc/q+t (slow)	Dlu A fall	TFL TSC TTLo	Dlo Dlo Sp Dfc fct	6fc fas Lb++ cSlb bs lt	Fw BSP FSPB Turn Fw slow ↓		4.5	4.7	9.2	9
8 black/orange	Ct strong m+7	DA turnout Dlu DFL Dlo	TSC af TIL4	DA 3 DTL	6et Lbtc fast cSlb Eds cs4b AW IRA	SE/SE/SE/SE EB/EB Fw con (2F) sp-lu		4.8	4.9	9.7	6
	blue royal silver	open strong -ofas ran into boards	DA DFL DSC	T	DA DTL TTL STL	fc bs cjbs 6/6 w rcc6/6+ Lb 8+ cSlb bs 10t	↗ t+ to music moves slow compa spt/ Fw to music		4.7	4.8	9.5	8

USFSA #53 (Rev 9/96)

1 A double Axel with good length.

2 P-popped, or missed, the triple loop.

TLu=Triple Lutz. The long slash through the TLu means that Skater #2 did not complete the jump, i.e., she fell or otherwise didn't finish the move. A smaller slash such as the one here for Skater #3's Triple Salchow (TSC) means that there was a mistake such as a hand touch in the landing, which requires a deduction, but the jump itself was completed.

3 lb??=A layback spin of questionable quality.

4 The judge makes notes on the costume of each skater to refresh his or her memory.

5 Not a great night for Skater #7. She fell on her double Lutz, touched on her triple toe loop, and bombed on her triple Salchow and second triple toe loop.

6 8fc+=A flying camel with eight revolutions, performed well by Skater #9.

7 A serpentine spiral sequence or footwork pattern.

8 Skater #3 is a fine spinner; all of her spins have 8 to 10 revolutions.

how they arrived at both marks for each skater. The group discusses any scores that appear to be out of step with the rest of the panel, and they ask judges who were in disagreement to explain the reasons for their scores. At the international level, the referee may ask a judge to submit a letter to justify a score that does not agree with the panel.

WHAT THE JUDGES LOOK FOR

The judges must watch for dozens of details in each program. In the singles and pairs short program, they are looking first and foremost for technical accuracy. The program must be within the prescribed length and must contain all of the required elements. If an element is missing, if a mistake is made, or if there are extra elements that are not required, points are deducted from the skater's base mark. The judges scrutinize each required element as follows.

FIVE-TIME U.S. CHAMPION TODD ELDREDGE TUCKS INTO A SIT SPIN WITH THE LEG EXTENSION THAT JUDGES LOOK FOR IN THIS MOVE.

> JUMPS: The judges evaluate the height and distance across the ice of each jump and jump combination, as well as whether the takeoffs and landings were clean. If a skater omits a required jump or jump combination, the judge deducts up to 0.5 from the skater's base mark. If the skater makes a mistake on a jump, such as putting a hand down on the ice or falling, the judge deducts between 0.1 and 0.4, depending on the severity of the mistake. These mistakes may also be reflected in the mark for presentation if they disrupt the flow of the program.

> SPINS: The judges count the revolutions in each spin to make sure they have the minimum number for singles in championship events (eight revolutions for individual spins, eight revolutions for flying spins, and twelve total revolutions for combination spins, with at least six revolutions on each foot). They also look for strength, control, speed, and whether the spin is centered. For flying spins, they look for the height of the jump into the spin. If a skater omits a required spin, the judge deducts up to 0.5 from the base mark. As with the jumps, the judges must deduct points for mistakes, such as not completing the required revolutions, or, in spins, traveling across the ice rather than staying centered. The points deducted range between 0.1 and 0.4, depending on the severity of the mistake.

> STEP AND SPIRAL SEQUENCES: The judges want to see intricacy in the footwork, good swing, carriage, and flow, as well as conformity with a circular, serpentine, or straight-line pattern. If the skater omits a step or spiral sequence, the judge deducts 0.4 from the base mark, and if the skater makes a mistake such as tripping or failing to complete a pattern, the judges deduct between 0.1 and 0.3 points.

RUSSIAN ILIA KULIK TOOK AN EARLY LEAD IN THE MEN'S COMPETITION AT NAGANO AND HELD ON TO WIN THE GOLD MEDAL.

Points are also deducted if the skater adds extra elements (0.1 to 0.2 deduction) or repeats a jump (0.3 deduction).

In the free skate, there are no required elements, thus no required deductions for omissions or mistakes in the program. The judges give credit for the technical difficulty of the program, the variety of moves executed, and the cleanness and sureness of the skater's execution of the moves. The USFSA rule book provides guidelines for what a well-balanced Senior free skate should contain; these include a number of different double or triple jumps (although only two given jumps may be repeated, and then only once and in combination); at least one jump combination or sequence, four different spins, with at least one a spin combination, and one a flying spin; two different kinds of step sequences for men; and a step sequence and a spiral or free-skating move sequence for women.

In addition to evaluating the technical elements, the judges must evaluate the presentation. For both the short program and the free skate, the judges arrive at their marks for presentation by evaluating: the overall balance of the program's composition, and whether it harmoniously conforms with the chosen music; the difficulty of the connecting steps; the skater's speed; the utilization of the ice surface; the skater's ease of movement and timing with the music; the skater's carriage and style; originality; and the skater's expression of the character of the music.

THE SCORES

The scores are based on a 6.0 scale: 0 means the program was not skated; 1.0 means it was skated very poorly; 2.0 means it was poor; 3.0 means it was mediocre; 4.0 means it was good; 5.0 means it was very good; and 6.0 means it was perfect and faultless. The most important factor is how each judge ranks the skaters relative to one another, not whether they thought the program was a "very good" 5.0. That's why a score of 5.2 by one judge may actually place that skater higher than another judge's score of 5.6.

In singles and pairs skating, the short program counts for one-third of the total score and the free skate counts for two-thirds. In ice dancing, there are generally two compulsory dances, an original dance, and a free dance. The two compulsory dances each count for 10 percent of the overall score, the original dance counts for 30 percent, and the free dance counts for 50 percent.

Each judge assigns two scores for every program and dance. In the pairs and singles short program, there is one score for required elements and one score for presentation, and in the free skate, one score for technical merit and another for presentation. Each judge then adds those two scores together to arrive at one total score for each performance.

The Men's competition from the 1998 Olympic Winter Games in Nagano will illustrate how this works. Below are the judges' short program scores for the top five skaters:

REQUIRED ELEMENT AND PRESENTATION SCORES PLUS TOTAL SCORES	GBR	UKR	CAN	ROM	JPN	RUS	AZE	USA	FRA
ILIA KULIK									
Required Elem.	5.7	5.8	5.7	5.8	5.8	5.8	5.8	5.7	5.8
Presentation	5.8	5.9	5.9	5.9	5.8	5.8	5.8	5.9	5.9
Total Score	11.5	11.7	11.6	11.7	11.6	11.6	11.6	11.6	11.7
PHILIPPE CANDELORO									
Required Elem.	5.3	5.4	5.4	5.1	5.5	5.5	5.3	5.2	5.6
Presentation	5.4	5.7	5.6	5.4	5.7	5.7	5.5	5.5	5.7
Total Score	10.7	11.1	11.0	10.5	11.2	11.2	10.8	10.7	11.3
ALEXEI YAGUDIN									
Required Elem.	5.9	5.7	5.6	5.5	5.7	5.7	5.7	5.5	5.7
Presentation	5.7	5.8	5.7	5.7	5.7	5.7	5.7	5.7	5.7
Total Score	11.6	11.5	11.3	11.2	11.4	11.4	11.4	11.2	11.4
TODD ELDREDGE									
Required Elem.	5.9	5.8	5.8	5.8	5.7	5.7	5.8	5.8	5.8
Presentation	5.8	5.8	5.7	5.8	5.8	5.8	5.9	5.8	5.8
Total Score	11.7	11.6	11.5	11.6	11.5	11.5	11.7	11.6	11.6
ELVIS STOJKO									
Required Elem.	5.7	5.9	5.8	5.9	5.8	5.8	5.8	5.8	5.9
Presentation	5.6	5.9	6.0	5.7	5.7	5.7	5.7	5.7	5.7
Total Score	11.3	11.8	11.8	11.6	11.5	11.5	11.5	11.5	11.6

PHILIPPE CANDELORO'S DRAMATIC FREE-SKATING PERFORMANCE AT THE NAGANO OLYMPICS PUSHED HIM PAST TODD ELDREDGE FOR THE MEN'S BRONZE MEDAL.

The total scores are then converted into what are called ordinals. An ordinal represents the numbered placement of each skater from first to last. Each judge's marks are placed in order from the highest total score down to the lowest, and ordinal number 1 goes to the highest total score.

Sometimes a judge gives the same total score to two or more skaters. For example, below you'll see that the U.S. judge assigned a total score of 11.6 to both Ilia Kulik and Todd Eldredge. Because this is the short program, the judge broke the tie by giving the higher-valued ordinal to the skater with the higher mark for required elements. (It is not necessary for a tie to be broken, but it is obviously desirable to do so.) In the previous chart you can see that the U.S. judge gave Todd a higher mark for required elements than he gave Ilia, so Todd got the U.S. judge's first-place ordinal. The other ties were broken in the same way.

TOTAL SCORES AND ORDINALS	GBR	UKR	CAN	ROM	JPN	RUS	AZE	USA	FRA
ILIA KULIK									
Total Score	11.5	11.7	11.6	11.7	11.6	11.6	11.6	11.6	11.7
Ordinal	3	2	2	1	1	1	2	2	1
PHILIPPE CANDELORO									
Total Score	10.7	11.1	11.0	10.5	11.2	11.2	10.8	10.7	11.3
Ordinal	5	5	5	5	5	5	5	5	5
ALEXEI YAGUDIN									
Total Score	11.6	11.5	11.3	11.2	11.4	11.4	11.4	11.2	11.4
Ordinal	2	4	4	4	4	4	4	4	4
TODD ELDREDGE									
Total Score	11.7	11.6	11.5	11.6	11.5	11.5	11.7	11.6	11.6
Ordinal	1	3	3	3	3	3	1	1	3
ELVIS STOJKO									
Total Score	11.3	11.8	11.8	11.6	11.5	11.5	11.5	11.5	11.6
Ordinal	4	1	1	2	2	2	3	3	2

Elvis Stojko of Canada (above) skated a memorable free-skating program, even though he was suffering from an injury. Despite a strong short program, Todd Eldredge (below) was not able to fend off Philippe Candeloro in the free skate.

Next the ordinals were counted. The skater with the absolute majority (five out of nine) of first-place ordinals won first place for the short, and so on down the list. In this case, there was no absolute majority of first-place ordinals—Ilia had four, Todd had three, and Elvis had two. When this happens, the skater with the most first- and second-place ordinals wins first place. Ilia had the most first- and second-place ordinals (eight total), so he won first- place for the short program.

When counting ordinals for second place and below, any ordinals that are higher in value than the placement being considered are counted toward the majority for that placement. For example, Elvis had six second-place or better ordinals (two first-place and four second-place), so he won second place. Todd got third place with nine third-place or better ordinals (three first and six third), and so on.

Remember, the short program counts for only one-third of the overall competition score. Once the placement in the short program has been determined, it is then multiplied by 0.5 to give it the proper weight in the overall competition score. The resulting number is called the factored placement.

ORDINALS									
	GBR	UKR	CAN	ROM	JPN	RUS	AZE	USA	FRA
ILIA KULIK									
Ordinal	3	2	2	1	1	1	2	2	1
PHILIPPE CANDELORO									
Ordinal	5	5	5	5	5	5	5	5	5
ALEXEI YAGUDIN									
Ordinal	2	4	4	4	4	4	4	4	4
TODD ELDREDGE									
Ordinal	1	3	3	3	3	3	1	1	3
ELVIS STOJKO									
Ordinal	4	1	1	2	2	2	3	3	2

FACTORED PLACEMENTS		
PLACEMENT	SKATER	FACTORED PLACEMENT (placement × .5)
1	Ilia Kulik	0.5
2	Elvis Stojko	1.0
3	Todd Eldredge	1.5
4	Alexei Yagudin	2.0
5	Philippe Candeloro	2.5

After the skaters have performed their free skates, those scores are added and assigned ordinals just like the short program scores. Here are the free-skate scores and ordinals for the top five men from the 1998 Olympics:

	GBR	UKR	CAN	ROM	JPN	RUS	AZE	USA	FRA
ILIA KULIK									
Technical Merit	5.7	5.9	5.8	5.9	5.9	5.8	5.8	5.8	5.8
Presentation	5.9	5.9	5.8	5.8	5.9	5.9	5.9	5.9	5.9
Total Score	11.6	11.8	11.6	11.7	11.8	11.7	11.7	11.7	11.7
Ordinal	1	1	1	1	1	1	1	1	1
TODD ELDREDGE									
Technical Merit	5.6	5.7	5.6	5.6	5.7	5.7	5.6	5.7	5.7
Presentation	5.7	5.8	5.8	5.7	5.8	5.7	5.7	5.8	5.8
Total Score	11.3	11.5	11.4	11.3	11.5	11.4	11.3	11.5	11.5
Ordinal	2	4	4	4	3	5	4	3	3
ALEXEI YAGUDIN									
Technical Merit	5.6	5.6	5.5	5.5	5.7	5.8	5.6	5.4	5.6
Presentation	5.6	5.6	5.5	5.4	5.7	5.7	5.6	5.7	5.5
Total Score	11.2	11.2	11.0	10.9	11.4	11.5	11.2	11.1	11.1
Ordinal	4	5	5	5	5	Tied 3	5	5	5
PHILIPPE CANDELORO									
Technical Merit	5.5	5.6	5.5	5.7	5.7	5.8	5.6	5.6	5.6
Presentation	5.7	5.9	5.9	5.8	5.9	5.8	5.8	5.8	6.0
Total Score	11.2	11.5	11.4	11.5	11.6	11.6	11.4	11.4	11.6
Ordinal	3	3	3	2	2	2	3	4	2
ELVIS STOJKO									
Technical Merit	5.7	5.8	5.8	5.8	5.8	5.8	5.8	5.8	5.8
Presentation	5.5	5.8	5.7	5.7	5.7	5.7	5.7	5.8	5.7
Total Score	11.2	11.6	11.5	11.5	11.5	11.5	11.5	11.6	11.5
Ordinal	5	2	2	3	4	Tied 3	2	2	4

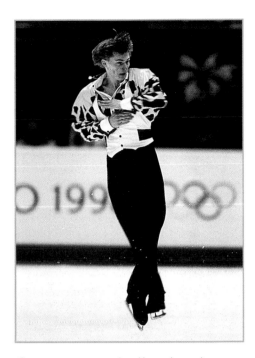

GOLD MEDAL WINNER ILIA KULIK (ABOVE) LANDED A QUADRUPLE JUMP IN HIS FREE-SKATING PROGRAM. (BELOW) KULIK ACCEPTS HIS MEDAL ALONG WITH SILVER MEDALIST ELVIS STOJKO (LEFT) AND BRONZE MEDALIST PHILIPPE CANDELORO (RIGHT).

Once again there were several ties that had to be broken. The judge from Great Britain gave the same total score to three different skaters—Alexei Yagudin, Philippe Candeloro, and Elvis Stojko. If a judge gives the same total score to two or more skaters in the free skate, the skater with the higher presentation mark wins the judge's higher-valued ordinal. Philippe had the highest presentation mark and got the third-place ordinal from the British judge, Alexei had the next highest presentation score and got the fourth-place ordinal, and Elvis got the fifth-place ordinal.

The Russian judge also tied two skaters, but the tie could not be broken. That judge gave the same total score to Alexei Yagudin and Elvis Stojko, with identical marks for both skaters for technical merit and presentation. Since neither skater had a higher presentation mark from the Russian judge, they remained tied for the judge's third-place ordinal. In that situation, the Russian judge's fourth-place ordinal was not assigned; the next ordinal assigned was the fifth-place ordinal.

Next, the free-skate ordinals were counted to determine who won the free skate. Ilia received first-place ordinals from all nine judges, unanimously winning first place. There was no absolute majority of second-place votes, so we count who has the most second- and third-place votes. Philippe had the most with eight (four second and four third) giving him second-place for the long, and Elvis had six (four second and two third) giving him third. Todd had the majority of fourth-place or better ordinals, and Alexei had the majority of fifth-place or better ordinals.

After the free-skate placements were determined, the short-program factored placements were added to the free skate factored placements. The skater with the lowest combined factored placement number wins.

FACTORED PLACEMENTS FROM SHORT PLUS LONG PLACEMENTS					
SKATER	SHORT	FACTORED	FREE SKATE	S + FS	FINISH
		(placement × .5)			
Ilia Kulik	1	0.5	1	1.5	1
Elvis Stojko	2	1.0	3	4.0	2
Todd Eldredge	3	1.5	4	5.5	4
Alexei Yagudin	4	2.0	5	7.0	5
Philippe Candeloro	5	2.5	2	4.5	3

As you can see, although Philippe placed higher than Elvis in the free skate, he placed third overall because his higher short-program factored placement brought his overall placement lower than Elvis's overall placement.

Don't worry if your head spins trying to follow all this. The USFSA uses official accountants to keep track of this process during each competition, and they use a specially designed computer program to help them do it quickly.

There is one interesting scoring phenomenon in figure skating that bears noting. Sometimes it's possible for a skater to beat another skater in the standings but then get knocked below them based on how a third skater is scored. One such situation occurred in the Ladies' free skate of the 1997 U.S. Championships. The standings entering the free skate had Michelle Kwan first, Tara Lipinski second, and Tonia Kwiatkowski third, followed by Amber Corwin in fourth, Angela Nikodinov in fifth and Nicole Bobek in sixth.

Nicole Bobek skated an excellent free skate which put her in first place before the final group of five skaters took the ice. Tonia Kwiatkowski skated next and stayed ahead of Nicole Bobek in the standings based on the skaters who had competed thus far. Tonia and Nicole's scores and placements looked like this:

	1	2	3	4	5	6	7	8	9
NICOLE BOBEK									
Technical Merit	5.4	5.7	5.8	5.5	5.4	5.6	5.6	5.6	5.7
Presentation	5.6	5.8	5.8	5.6	5.6	5.8	5.8	5.8	5.8
Total Score	11.0	11.5	11.6	11.1	11.0	11.4	11.4	11.4	11.5
Ordinal	1	1	1	1	1	1	1	1	1

Short Program Factored Placement = 3   Current Combined Placement = 4.0
Current Long Program Placement = 1   Current Overall Placement = 2

	1	2	3	4	5	6	7	8	9
TONIA KWIATKOWSKI									
Technical Merit	5.2	5.4	5.4	5.4	5.3	5.3	5.4	4.9	5.4
Presentation	5.4	5.7	5.6	5.5	5.5	5.6	5.6	4.8	5.5
Total Score	10.6	11.1	11.0	10.9	10.8	10.9	11.0	9.7	10.9
Ordinal	2	2	2	2	2	2	2	2	2

Short Program Factored Placement = 1.5   Current Combined Placement = 3.5
Current Long Program Placement = 2   Current Overall Placement = 1

Angela Nikodinov skated next and her scores put her in second place. But the interesting thing about Angela's scores was that they bumped Tonia out of first place down to third, and boosted Nicole up from second to first place. The following shows how the scores, ordinals, and placements shifted:

A QUIRK IN SCORING CALCULATIONS PUT TONIA KWIATKOWSKI (ABOVE) DOWN FROM FIRST TO THIRD PLACE AT THE 1997 U.S. CHAMPIONSHIPS AND NICOLE BOBEK (OPPOSITE) UP FROM SECOND PLACE TO FIRST, ALL BECAUSE OF ANOTHER SKATER'S PERFORMANCE.

	1	2	3	4	5	6	7	8	9
NICOLE BOBEK									
Technical Merit	5.4	5.7	5.8	5.5	5.4	5.6	5.6	5.6	5.7
Presentation	5.6	5.8	5.8	5.6	5.6	5.8	5.8	5.8	5.8
Total Score	11.0	11.5	11.6	11.1	11.0	11.4	11.4	11.4	11.5
Ordinal	1	1	1	2	2	1	1	2	1

Short Program Factored Placement = 3
Current Long Program Placement = 1

Current Combined Placement = 4.0
Current Overall Placement = 1

	1	2	3	4	5	6	7	8	9
TONIA KWIATKOWSKI									
Technical Merit	5.2	5.4	5.4	5.4	5.3	5.3	5.4	4.9	5.4
Presentation	5.4	5.7	5.6	5.5	5.5	5.6	5.6	4.8	5.5
Total Score	10.6	11.1	11.0	10.9	10.8	10.9	11.0	9.7	10.9
Ordinal	3	3	3	3	3	3	3	3	3

Short Program Factored Placement = 1.5
Current Long Program Placement = 3

Current Combined Placement = 4.5
Current Overall Placement = 1

	1	2	3	4	5	6	7	8	9
ANGELA NIKODINOV									
Technical Merit	5.5	5.7	5.6	5.6	5.6	5.7	5.7	5.8	5.6
Presentation	5.4	5.6	5.6	5.7	5.8	5.5	5.7	5.7	5.4
Total Score	10.9	11.3	11.2	11.3	11.4	11.2	11.4	11.5	11.0
Ordinal	2	2	2	1	1	2	2	1	2

Short Program Factored Placement = 2.5
Current Long Program Placement = 2

Current Combined Placement = 4.5
Current Overall Placement = 1

Although they had the same total combined placement (4.5), the tie was broken in favor of the skater who had the better long-program placement, which in this case was Angela. The ISU is exploring ways to remedy this kind of result.

HOW THE JUDGES ARE JUDGED

Evaluated throughout their career, judges must comply with regular continuing education requirements to keep up with the evolving rules of the sport, and must pass an annual exam. In addition, scoring is monitored to maintain conformity. There will seldom be 100 percent consensus as to the exact ranking of all of the skaters, but there should be a great deal of agreement. If a judge consistently falls outside the consensus, he or she will not be invited back to judge future competitions.

At international competitions, a Technical Committee monitors the judges' scoring for problems such as national bias or block voting. Judges will be asked to justify themselves if they have placed a member of their nation's team in first place with no agreement from the panel. In addition, if a group of judges appears to be ranking the skaters the same way, but the remaining judges have given noticeably different rankings, the Technical Committee will investigate whether the group has essentially conspired ahead of time to vote a certain way. The severest penalty would be that a judge is banned from judging future competitions. Block judging is relatively uncommon at major events today, due in large part to the greater accountability demanded now of judges as well as the increased scrutiny that comes with broader television coverage.

Judging requires a lot of time, a lot of study, a keen eye, and perhaps most of all a lot of guts. The competitors may be under the critical eye of the judges, but the judges are under the critical eye of the increasingly figure skating–savvy public. The more the public understands about the judging system, the more judges will be held accountable for their scores, making the system as fair as it can be. ✳

PAUL WYLIE

"Making peace with my career."

In the year leading up to the 1992 Olympics in Albertville, judges, coaches, journalists, and other skaters all said Paul Wylie should give up skating. One journalist called him a "pathetic figure" and, at a press conference during the U.S. Championships, asked him: "What are you doing here?"

"Everybody wanted me to be gone," Wylie says, "and I don't know why."

When the nationals got under way, Wylie's performance was as disappointing as had been predicted. He tried two triple Axels, but stepped out of both. His marks were not great, and there were three skaters left to go. Thinking his chances for making the Olympic team were gone, Wylie went to the dressing room and started changing into his street clothes.

"In that moment I started making peace with my career," he explains. "I was thinking about how thankful I was for the fun I did have, and that I had done my best. Then I started to think ahead to my future, about the possibility of going to law school. By the time I finished that thought, someone rushed in and said, 'What are you doing? You made the Olympic team, get your clothes on and get on the podium.'"

Paul Wylie, who was supposedly washed-up as a skater, had just five weeks to prepare for the Olympics. "I had a total change of attitude," he says. "I really went for it in training and started focusing on everything positive."

In the short program at Albertville, Wylie completed both the difficult triple Axel combination and the triple flip. It was the best performance of his career.

"I was the guy who had not even made the advance publicity in the *New York Times*, and suddenly I was in third place going into the long program," Wylie says. "The next day I went to the team sports psychologist and asked how I could keep from choking in the long. If I had choked, I could have gone down in history as that 'pathetic figure,' and I really didn't want that." The psychologist told Paul to allow himself to indulge in an embellished visualization of all the positive things a medal would do for his career, and then to forget about the aftermath and concentrate on the free skate itself.

Wylie took the advice and gave a performance he could be proud of as the last of his eligible career. "I had this huge smile on my face because I knew I would never have to face that kind of pressure in front of those judges again. It had been a long and very painful career, with a lot of bad memories mixed in with the good. I was thrilled to be on the other side of all of that. When the last beat of my music ended, I felt so relieved."

No one was more shocked than Wylie when he learned he had won the silver medal. "That moment totally rewrote the ending of my story." ✳

PAUL WYLIE ENDED HIS ELIGIBLE CAREER WITH A

MEMORABLE TRIUMPH.

RUDY GALINDO

"It was like a dream."

Of Rudy Galindo's many achievements—winning the World Junior Men's title, being the first U.S. pairs team (with Kristi Yamaguchi) to win the World Junior Pairs title, and winning the U.S. Senior Pairs title—his most memorable by far was his victory at the 1996 U.S. Men's Championship.

Galindo had been seriously considering quitting the sport. He was struggling financially. To make ends meet, he taught skating to young kids at his local rink. "I remember seeing a poster announcing that the next nationals would be held in San Jose," Galindo recalls. "It's so rare for nationals to come to a skater's home town that I decided to give it one more year. I thought it would be a fun way to go out—in my home town."

Galindo's car broke down early in the summer, but since he was saving his teaching money for training and costumes, he decided to ride his bike to and from the rink every day instead. "It was great exercise," he says. "It got me into great shape."

At an early-season qualifying competition, friends and advisors told him that his skating was good enough to qualify for the World team. "So after I won sectionals," Galindo recounts, "I kept up the same training habits, riding my bike to practice and to the gym, even through the rain. But I couldn't help wondering if anything would really come of it."

When the week of the U.S. Championships arrived, Galindo was skating better than ever. He was third after the short program. "I remember the crowd booing the judges' marks," he says. "I had been the only one who did a triple/triple combination. So I thought, 'Oh, it's going to be one of those competitions where they're not going to give me the marks anyway, so just have fun.'"

That night Galindo sat home alone. "I knew it could go either way—I could get third and make the World team, or get fourth and just miss it. I realized it wasn't just about fun anymore. I had to get serious for the long program because I had a real chance."

The free skate the next day was one of the most extraordinary experiences of his life. "When I stepped on the ice," he says, "I felt like I was in a harness and someone was helping me through it." The next thing he remembers is being in the press room wearing a gold medal. He had come full circle—from the top of the sport with Kristi Yamaguchi to not knowing if he would ever find his place again when she quit pairs and now back, many years later, to the top again.

"It was so weird," he says. "I had been national champion with Kristi, and now here I was national champion again so many years later. People kept asking me how I felt—it was like a dream." ✳

RUDY GALINDO'S LAST TRY FOR A U.S. CHAMPIONSHIP WAS HIS FINEST. HE WON THE 1996 U.S. TITLE BEFORE A HOME TOWN CROWD IN SAN JOSE.

MEN'S GOLD MEDALISTS

1914	New Haven, CT	Norman M. Scott
1915-1917	No Competition Held	
1918	New York, NY	Nathaniel Niles
1919	No Competition Held	
1920	New York, NY	Sherwin Badger
1921	Philadelphia, PA	Sherwin Badger
1922	Boston, MA	Sherwin Badger
1923	New Haven, CT	Sherwin Badger
1924	Philadelphia, PA	Sherwin Badger
1925	New York, NY	Nathaniel Niles
1926	Boston, MA	Chris Christenson
1927	New York, NY	Nathaniel Niles
1928	New Haven, CT	Roger Turner
1929	New York, NY	Roger Turner
1930	Providence, RI	Roger Turner
1931	Boston, MA	Roger Turner
1932	New York, NY	Roger Turner
1933	New Haven, CT	Roger Turner
1934	Philadelphia, PA	Roger Turner
1935	New Haven, CT	Robin Lee
1936	New York, NY	Robin Lee
1937	Chicago, IL	Robin Lee
1938	Philadelphia, PA	Robin Lee
1939	St. Paul, MN	Robin Lee
1940	Cleveland, OH	Eugene Turner
1941	Boston, MA	Eugene Turner
1942	Chicago, IL	Bobby Specht
1943	New York, NY	Arthur R. Vaughn, Jr.
1944-1945	No Competition Held	
1946	Chicago, IL	Richard Button
1947	Berkeley, CA	Richard Button
1948	Colo. Springs, CO	Richard Button
1949	Colo. Springs, CO	Richard Button
1950	Washington, D.C.	Richard Button
1951	Seattle, WA	Richard Button
1952	Colo. Springs, CO	Richard Button
1953	Hershey, PA	Hayes A. Jenkins
1954	Los Angeles, CA	Hayes A. Jenkins
1955	Colo. Springs, CO	Hayes A. Jenkins
1956	Philadelphia, PA	Hayes A. Jenkins
1957	Berkeley, CA	David Jenkins
1958	Minneapolis, MN	David Jenkins
1959	Rochester, NY	David Jenkins
1960	Seattle, WA	David Jenkins
1961	Colo. Springs, CO	Bradley Lord
1962	Boston, MA	Monty Hoyt
1963	Long Beach, CA	Thomas Litz
1964	Cleveland, OH	Scott Allen
1965	Lake Placid, NY	Gary Visconti
1966	Berkeley, CA	Scott Allen
1967	Omaha, NE	Gary Visconti
1968	Philadelphia, PA	Tim Wood
1969	Seattle, WA	Tim Wood

1970	Tulsa, OK	Tim Wood
1971	Buffalo, NY	John Misha Petkevich
1972	Long Beach, CA	Kenneth Shelley
1973	Minneapolis, MN	Gordon McKellen, Jr.
1974	Providence, RI	Gordon McKellen, Jr.
1975	Oakland, CA	Gordon McKellen, Jr.
1976	Colo. Springs, CO	Terry Kubicka
1977	Hartford, CT	Charles Tickner
1978	Portland, OR	Charles Tickner
1979	Cincinnati, OH	Charles Tickner
1980	Atlanta, GA	Charles Tickner
1981	San Diego, CA	Scott Hamilton
1982	Indianapolis, IN	Scott Hamilton
1983	Pittsburgh, PA	Scott Hamilton
1984	Salt Lake City, UT	Scott Hamilton
1985	Kansas City, MO	Brian Boitano
1986	Long Island, NY	Brian Boitano
1987	Tacoma, WA	Brian Boitano
1988	Denver, CO	Brian Boitano
1989	Baltimore, MD	Christopher Bowman
1990	Salt Lake City, UT	Todd Eldredge
1991	Minneapolis, MN	Todd Eldredge
1992	Orlando, FL	Christopher Bowman
1993	Phoenix, AZ	Scott Davis
1994	Detroit, MI	Scott Davis
1995	Providence, RI	Todd Eldredge
1996	San Jose, CA	Rudy Galindo
1997	Nashville, TN	Todd Eldredge
1998	Philadelphia, PA	Todd Eldredge

LADIES' GOLD MEDALISTS

1914	New Haven, CT	Theresa Weld
1915-1917	No Competition Held	
1918	New York, NY	Rosemary Beresford
1919	No Competition Held	
1920	New York, NY	Theresa Weld
1921	Philadelphia, PA	Theresa Weld Blanchard
1922	Boston, MA	Theresa Weld Blanchard
1923	New Haven, CT	Theresa Weld Blanchard
1924	Philadelphia, PA	Theresa Weld Blanchard
1925	New York, NY	Beatrix Loughran
1926	Boston, MA	Beatrix Loughran
1927	New York, NY	Beatrix Loughran
1928	New Haven, CT	Maribel Vinson
1929	New York, NY	Maribel Vinson
1930	Providence, RI	Maribel Vinson
1931	Boston, MA	Maribel Vinson
1932	New York, NY	Maribel Vinson
1933	New Haven, CT	Maribel Vinson
1934	Philadelphia, PA	Suzanne Davis
1935	New Haven, CT	Maribel Vinson
1936	New York, NY	Maribel Vinson
1937	Chicago, IL	Maribel Vinson
1938	Philadelphia, PA	Joan Tozzer
1939	St. Paul, MN	Joan Tozzer
1940	Cleveland, OH	Joan Tozzer
1941	Boston, MA	Jane Vaughn
1942	Chicago, IL	Jane Vaughn Sullivan
1943	New York, NY	Gretchen Merrill
1944	Minneapolis, MN	Gretchen Merrill
1945	New York, NY	Gretchen Merrill
1946	Chicago, IL	Gretchen Merrill
1947	Berkeley, CA	Gretchen Merrill
1948	Colo. Springs, CO	Gretchen Merrill
1949	Colo. Springs, CO	Yvonne C. Sherman
1950	Washington, D.C.	Yvonne C. Sherman
1951	Seattle, WA	Sonya Klopfer
1952	Colo. Springs, CO	Tenley Albright
1953	Hershey, PA	Tenley Albright
1954	Los Angeles, CA	Tenley Albright
1955	Colo. Springs, CO	Tenley Albright
1956	Philadelphia, PA	Tenley Albright
1957	Berkeley, CA	Carol Heiss
1958	Minneapolis, MN	Carol Heiss

TARA LIPINSKI

1959	Rochester, NY	Carol Heiss
1960	Seattle, WA	Carol Heiss
1961	Colo. Springs, CO	Laurence Owen
1962	Boston, MA	Barbara Roles
1963	Long Beach, CA	Lorraine Hanlon
1964	Cleveland, OH	Peggy Fleming
1965	Lake Placid, NY	Peggy Fleming
1966	Berkeley, CA	Peggy Fleming
1967	Omaha, NE	Peggy Fleming
1968	Philadelphia, PA	Peggy Fleming
1969	Seattle, WA	Janet Lynn
1970	Tulsa, OK	Janet Lynn
1971	Buffalo, NY	Janet Lynn
1972	Long Beach, CA	Janet Lynn
1973	Minneapolis, MN	Janet Lynn
1974	Providence, RI	Dorothy Hamill
1975	Oakland, CA	Dorothy Hamill
1976	Colo. Springs, CO	Dorothy Hamill
1977	Hartford, CT	Linda Fratianne
1978	Portland, OR	Linda Fratianne
1979	Cincinnati, OH	Linda Fratianne
1980	Atlanta, GA	Linda Fratianne
1981	San Diego, CA	Elaine Zayak
1982	Indianapolis, IN	Rosalynn Sumners
1983	Pittsburgh, PA	Rosalynn Sumners
1984	Salt Lake City, UT	Rosalynn Sumners
1985	Kansas City, MO	Tiffany Chin
1986	Long Island, NY	Debi Thomas
1987	Tacoma, WA	Jill Trenary
1988	Denver, CO	Debi Thomas
1989	Baltimore, MD	Jill Trenary
1990	Salt Lake City, UT	Jill Trenary
1991	Minneapolis, MN	Tonya Harding
1992	Orlando, FL	Kristi Yamaguchi
1993	Phoenix, AZ	Nancy Kerrigan
1994	Detroit, MI	Vacant*
1995	Providence, RI	Nicole Bobek
1996	San Jose, CA	Michelle Kwan
1997	Nashville, TN	Tara Lipinski
1998	Philadelphia, PA	Michelle Kwan

* In June 1994, a USFSA Hearing Panel stripped Tonya Harding of the 1994 U.S. Ladies' title for her involvement in the Jan. 6, 1994, attack on Nancy Kerrigan. In August 1994, the USFSA Executive Committee voted to leave the title vacant.

"THE KING PIVOT"

Pairs Gold Medalists

1914	New Haven, CT	Jeanne Chevalier Norman M. Scott
1915-1917	No Competition Held	
1918	New York, NY	Theresa Weld Nathaniel Niles
1919	No Competition Held	
1920	New York, NY	Theresa Weld Nathaniel Niles
1921	Philadelphia, PA	Theresa Weld Blanchard Nathaniel Niles
1922	Boston, MA	Theresa Weld Blanchard Nathaniel Niles
1923	New Haven, CT	Theresa Weld Blanchard Nathaniel Niles
1924	Philadelphia, PA	Theresa Weld Blanchard Nathaniel Niles
1925	New York, NY	Theresa Weld Blanchard Nathaniel Niles
1926	Boston, MA	Theresa Weld Blanchard Nathaniel Niles
1927	New York, NY	Theresa Weld Blanchard Nathaniel Niles
1928	New Haven, CT	Maribel Vinson Thornton Coolidge
1929	New York, NY	Maribel Vinson Thornton Coolidge
1930	Providence, RI	Beatrix Loughran Sherwin Badger
1931	Boston, MA	Beatrix Loughran Sherwin Badger
1932	New York, NY	Beatrix Loughran Sherwin Badger
1933	New Haven, CT	Maribel Vinson George Hill
1934	Philadelphia, PA	Grace Madden James L. Madden
1935	New Haven, CT	Maribel Vinson George Hill
1936	New York, NY	Maribel Vinson George Hill
1937	Chicago, IL	Maribel Vinson George Hill
1938	Philadelphia, PA	Joan Tozzer Bernard Fox
1939	St. Paul, MN	Joan Tozzer Bernard Fox
1940	Cleveland, OH	Joan Tozzer Bernard Fox
1941	Boston, MA	Donna Atwood Eugene Turner
1942	Chicago, IL	Doris Schubach Walter Noffke
1943	New York, NY	Doris Schubach Walter Noffke
1944	Minneapolis, MN	Doris Schubach Walter Noffke
1945	New York, NY	Donna J. Pospisil Jean P. Brunet
1946	Chicago, IL	Donna J. Pospisil Jean P. Brunet
1947	Berkeley, CA	Yvonne Sherman Robert Swenning
1948	Colo. Springs, CO	Karol Kennedy Peter Kennedy
1949	Colo. Springs, CO	Karol Kennedy Peter Kennedy
1950	Washington, D.C.	Karol Kennedy Peter Kennedy
1951	Seattle, WA	Karol Kennedy Peter Kennedy
1952	Colo. Springs, CO	Karol Kennedy Peter Kennedy
1953	Hershey, PA	Carole Ormaca Robin Greiner
1954	Los Angeles, CA	Carole Ormaca Robin Greiner
1955	Colo. Springs, CO	Carole Ormaca Robin Greiner
1956	Philadelphia, PA	Carole Ormaca Robin Greiner
1957	Berkeley, CA	Nancy Rouillard Ronald Ludington
1958	Minneapolis, MN	Nancy Ludington Ronald Ludington
1959	Rochester, NY	Nancy Ludington Ronald Ludington
1960	Seattle, WA	Nancy Ludington Ronald Ludington
1961	Colo. Springs, CO	Maribel Owen Dudley Richards
1962	Boston, MA	Dorothyann Nelson Pieter Kollen
1963	Long Beach, CA	Judianne Fotheringill Jerry Fotheringill
1964	Cleveland, OH	Judianne Fotheringill Jerry Fotheringill
1965	Lake Placid, NY	Vivian Joseph Ronald Joseph
1966	Berkeley, CA	Cynthia Kauffman Ronald Kauffman
1967	Omaha, NE	Cynthia Kauffman Ronald Kauffman
1968	Philadelphia, PA	Cynthia Kauffman Ronald Kauffman
1969	Seattle, WA	Cynthia Kauffman Ronald Kauffman
1970	Tulsa, OK	JoJo Starbuck Kenneth Shelley
1971	Buffalo, NY	JoJo Starbuck Kenneth Shelley
1972	Long Beach, CA	JoJo Starbuck Kenneth Shelley
1973	Minneapolis, MN	Melissa Militano Mark Militano
1974	Providence, RI	Melissa Militano Johnny Johns
1975	Oakland, CA	Melissa Militano Johnny Johns
1976	Colo. Springs, CO	Tai Babilonia Randy Gardner
1977	Hartford, CT	Tai Babilonia Randy Gardner
1978	Portland, OR	Tai Babilonia Randy Gardner
1979	Cincinnati, OH	Tai Babilonia Randy Gardner
1980	Atlanta, GA	Tai Babilonia Randy Gardner
1981	San Diego, CA	Caitlin Carruthers Peter Carruthers
1982	Indianapolis, IN	Caitlin Carruthers Peter Carruthers
1983	Pittsburgh, PA	Caitlin Carruthers Peter Carruthers
1984	Salt Lake City, UT	Caitlin Carruthers Peter Carruthers
1985	Kansas City, MO	Jill Watson Peter Oppegard
1986	Long Island, NY	Gillian Wachsman Todd Waggoner
1987	Tacoma, WA	Jill Watson Peter Oppegard
1988	Denver, CO	Jill Watson Peter Oppegard
1989	Baltimore, MD	Kristi Yamaguchi Rudy Galindo
1990	Salt Lake City, UT	Kristi Yamaguchi Rudy Galindo
1991	Minneapolis, MN	Natasha Kuchiki Todd Sand
1992	Orlando, FL	Calla Urbanski Rocky Marval
1993	Phoenix, AZ	Calla Urbanski Rocky Marval
1994	Detroit, MI	Jenni Meno Todd Sand
1995	Providence, RI	Jenni Meno Todd Sand
1996	San Jose, CA	Jenni Meno Todd Sand
1997	Nashville, TN	Kyoko Ina Jason Dungjen
1998	Philadelphia, PA	Kyoko Ina Jason Dungjen

TODD ELDREDGE

Ice Dancing Gold Medalists

1914	New Haven, CT		
	Waltz		Theresa Weld Nathaniel Niles
1915-1919	No Competition Held		
1920	New York, NY		
	Waltz		Theresa Weld Nathaniel Niles
	Ten Step		Gertrude Cheever Porter Irving Brokaw
1921	Philadelphia, PA		
	Waltz		Theresa Weld Blanchard Nathaniel Niles
	Fourteen Step		Theresa Weld Blanchard Nathaniel Niles
1922	Boston, MA		
	Waltz		Beatrix Loughran Edward Howland
	Fourteen Step		Theresa Weld Blanchard Nathaniel Niles

BABILONIA AND GARDNER

1923	New Haven, CT	
	Waltz	Mrs. Henry Howe
		Mr. Henry Howe
	Fourteen Step	Sydney Goode
		James Greene
1924	Philadelphia, PA	
	Waltz	Rosalie Dunn
		Fredrick Gabel
	Fourteen Step	Sydney Goode
		James Greene
1925	New York, NY	
	Waltz	Virginia Slattery
		Ferrier Martin
	Fourteen Step	Virginia Slattery
		Ferrier Martin
1926	Boston, MA	
	Waltz	Rosalie Dunn
		Joseph Savage
	Fourteen Step	Sydney Goode
		James Greene
1927	New York, NY	
	Waltz	Rosalie Dunn
		Joseph Savage
	Fourteen Step	Rosalie Dunn
		Joseph Savage
1928	New Haven, CT	
	Waltz	Rosalie Dunn
		Joseph Savage
	Fourteen Step	Ada Baumann Kelly
		George Braakman
1929	New York, NY	
	Waltz & Original	Edith Secord
	Dance Combined	Joseph Savage
1930	Providence, RI	
	Waltz	Edith Secord
		Joseph Savage
	Original Dance	Clara Frothingham
		George Hill
1931	Boston, MA	
	Waltz	Edith Secord
		Ferrier Martin
	Original Dance	Theresa Weld Blanchard
		Nathaniel Niles
1932	New York, NY	
	Waltz	Edith Secord
		Joseph Savage
	Original Dance	Clara Frothingham
		George Hill
1933	New Haven, CT	
	Waltz	Ilse Twaroschk
		Fred Fleischman
	Original Dance	Suzanne Davis
		Frederick Goodridge
1934	Philadelphia, PA	
	Waltz	Nettie Prantell
		Roy Hunt
	Original Dance	Suzanne Davis
		Frederick Goodridge
1935	New Haven, CT	
	Waltz	Nettie Prantell
		Roy Hunt
1936	Boston, MA	Marjorie Parker
		Joseph Savage
1937	Chicago, IL	Nettie Prantell
		Harold Hartshorne
1938	Philadelphia, PA	Nettie Prantel
		Harold Hartshorne
1939	St. Paul, MN	Sandy MacDonald
		Harold Hartshorne
1940	Cleveland, OH	Sandy MacDonald
		Harold Hartshorne
1941	Boston, MA	Sandy MacDonald
		Harold Hartshorne
1942	Chicago, IL	Edith Whetstone
		Alfred Richards

LADIES' MEDALISTS AT THE 1998 U.S. CHAMPIONSHIPS

1943	New York, NY	Marcella May
		James Lochead
1944	Minneapolis, MN	Marcella May
		James Lochead
1945	New York, NY	Kathe Williams
		Robert Swenning
1946	Chicago, IL	Anne Davies
		Carleton Hoffner
1947	Berkeley, CA	Lois Waring
		Walter Bainbridge
1948	Colo. Springs, CO	Lois Waring
		Walter Bainbridge
1949	Colo. Springs, CO	Lois Waring
		Walter Bainbridge
1950	Washington, D.C.	Lois Waring
		Michael McGean
1951	Seattle, WA	Carmel Bodel
		Edward Bodel
1952	Colo. Springs, CO	Lois Waring
		Michael McGean
1953	Hershey, PA	Carol Ann Peters
		Daniel Ryan
1954	Los Angeles, CA	Carmel Bodel
		Edward Bodel
1955	Colo. Springs, CO	Carmel Bodel
		Edward Bodel
1956	Philadelphia, PA	Joan Zamboni
		Roland Junso
1957	Berkeley, CA	Sharon McKenzie
		Bert Wright
1958	Minneapolis, MN	Andree Anderson
		Donald Jacoby
1959	Rochester, NY	Andree Jacoby
		Donald Jacoby
1960	Seattle, WA	Margie Ackles
		Charles Phillips
1961	Colo. Springs, CO	Dianne Sherbloom
		Larry Pierce
1962	Boston, MA	Yvonne Littlefield
		Peter Betts
1963	Long Beach, CA	Sally Schantz
		Stanley Urban
1964	Cleveland, OH	Darlene Streich
		Charles Fetter
1965	Lake Placid, NY	Kristin Fortune
		Dennis Sveum

1966	Berkeley, CA	Kristin Fortune
		Dennis Sveum
1967	Omaha, NE	Lorna Dyer
		John Carrell
1968	Philadelphia, PA	Judy Schwomeyer
		James Sladky
1969	Seattle, WA	Judy Schwomeyer
		James Sladky
1970	Tulsa, OK	Judy Schwomeyer
		James Sladky
1971	Buffalo, NY	Judy Schwomeyer
		James Sladky
1972	Long Beach, CA	Judy Schwomeyer
		James Sladky
1973	Minneapolis, MN	Mary Campbell
		Johnny Johns
1974	Providence, RI	Colleen O'Connor
		Jim Millns
1975	Oakland, CA	Colleen O'Connor
		Jim Millns
1976	Colo. Springs, CO	Colleen O'Connor
		Jim Millns
1977	Hartford, CT	Judy Genovesi
		Kent Weigle
1978	Portland, OR	Stacey Smith
		John Summers
1979	Cincinnati, OH	Stacey Smith
		John Summers
1980	Atlanta, GA	Stacey Smith
		John Summers
1981	San Diego, CA	Judy Blumberg
		Michael Seibert
1982	Indianapolis, IN	Judy Blumberg
		Michael Seibert
1983	Pittsburgh, PA	Judy Blumberg
		Michael Seibert
1984	Salt Lake City, UT	Judy Blumberg
		Michael Seibert
1985	Kansas City, MO	Judy Blumberg
		Michael Seibert
1986	Long Island, NY	Renee Roca
		Donald Adair
1987	Tacoma, WA	Suzanne Semanick
		Scott Gregory
1988	Denver, CO	Suzanne Semanick
		Scott Gregory
1989	Baltimore, MD	Susan Wynne
		Joseph Druar
1990	Salt Lake City, UT	Susan Wynne
		Joseph Druar
1991	Minneapolis, MN	Elizabeth Punsalan
		Jerod Swallow
1992	Orlando, FL	April Sargent
		Russ Witherby
1993	Phoenix, AZ	Renee Roca
		Gorsha Sur
1994	Detroit, MI	Elizabeth Punsalan
		Jerod Swallow
1995	Providence, RI	Renee Roca
		Gorsha Sur
1996	San Jose, CA	Elizabeth Punsalan
		Jerod Swallow
1997	Nashville, TN	Elizabeth Punsalan
		Jerod Swallow
1998	Philadelphia, PA	Elizabeth Punsalan
		Jerod Swallow

OLYMPIC CHAMPIONS

SKATING IN JAPAN

MEN'S GOLD MEDAL WINNERS

1908	London, GBR	Ulrich Salchow (SWE)
1920	Antwerp, BEL	Gillis Grafstrom (SWE)
1924	Chamonix, FRA	Gillis Grafstrom (SWE)
1928	St. Moritz, SWI	Gillis Grafstrom (SWE)
1932	Lake Placid, USA	Karl Schafer (AUT)
1936	Garmisch, GER	Karl Schafer (AUT)
1940, 1944	No Olympic Games Held	
1948	St. Moritz, SWI	Richard Button (USA)
1952	Oslo, NOR	Richard Button (USA)
1956	Cortina, ITA	Hayes A. Jenkins (USA)
1960	Squaw Valley, USA	David Jenkins (USA)
1964	Innsbruck, AUT	Manfred Schnelldorfer (FRG)
1968	Grenoble, FRA	Wolfgang Schwarz (AUT)
1972	Sapporo, JPN	Ondrej Nepela (CZE)
1976	Innsbruck, AUT	John Curry (GBR)
1980	Lake Placid, USA	Robin Cousins (GBR)
1984	Sarajevo, YUG	Scott Hamilton (USA)
1988	Calgary, CAN	Brian Boitano (USA)
1992	Albertville, FRA	Viktor Petrenko (EUN)
1994	Lillehammer, NOR	Alexei Urmanov (RUS)
1998	Nagano, JPN	Ilia Kulik (RUS)

LADIES' GOLD MEDAL WINNERS

1908	London, GBR	Madge Syers (GBR)
1920	Antwerp, BEL	Magda Julin-Mauroy (SWE)
1924	Chamonix, FRA	Herma Plank-Szabo (AUT)
1928	St. Moritz, SWI	Sonja Henie (NOR)
1932	Lake Placid, USA	Sonja Henie (NOR)
1936	Garmisch, GER	Sonja Henie (NOR)
1940, 1944	No Olympic Games Held	
1948	St. Moritz, SWI	Barbara Ann Scott (CAN)
1952	Oslo, NOR	Jeannette Altwegg (GBR)
1956	Cortina, ITA	Tenley Albright (USA)
1960	Squaw Valley, USA	Carol Heiss (USA)
1964	Innsbruck, AUT	Sjoukje Dijkstra (HOL)
1968	Grenoble, FRA	Peggy Fleming (USA)
1972	Sapporo, JPN	Beatrix Schuba (AUT)
1976	Innsbruck, AUT	Dorothy Hamill (USA)
1980	Lake Placid, USA	Anett Poetzsch (GDR)
1984	Sarajevo, YUG	Katarina Witt (GDR)
1988	Calgary, CAN	Katarina Witt (GDR)
1992	Albertville, FRA	Kristi Yamaguchi (USA)
1994	Lillehammer, NOR	Oksana Baiul (UKR)
1998	Nagano, JPN	Tara Lipinski (USA)

PAIRS' GOLD MEDAL WINNERS

1908	London, GBR	Anna Hubler (GER)
		Heinrich Burger
1920	Antwerp, BEL	Ludowika Jakobsson (FIN)
		Walter Jakobsson
1924	Chamonix, FRA	Helene Engelmann (AUT)
		Alfred Berger
1928	St. Moritz, SWI	Andrée Brunet (FRA)
		Pierre Brunet
1932	Lake Placid, USA	Andrée Brunet (FRA)
		Pierre Brunet
1936	Garmisch, GER	Maxie Herber (GER)
		Ernst Baier
1940, 1944	No Olympic Games Held	
1948	St. Moritz, SWI	Micheline Lannoy (BEL)
		Pierre Baugniet
1952	Oslo, NOR	Ria Falk (FRG)
		Paul Falk
1956	Cortina, ITA	Elisabeth Schwarz (AUT)
		Kurt Oppelt
1960	Squaw Valley, USA	Barbara Wagner (CAN)
		Robert Paul
1964	Innsbruck, AUT	Ludmila Belousova (URS)
		Oleg Protopopov
1968	Grenoble, FRA	Ludmila Protopopov (URS)
		Oleg Protopopov
1972	Sapporo, JPN	Irina Rodnina (URS)
		Alexsei Ulanov
1976	Innsbruck, AUT	Irina Rodnina (URS)
		Aleksandr Zaitsev
1980	Lake Placid, USA	Irina Rodnina (URS)
		Aleksandr Zaitsev
1984	Sarajevo, YUG	Elena Valova (URS)
		Oleg Vassiliev
1988	Calgary, CAN	Ekaterina Gordeeva (URS)
		Sergei Grinkov
1992	Albertville, FRA	Natalia Mishkutenok (EUN)
		Artur Dmitriev
1994	Lillehammer, NOR	Ekaterina Gordeeva (RUS)
		Sergei Grinkov
1998	Nagano, JPN	Oksana Kazakova (RUS)
		Artur Dmitriev

ICE DANCING GOLD MEDAL WINNERS

1976	Innsbruck, AUT	Liudmila Pakhomova (URS)
		Aleksandr Gorshkov
1980	Lake Placid, USA	Natalia Linichuk (URS)
		Gennadi Karponosov
1984	Sarajevo, YUG	Jayne Torvill (GBR)
		Christopher Dean
1988	Calgary, CAN	Natalia Bestemianova (URS)
		Andrei Bukin
1992	Albertville, FRA	Marina Klimova (EUN)
		Sergei Ponomarenko
1994	Lillehammer, NOR	Oksana Grishuk (RUS)
		Evgeny Platov
1998	Nagano, JPN	Pasha Grishuk (RUS)
		Evgeny Platov

TORVILL AND DEAN

MEN'S GOLD MEDALISTS

1896	St. Petersburg, RUS	Gilbert Fuchs (GER)
1897	Stockholm, SWE	Gustav Hugel (AUT)
1898	London, GBR	Henning Grenander (SWE)
1899	Davos, SWI	Gustav Hugel (AUT)
1900	Davos, SWI	Gustav Hugel (AUT)
1901	Stockholm, SWE	Ulrich Salchow (SWE)
1902	London, GBR	Ulrich Salchow (SWE)
1903	St. Petersburg, RUS	Ulrich Salchow (SWE)
1904	Berlin, GER	Ulrich Salchow (SWE)
1905	Stockholm, SWE	Ulrich Salchow (SWE)
1906	Munich, GER	Gilbert Fuchs (GER)
1907	Vienna, AUT	Ulrich Salchow (SWE)
1908	Troppau, CZE	Ulrich Salchow (SWE)
1909	Stockholm, SWE	Ulrich Salchow (SWE)
1910	Davos, SWI	Ulrich Salchow (SWE)
1911	Berlin, GER	Ulrich Salchow (SWE)
1912	Manchester, GBR	Fritz Kachler (AUT)
1913	Vienna, AUT	Fritz Kachler (AUT)
1914	Helsinki, FIN	Gosta Sandahl (SWE)
1915-1921	No Championship Held	
1922	Stockholm, SWE	Gillis Grafstrom (SWE)
1923	Vienna, AUT	Fritz Kachler (AUT)
1924	Manchester, GBR	Gillis Grafstrom (SWE)
1925	Vienna, AUT	Willy Boeckl (AUT)
1926	Berlin, GER	Willy Boeckl (AUT)
1927	Davos, SWI	Willy Boeckl (AUT)
1928	Berlin, GER	Willy Boeckl (AUT)
1929	London, GBR	Gillis Grafstrom (SWE)
1930	New York, USA	Karl Schafer (AUT)
1931	Berlin, GER	Karl Schafer (AUT)
1932	Montreal, CAN	Karl Schafer (AUT)
1933	Zurich, SWI	Karl Schafer (AUT)
1934	Stockholm, SWE	Karl Schafer (AUT)
1935	Budapest, HUN	Karl Schafer (AUT)
1936	Paris, FRA	Karl Schafer (AUT)
1937	Vienna, AUT	Felix Kaspar (AUT)
1938	Berlin, GER	Felix Kaspar (AUT)
1939	Budapest, HUN	Graham Sharp (GBR)
1940-1946	No Championship Held	
1947	Stockholm, SWE	Hans Gerschwiler (SWI)
1948	Davos, SWI	Richard Button (USA)
1949	Paris, FRA	Richard Button (USA)
1950	London, GBR	Richard Button (USA)
1951	Milan, ITA	Richard Button (USA)
1952	Paris, FRA	Richard Button (USA)
1953	Davos, SWI	Hayes A. Jenkins (USA)
1954	Oslo, NOR	Hayes A. Jenkins (USA)
1955	Vienna, AUT	Hayes A. Jenkins (USA)
1956	Garmisch, FRG	Hayes A. Jenkins (USA)
1957	Colo. Springs, USA	David Jenkins (USA)
1958	Paris, FRA	David Jenkins (USA)
1959	Colo. Springs, USA	David Jenkins (USA)
1960	Vancouver, CAN	Alain Giletti (FRA)
1961	No Championship Held	
1962	Prague, CZE	Donald Jackson (CAN)
1963	Cortina, ITA	Donald McPherson (CAN)
1964	Dortmund, FRG	Manfred Schnelldorfer (FRG)
1965	Colo. Springs, USA	Alain Calmat (FRA)
1966	Davos, SWI	Emmerich Danzer (AUT)
1967	Vienna, AUT	Emmerich Danzer (AUT)
1968	Geneva, SWI	Emmerich Danzer (AUT)
1969	Colo. Springs, USA	Tim Wood (USA)
1970	Ljubljana, YUG	Tim Wood (USA)
1971	Lyon, FRA	Ondrej Nepela (CZE)
1972	Calgary, CAN	Ondrej Nepela (CZE)
1973	Bratislava, CZE	Ondrej Nepela (CZE)
1974	Munich, FRG	Jan Hoffman (GDR)
1975	Colo. Springs, USA	Sergei Volkov (URS)
1976	Gothenberg, SWE	John Curry (GBR)
1977	Tokyo, JPN	Vladimir Kovalev (URS)
1978	Ottawa, CAN	Charles Tickner (USA)
1979	Vienna, AUT	Vladimir Kovalev (URS)
1980	Dortmund, FRG	Jan Hoffman (GDR)
1981	Hartford, USA	Scott Hamilton (USA)
1982	Copenhagen, DEN	Scott Hamilton (USA)
1983	Helsinki, FIN	Scott Hamilton (USA)
1984	Ottawa, CAN	Scott Hamilton (USA)
1985	Tokyo, JPN	Alexandr Fadeev (URS)
1986	Geneva, SWI	Brian Boitano (USA)
1987	Cincinnati, USA	Brian Orser (CAN)
1988	Budapest, HUN	Brian Boitano (USA)
1989	Paris, FRA	Kurt Browning (CAN)
1990	Halifax, CAN	Kurt Browning (CAN)
1991	Munich, GER	Kurt Browning (CAN)
1992	Oakland, USA	Viktor Petrenko (CIS)
1993	Prague, CZE	Kurt Browning (CAN)
1994	Chiba, JPN	Elvis Stojko (CAN)
1995	Birmingham, ENG	Elvis Stojko (CAN)
1996	Edmonton, CAN	Todd Eldredge (USA)
1997	Lausanne, SWI	Elvis Stojko (CAN)
1998	Minneapolis, USA	Alexei Yagudin (RUS)

* 1902 marked the first year a woman applied to compete in the World Championships. At that time there was no provision in the rules for such an occurrence and it was not until 1903 that the congress decided that ladies should not be permitted to compete at international men's championships. The Ladies' event was introduced at the 1906 World Championships.

LADIES' GOLD MEDALISTS

1906	Davos, SWI	Madge Syers (GBR)
1907	Vienna, AUT	Madge Syers (GBR)
1908	Troppau, CZE	Lily Kronberger (HUN)
1909	Budapest, HUN	Lily Kronberger (HUN)
1910	Berlin, GER	Lily Kronberger (HUN)
1911	Vienna, AUT	Lily Kronberger (HUN)
1912	Davos, SWI	Opika von Horvath (HUN)
1913	Stockholm, SWE	Opika von Horvath (HUN)
1914	St. Moritz, SWI	Opika von Horvath (HUN)
1915-1921	No Championship Held	
1922	Stockholm, SWE	Herma Plank-Szabo (AUT)
1923	Vienna, AUT	Herma Plank-Szabo (AUT)
1924	Oslo, NOR	Herma Plank-Szabo (AUT)
1925	Davos, SWI	Herma Jaross-Szabo (AUT)
1926	Stockholm, SWE	Herma Jaross-Szabo (AUT)
1927	Oslo, NOR	Sonja Henie (NOR)
1928	London, GBR	Sonja Henie (NOR)
1929	Budapest, HUN	Sonja Henie (NOR)
1930	New York, USA	Sonja Henie (NOR)
1931	Berlin, GER	Sonja Henie (NOR)
1932	Montreal, CAN	Sonja Henie (NOR)
1933	Stockholm, SWE	Sonja Henie (NOR)
1934	Oslo, NOR	Sonja Henie (NOR)
1935	Vienna, AUT	Sonja Henie (NOR)
1936	Paris, FRA	Sonja Henie (NOR)
1937	London, GBR	Cecilia Colledge (GBR)
1938	Stockholm, SWE	Megan Taylor (GBR)
1939	Prague, CZE	Megan Taylor (GBR)
1940-1946	No Championship Held	
1947	Stockholm, SWE	Barbara Ann Scott (CAN)
1948	Davos, SWI	Barbara Ann Scott (CAN)
1949	Paris, FRA	Alena Vrzanova (CZE)
1950	London, GBR	Alena Vrzanova (CZE)
1951	Milan, ITA	Jeannette Altwegg (GBR)
1952	Paris, FRA	Jacqueline du Bief (FRA)
1953	Davos, SWI	Tenley Albright (USA)
1954	Oslo, NOR	Gundi Busch (FRG)
1955	Vienna, AUT	Tenley Albright (USA)
1956	Garmisch, FRG	Carol Heiss (USA)
1957	Colo. Springs, USA	Carol Heiss (USA)
1958	Paris, FRA	Carol Heiss (USA)
1959	Colo. Springs, USA	Carol Heiss (USA)
1960	Vancouver, CAN	Carol Heiss (USA)
1961	No Championship Held	
1962	Prague, CZE	Sjoukje Dijkstra (HOL)
1963	Cortina, ITA	Sjoukje Dijkstra (HOL)
1964	Dortmund, FRG	Sjouke Dijkstra (HOL)
1965	Colo. Springs, USA	Petra Burka (CAN)
1966	Davos, SWI	Peggy Fleming (USA)
1967	Vienna, AUT	Peggy Fleming (USA)
1968	Geneva, SWI	Peggy Fleming (USA)
1969	Colo. Springs, USA	Gabriele Seyfert (GDR)
1970	Ljubljana, YUG	Gabriele Seyfert (GDR)
1971	Lyon, FRA	Beatrix Schuba (AUT)
1972	Calgary, CAN	Beatrix Schuba (AUT)
1973	Bratislava, CZE	Karen Magnussen (CAN)
1974	Munich, FRG	Christine Errath (GDR)
1975	Colo. Springs, USA	Dianne de Leeuw (HOL)
1976	Gothenberg, SWE	Dorothy Hamill (USA)
1977	Tokyo, JPN	Linda Fratianne (USA)
1978	Ottawa, CAN	Anett Pötzsch (GDR)
1979	Vienna, AUT	Linda Fratianne (USA)
1980	Dortmund, FRG	Anett Pötzsch (GDR)
1981	Hartford, USA	Denise Biellmann (SWI)
1982	Copenhagen, DEN	Elaine Zayak (USA)
1983	Helsinki, FIN	Rosalynn Sumners (USA)
1984	Ottawa, CAN	Katarina Witt (GDR)
1985	Tokyo, JPN	Katarina Witt (GDR)
1986	Geneva, SWI	Debi Thomas (USA)
1987	Cincinnati, USA	Katarina Witt (GDR)
1988	Budapest, HUN	Katarina Witt (GDR)
1989	Paris, FRA	Midori Ito (JPN)
1990	Halifax, CAN	Jill Trenary (USA)
1991	Munich, GER	Kristi Yamaguchi (USA)
1992	Oakland, USA	Kristi Yamaguchi (USA)
1993	Prague, CZE	Oksana Baiul (UKR)
1994	Chiba, JPN	Yuka Sato (JPN)
1995	Birmingham, ENG	Chen Lu (CHN)
1996	Edmonton, CAN	Michelle Kwan (USA)
1997	Lausanne, SWI	Tara Lipinski (USA)
1998	Minneapolis, USA	Michelle Kwan (USA)

PAIRS' GOLD MEDALISTS

1908	St. Petersburg, RUS	Anna Hubler (GER)
		Heinrich Burger
1909	Stockholm, SWE	Phyllis Johnson (GBR)
		James Johnson
1910	Berlin, GER	Anna Hubler (GER)
		Henrich Burger
1911	Vienna, AUT	Ludowika Eilers (FIN)
		Walter Jakobsson
1912	Manchester, GBR	Phyllis Johnson (GBR)
		James Johnson
1913	Stockholm, SWE	Helene Engelmann (AUT)
		Karl Mejstrik
1914	St. Moritz, SWI	Ludowika Jakobsson (FIN)
		Walter Jakobsson
1915-1921	No Championship Held	
1922	Davos, SWI	Helene Engelmann (AUT)
		Alfred Berger
1923	Oslo, NOR	Ludowika Jakobsson (FIN)
		Walter Jakobsson
1924	Manchester, GBR	Helene Engelmann (AUT)
		Alfred Berger
1925	Vienna, AUT	Herma Jaross-Szabo (AUT)
		Ludwig Wrede
1926	Berlin, GER	Andrée Brunet (FRA)
		Pierre Brunet
1927	Vienna, AUT	Herma Jaross-Szabo (AUT)
		Ludwig Wrede
1928	London, GBR	Andrée Brunet (FRA)
		Pierre Brunet
1929	Budapest, HUN	Lilly Scholz (AUT)
		Otto Kaiser
1930	New York, USA	Andrée Brunet (FRA)
		Pierre Brunet
1931	Berlin, GER	Emilie Rotter (HUN)
		Laszlo Szollas
1932	Montreal, CAN	Andrée Brunet (FRA)
		Pierre Brunet

1933	Stockholm, SWE	Emilie Rotter (HUN) Laszlo Szollas
1934	Helsinki, FIN	Emilie Rotter (HUN) Laszlo Szollas
1935	Budapest, HUN	Emilie Rotter (HUN) Laszlo Szollas
1936	Paris, FRA	Maxi Herber (GER) Ernst Baier
1937	London, GBR	Maxi Herber (GER) Ernst Baier
1938	Berlin, GER	Maxi Herber (GER) Ernst Baier
1939	Budapest, HUN	Maxi Herber (GER) Ernst Baier
1940-1946	No Championship Held	
1947	Stockholm, SWE	Micheline Lannoy (BEL) Pierre Baugniet
1948	Davos, SWI	Micheline Lannoy (BEL) Pierre Baugniet
1949	Paris, FRA	Andrea Kekesy (HUN) Ede Kiraly
1950	London, GBR	Karol Kennedy (USA) Peter Kennedy
1951	Milan, ITA	Ria Falk (FRG) Paul Falk
1952	Paris, FRA	Ria Falk (FRG) Paul Falk
1953	Davos, SWI	Jennifer Nicks (GBR) John Nicks
1954	Oslo, NOR	Frances Dafoe (CAN) Norris Bowden
1955	Vienna, AUT	Frances Dafoe (CAN) Norris Bowden
1956	Garmisch, FRG	Elisabeth Schwarz (AUT) Kurt Oppelt
1957	Colo. Springs, USA	Barbara Wagner (CAN) Robert Paul
1958	Paris, FRA	Barbara Wagner (CAN) Robert Paul
1959	Colo. Springs, USA	Barbara Wagner (CAN) Robert Paul
1960	Vancouver, CAN	Barbara Wagner (CAN) Robert Paul
1961	No Championship Held	
1962	Prague, CZE	Maria Jelinek (CAN) Otto Jelinek
1963	Cortina, ITA	Marika Kilius (FRG) Hans Baumler
1964	Dortmund, FRG	Marika Kilius (FRG) Hans Baumler
1965	Colo. Springs, USA	Ludmila Belousova (URS) Oleg Protopopov
1966	Davos, SWI	Ludmila Belousova (URS) Oleg Protopopov
1967	Vienna, AUT	Ludmila Belousova (URS) Oleg Protopopov
1968	Geneva, SWI	Ludmila Belousova (URS) Oleg Protopopov
1969	Colo. Springs, USA	Irina Rodnina (URS) Alexsei Ulanov
1970	Ljubljana, YUG	Irina Rodnina (URS) Alexsei Ulanov
1971	Lyon, FRA	Irina Rodnina (URS) Alexsei Ulanov
1972	Calgary, CAN	Irina Rodnina (URS) Alexsei Ulanov
1973	Bratislava, CZE	Irina Rodnina (URS) Alexandr Zaitsev
1974	Munich, FRG	Irina Rodnina (URS) Alexandr Zaitsev
1975	Colo. Springs, USA	Irina Rodnina (URS) Alexandr Zaitsev
1976	Gothenberg, SWE	Irina Rodnina (URS) Alexandr Zaitsev
1977	Tokyo, JPN	Irina Rodnina (URS)
1978	Ottawa, CAN	Alexandr Zaitsev Irina Rodnina (URS) Alexandr Zaitsev
1979	Vienna, AUT	Tai Babilonia (USA) Randy Gardner
1980	Dortmund, FRG	Marina Cherkasova (URS) Sergei Shakhrai
1981	Hartford, USA	Irina Vorobieva (URS) Igor Lisovsky
1982	Copenhagen, DEN	Sabine Baess (GDR) Tassilo Thierbach
1983	Helsinki, FIN	Elena Valova (URS) Oleg Vassiliev
1984	Ottawa, CAN	Barbara Underhill (CAN) Paul Martini
1985	Tokyo, JPN	Elena Valova (URS) Oleg Vassiliev
1986	Geneva, SWI	Ekaterina Gordeeva (URS) Sergei Grinkov
1987	Cincinnati, USA	Ekaterina Gordeeva (URS) Sergei Grinkov
1988	Budapest, HUN	Elena Valova (URS) Oleg Vassiliev
1989	Paris, FRA	Ekaterina Gordeeva (URS) Sergei Grinkov
1990	Halifax, CAN	Ekaterina Gordeeva (URS) Sergei Grinkov
1991	Munich, GER	Natalia Mishkutenok (URS) Artur Dmitriev
1992	Oakland, USA	Natalia Mishkutenok (CIS) Artur Dmitriev
1993	Prague, CZE	Isabelle Brasseur (CAN) Lloyd Eisler
1994	Chiba, JPN	Evgenia Shishkova (RUS) Vadim Naumov
1995	Birmingham, ENG	Radka Kovarikova (CZE) Rene Novotny
1996	Edmonton, CAN	Marina Eltsova (RUS) Andrei Bushkov
1997	Lausanne, SWI	Mandy Wotzel (GER) Ingo Steuer
1998	Minneapolis, USA	Elena Berezhnaya (RUS) Anton Sikharulidze

ICE DANCING GOLD

1952	Paris, FRA	Jean Westwood (GBR) Lawrence Demmy
1953	Davos, SWI	Jean Westwood (GBR) Lawrence Demmy
1954	Oslo, NOR	Jean Westwood (GBR) Lawrence Demmy
1955	Vienna, AUT	Jean Westwood (GBR) Lawrence Demmy
1956	Garmisch, FRG	Pamela Weight (GBR) Paul Thomas
1957	Colo. Springs, USA	June Markham (GBR) Courtney Jones
1958	Paris, FRA	June Markham (GBR) Courtney Jones
1959	Colo. Springs, USA	Doreen Denny (GBR) Courtney Jones
1960	Vancouver, CAN	Doreen Denny (GBR) Courtney Jones
1961	No Competition Held	
1962	Prague, CZE	Eva Romanova (CZE) Pavel Roman
1963	Cortina, ITA	Eva Romanova (CZE) Pavel Roman
1964	Dortmund, FRG	Eva Romanova (CZE) Pavel Roman
1965	Colo. Springs, USA	Eva Romanova (CZE) Pavel Roman
1966	Davos, SWI	Diane Towler (GBR) Bernard Ford
1967	Vienna, AUT	Diane Towler (GBR) Bernard Ford
1968	Geneva, SWI	Diane Towler (GBR) Bernard Ford
1969	Colo. Springs, USA	Diane Towler (GBR) Bernard Ford
1970	Ljubljana, YUG	Liudmilla Pakhomova (URS) Aleksandr Gorshkov
1971	Lyon, FRA	Liudmilla Pakhomova (URS) Aleksandr Gorshkov
1972	Calgary, CAN	Liudmilla Pakhomova (URS) Aleksandr Gorschkov
1973	Bratislava, CZE	Liudmilla Pakhomova (URS) Aleksandr Gorshkov
1974	Munich, FRG	Liudmilla Pakhomova (URS) Aleksandr Gorshkov
1975	Colo. Springs, USA	Irina Moiseeva (URS) Andrei Minenkov
1976	Gothenberg, SWE	Liudmilla Pakhomova (URS) Aleksandr Gorshkov
1977	Tokyo, JPN	Irina Moiseeva (URS) Andrei Minenkov
1978	Ottawa, CAN	Natalia Linichuk (URS) Gennadi Karponosov
1979	Vienna, AUT	Natalia Linichuk (URS) Gennadi Karponosov
1980	Dortmund, FRG	Krisztina Regoeczy (HUN) Andras Sallay
1981	Hartford, USA	Jayne Torvill (GBR) Christopher Dean
1982	Copenhagen, DEN	Jayne Torvill (GBR) Christopher Dean
1983	Helsinki, FIN	Jayne Torvill (GBR) Christopher Dean
1984	Ottawa, CAN	Jayne Torvill (GBR) Christopher Dean
1985	Tokyo, JPN	Natalia Bestemianova (URS) Andrei Bukin
1986	Geneva, SWI	Natalia Bestemianova (URS) Andrei Bukin
1987	Cincinnati, USA	Natalia Bestemianova (URS) Andrei Bukin
1988	Budapest, HUN	Natalia Bestemianova (URS) Andrei Bukin
1989	Paris, FRA	Marina Klimova (URS) Sergei Ponomarenko
1990	Halifax, CAN	Marina Klimova (URS) Sergei Ponomarenko
1991	Munich, GER	Isabelle Duchesnay (FRA) Paul Duchesnay
1992	Oakland, USA	Marina Klimova (CIS) Sergei Ponomarenko
1993	Prague, CZE	Maia Usova (RUS) Alexander Zhulin
1994	Chiba, JPN	Oksana Grishuk (RUS) Evgeny Platov
1995	Birmingham, ENG	Oksana Grishuk (RUS) Evgeny Platov
1996	Edmonton, CAN	Oksana Grishuk (RUS) Evgeny Platov
1997	Lausanne, SWI	Oksana Grishuk (RUS) Evgeny Platov
1998	Minneapolis, USA	Anjelika Krylova (RUS) Oleg Ovsiannikov

FIGURE SKATING CLUBS OF THE UNITED STATES

ALABAMA
BIRMINGHAM FSC, INC.
Alpine Ice Arena, 160 Oxmoor Road,
Birmingham, AL 35209;
Rink: 205/942-0223

HUNTSVILLE FSC
Benton H. Wilcoxon Municipal Ice
Complex, 3185 Leeman Ferry Road,
Huntsville, AL 35805; Rink: 205/883-3773

ALASKA
ALASKA ASSOC OF FIGURE SKATERS
Ben Boeke Ice Arena, 334 E. 16th
Avenue, Anchorage, AK 99520;
Rink: 907/274-2767

ANCHORAGE FSC
University of Alaska Ice Rink, 2801
Providence Drive, Anchorage, AK 99508;
Rink: 907/786-1231

DENALI ICE CLUB, INC.
Central Peninsula Sports Ctr., 538 Arena
Drive, Soldotna, AK 99669;
Rink: 907/262-3151

FAIRBANKS FSC
Big Dipper Ice Rink, 19th & Lathrop
streets, Fairbanks, AK 99701;
Rink: 907/459-1071

ARIZONA
COYOTES SC OF ARIZONA
The Ice Den, 9375 E. Bell Road, Scotts-
dale, AZ, 85260; Rink: 602/267-0591

SC OF PHOENIX
Oceanside Ice Arena, 1520 N.
McClintock Road, Tempe, AZ 85281;
Rink: 602/941-0944

TUCSON FSC
Iceoplex, 7333 E. Rosewood Street,
Tucson, AZ, 85701; Rink: 520/290-8800

ARKANSAS
DIAMOND EDGE FSC
Little Rock Skating Arena, 1311 Bowman
Road, Little Rock, AR 72211;
Rink: 501/227-4333

OZARK FSC
Harvey and Bernice Jones Center for
Families, 922 S. Emma, Springdale, AR
72765; Rink: 501/227-4333

CALIFORNIA
ALL YEAR FSC
Culver Ice Arena, 4545 Sepulveda
Boulevard, Culver City, CA 90230;
Rink: 310/398-5719

ARCTIC BLADES FSC
Iceland Arena, 8041 Jackson Street, Para-
mount, CA 90723; Rink: 562/633-1172

ARROWHEAD FSC
Ontario Ice Skating Center, 1225 W.
Holt Boulevard, Ontario, CA 91761;
Rink: 909/986-0793

CAPITAL CITY FSC, INC.
Iceland Skating Arena, 1430 Del Paso
Blvd, Sacramento, CA 95815;
Rink: 916/925-3529

ESCONDIDO FSC
Iceoplex, 555 N. Tulip Street, Escondido,
CA 92025

ISC OF FRESNO
Iceoplex, 2473 N. Marks Avenue, Fresno,
CA 93722

GLACIER FALLS FSC, INC.
Disney Ice Arena, 300 W. Lincoln
Avenue, Anaheim, CA 92805;
Rink: 714/535-7465

GOLDEN STATE FSC
Norwalk Ice Arena, 14100 S. Shoemaker
Avenue, Norwalk, CA 90650;
Rink: 562/921-5391

LA JOLLA FSC
Ice Chalet, 4545 La Jolla Village Drive, San
Diego, CA 92122; Rink: 619/452-9110

LOS ANGELES FSC
Pickwick Ice Arena, 1001 Riverside
Drive, Burbank, CA 91506;
Rink: 818/846-0035

NORTH HILLS FSC
Iceoplex, 8345-C Havenhurst Place,
North Hills, CA 91343;
Rink: 818/893-1784

ORANGE COUNTY FSC
Ice Chalet, 2701 Harbor Blvd, Costa
Mesa, CA 92626; Rink: 714/979-8880

PALM DESERT FSC
Palm Desert Ice Capades, 72-840
Highway 111 Suite A, Palm Desert, CA
92260; Rink: 619/340-4412

PALOMARES FSC
Ice Oasis, 3140 Bay Road, Redwood
City, CA 94063; Rink: 650/364-8091

PASADENA FSC
Pasadena Ice Skating Center, 300 E.
Green Street, Pasadena, CA 91101;
Rink: 818/578-0801

PENINSULA SC
The Ice Centre of San Jose, 1500 S.
Tenth Street, San Jose, CA 95112;
Rink: 408/279-6000

RIM OF THE WORLD FSC
Blue Jay Ice Castle, 27307 Highway 189,
Blue Jay, CA 92317; Rink: 909/336-4085

SAN DIEGO FSC
San Diego Ice Arena, 11048 Ice Skate
Place, San Diego, CA 92126;
Rink: 619/530-1825

THE SC OF SAN FRANCISCO
Eleanor S. Woodbury, 1121 Stanyan
Street, San Francisco, CA, 94127.

THE SAN JOSE FSC
Eastridge Ice Arena, 2190 A Tully Road,
San Jose, CA 95122; Rink: 408/238-0440

SANTA ROSA FSC
Redwood Empire Ice Arena, 1667 W.
Steele Lane, Santa Rosa, CA 95403;
Rink: 707/546-7147

SIERRA NEVADA FSC
Olympic Ice Pavilion, Squaw Valley USA,
1960 Squaw Valley Road, Olympic Valley,
CA 96146; Rink: 916/581-5518

SOUTH BAY FSC, INC.
Skating Edge Ice Arena, 23770 S.

Western Avenue, Harbor City, CA
90710; Rink: 310/325-4475

ST. MORITZ ISC, INC.
Eastbay Iceland, Inc., 2727 Milvia Street,
Berkeley, CA 94703; Rink: 510/843-8800

STOCKTON FSC
Oak Park Ice Arena, 3545 N Alvarado
Street, Stockton, CA 95204;
Rink: 209/937-7432

TRI-VALLEY FSC
Easy Street Arena, 131 W. Easy Street,
Simi Valley, CA 93065; Rink: 805/520-7465

UNIVERSITY ISC OF SAN JOSE
Ice Capades Chalet, 10123 N Wolfe
Road, Cupertino, CA 95014;
Rink: 408/446-2906

THE SC OF VAN NUYS
Van Nuys Iceland, 14318 Calvert Street,
Van Nuys, CA 91401; Rink: 818/785-2171

COLORADO
ALPINE SC
7278 S. Iris Court, Littleton, CO 80123

ARAPAHOE HIGH SCHOOL (SA)
Allyson Ritchie, 2201 E. Day Creek
Road, Littleton, CO 80122

ARVADA WEST HIGH SCHOOL (SA)
Susan Melton, 11325 Allendale Drive,
Arvada, CO 80021

ASPEN SC
Aspen Ice Garden, 233 W. Hyman
Avenue, Aspen, CO 81611

ASPEN SKIERS SC (SA)
Aspen Ice Garden, 233 W. Hyman,
Aspen, CO 81611

BOULDER HIGH SCHOOL (SA)
1604 Arapahoe Avenue, Boulder, CO
80302

BROADMOOR SC, INC.
Colorado Springs World Arena, 3205
Venetucci Blvd, Colorado Springs, CO
80906; Rink: 719/5479-8014

CENTENNIAL SC
Mark 'Pa' Sertich Ice Center, 1705 E.
Pikes Peak Avenue, Colorado Springs,
CO 80909; Rink: 719/578-6883

CHATFIELD HIGH SCHOOL (SA)
Carol Zeles, 7227 S. Simms Street,
Littleton, CO 80127

CHERRY CREEK HIGH SCHOOL (SA)
Carol Palmer, 9300 E. Union Avenue,
Englewood, CO 80111

CHEYENNE MOUNTAIN HIGH
SCHOOL (SA)
Ellen Bishop, 1200 Cresta Road,
Colorado Springs, CO 80906

COLORADO SC
South Suburban Ice Arena, 6580 S. Vine
Street, Littleton, CO 80121;
Rink: 303/798-7881

COLORADO ACADEMY (SA)
Edna Chang-Grant, 3800 S. Pierce Street,
Denver, CO 80235

UNIVERSITY OF COLORADO , CU (CC)
Student Rec/Ice Arena, Campus Box 355,
Boulder, CO 80309; Rink: 303/492-7255

COLUMBINE FSC
North Jeffco Ice Arena, 9101 Ralston
Road, Arvada, CO 80002-2297;
Rink: 303/421-1786

DENVER FSC
South Suburban Ice Arena, 6580 S. Vine
Street, Littleton, CO 80121;
Rink: 303/798-7881

EAST HIGH SCHOOL (SA)
Kathy Hayes, 1545 Detroit Street,
Denver, CO 80206

FAIRVIEW HIGH SCHOOL (SA)
Jackie Whelan, 1515 Greenbriar, Boulder,
CO 80303

ISC OF FORT COLLINS
Edora Pool and Ice Center, 1810
Riverside Avenue, Ft Collins, CO 80525;
Rink: 970/221-6684

FORT COLLINS HIGH SCHOOL (SA)
Marilyn Bonnette, 3400 Lambkin Way,
Fort Collins, CO 80525

FRONT RANGE FSC
Mark 'Pa' Sertich Ice Center, 1705 E.
Pikes Peak Avenue, Colorado Springs,
CO 80909

GREEN MOUNTAIN HIGH
SCHOOL (SA)
Sharon Ehler, 13175 W. Green Mountain
Drive, Lakewood, CO 80228

HIGHLANDS RANCH HIGH
SCHOOL (SA)
Beth Burket, 9375 S. Cresthill Lane,
Highlands Ranch, CO 80126

IVER C. RANUM HIGH SCHOOL (SA)
Cherry Harrison, 4860 W. 102nd
Avenue, Westminster, CO 80030

POMONA SR. HIGH SCHOOL (SA)
Ken Harrell, 1960 Zang Street, Golden,
CO 80401

PUEBLO FSC
Pueblo Plaza Ice Arena, 100 N. Grand Ave,
Pueblo, CO 81003; Rink: 719/542-8784

ROCKY MOUNTAIN FSC
Hyland Hills Ice Arena, 420 W. 94th
Avenue, Westminster, CO 80030;
Rink: 303/650-7552

SMOKY HILLS HIGH SCHOOL (SA)
Carol Gilmer, 16100 E. Smoky Hill Road,
Aurora, CO 80015

SOUTH HIGH SCHOOL (SA)
Margaret Bowe, 1700 E. Louisiana
Avenue, Denver, CO 80210

STEAMBOAT SPRINGS FSC
Howelsen Ice Arena, 243 River Road,
Steamboat Springs, CO 80487;
Rink: 970/879-0341

STEAMBOAT SPRINGS HIGH
SCHOOL (SA)
Kim Haggerty, 45 Maple, Steamboat
Springs, CO 80487

SC OF VAIL INC.
John A. Dobson Arena, 292 W. Meadow Drive, Vail, CO 81657;
Rink: 470/479-2271

WHEAT RIDGE SR. HIGH SCHOOL (SA)
Ken Harrell, 1960 Zang Street, Golden, CO 80401

CONNECTICUT
BOLTON FSC, INC.
The Bolton Ice Palace, 145 Hop River Road, Route #6, PO Box 9157, Bolton, CT 06043; Rink: 860/646-7851

BRIDGEPORT SC, INC.
Wonderland of Ice, 123 Glenwood Avenue, Bridgeport, CT 06610;
Rink: 203/576-8118

CHARTER OAK FSC
Int'l Skating Ctr of CT 1375 Hopmeadow Street, PO Box 577, Simsbury, CT 06070; Rink: 860/651-5400

CONNECTICUT COLLEGE (CC)
Connecticut College, Dayton Arena, Rt 32, New London, CT 06320

UNIV OF CONNECTICUT STUDENT SC (CC)
Univ Of Connecticut Ice Rink, U/78 Athletic Building, Storrs, CT 06268; Rink: 203/486-3808

DARIEN SC OF SOUTHERN CT
Darien Ice Rink, Old Kings Highway N., Darien, CT 06820; Rink: 203/655-8251

GREENWICH SC, INC.
Greenwich SC, Cardinal Road, Greenwich, CT 06830; Rink: 203/622-9503

GREENWICH HIGH SCHOOL (SA)
Carrie Starr, 10 Hillside Road, Greenwich, CT 06830

HAMDEN FIGURE SKATING ASSC INC
Hamden Memorial Ice Rink, Mix Avenue, Hamden, CT 06514; Rink: 203/248-3461

SC OF HARTFORD
Tri-Town Sports Center, Sebothe Road, Cromwell, CT 06416;
Rink: 203/632-2270

INSIDE EDGE FS ACADEMY
Enfield Twin Rinks, 1 Prior Road, Enfield, CT 06082

LAUREL RIDGE SC
Winter Garden Ice Rink, 11 Prospect Ridge Road, Ridgefield, CT 06877

NEW CANAAN WINTER CLUB
New Canaan Winter Club, PO Box 208, 604 Frogtown Road, New Canaan, CT 06840; Rink: 203/966-9030

NEW HAVEN SC, INC.
Milford Ice Pavilion, 291 Bic Drive, Milford, CT 06460; Rink: 203/878-6516

NORWICH FSC
Norwich Municipal Ice Rink, 641 New London Tpk, Norwich, CT 06360; Rink: 860/892-2555

SACRED HEART ACADEMY (SA)
Hamden Skating Rink, Mix Avenue, Hamden, CT 06514

SHORELINE FIGURE SKATERS
East Haven Veterans Memorial Ice Rink,
Hudson Street, East Haven, CT 06512; Rink: 203/468-3367

SPRINGDALE FSC
Stamford Twin Rinks, 1063 Hope Street, Stamford, CT 06907; Rink: 203/968-9000

STAPLES HIGH SCHOOL (SA)
Peter VanHagen, 70 North Avenue, Westport, CT 06880

WATERTOWN SC, INC.
Taft School Mays Rink, Guerseytown Road, Watertown, CT 06795;
Rink: 203/274-2516

WINDY HILL SC
Dorothy Hamill Skating Rink, 101 Field Point Road, Greenwich, CT 06836;
Rink: 914/234-0717

YALE FSC
Ingalls Rink, 73 Sachem Street, New Haven, CT 06520; Rink: 203/432-0877

DELAWARE
UNIVERSITY OF DELAWARE FSC (CC)
U of Delaware Ice Skating, Science Development Center, Blue Arena-South College Ave, Newark, DE 19716;
Rink: 302/831-2868

THE SC OF WILMINGTON, INC.
The SC of Wilmington, Inc., Carruthers Lane, off Weldin Rd, Wilmington, DE 19803-0307; Rink: 302/656-5007

FLORIDA
CITRUS FSC
Orlando Ice Skating Palace, 3123 W. Colonial Drive, Orlando, FL 32801;
Rink: 407/299-5440

THE SC OF FLORIDA, INC.
Incredible Ice, 3299 Sportsplex Dr., Coral Springs, FL 33363

FLORIDA SUNCOAST FSC, INC.
Sun Blades Ice Rink, 13940 Icot Blvd, Clearwater, FL 34620; Rink: 813/536-5843

FLORIDA GOLDCOAST FSC, INC.
Goldcoast Ice Arena, 4601 N. Federal Highway, Pompano Beach, FL 33064;
Rink: 954/943-1437

MIAMI ICE FSC, INC.
Miami Ice Arena, 14770 Biscayne Blvd., N. Miami Beach, FL 33181; Rink: 305/371-8846

SOUTH FLORIDA SILVER BLADES FSC
Miami Ice Arena, 14770 Biscayne Blvd, Miami Beach, FL 33181; Rink: 305/940-8222

SPACE COAST FSC
Space Coast Ice Plex, 720 Roy Wall Blvd., Rockledge, FL 32955

SC SUNRISE
Sunrise Ice Skating Center, Corner of Pine Island and Oakland Park Blvd, Sunrise, FL 33351; Rink: 305/741-2366

SUNSHINE STATE FSC
Rock On Ice!, 7500 Canada Avenue, Orlando, FL 32819; Rink: 407/352-9878

TAMPA BAY SC
Tampa Bay Skating Academy, 251 Lakeview Drive, Oldsmar, FL 34677;
Rink: 813/854-4009

VENICE FSC
Venice Ice Pavilion, 1266 US 41 Bypass S, Venice, FL 34292; Rink: 941/484-0080

GEORGIA
ATLANTA FSC
Parkaire Ice Rink, 4880 Lower Roswell Road NE, Suite 900, Marietta, GA 30068;
Rink: 404/973-0753

TARA FSC
Parkaire Ice Rink, 4880 Lower Roswell Road NE, Marietta, GA 30068

HAWAII
HAWAII FSC
The Ice Palace, 4510 Salt Lake Blvd, Honolulu, HI 96818; Rink: 808/487-9921

IDAHO
IDAHO FALLS FSC
J. Marmo & W. Lehto Ice Arena, Carnival Way, Tautphaus Park, Idaho Falls, ID 83402; Rink: 208/529-0941

SUN VALLEY FSC, INC.
Sun Valley Skate Center, Sun Valley Resort, Sun Valley, ID 83353;
Rink: 208/622-8020

ILLINOIS
CHICAGO FSC
Glenview Ice Arena, 1851 Landwehr Road, Glenview, IL 60025; Rink: 847/724-2800

DUPAGE FSC
Seven Bridges Ice Arena, 6690 S. Route 53, Woodridge, IL 60517; Rink: 630/271-4423

GLENWOOD FSC
Homewood Flossmoor Ice Arena, 777 Kedzie Ave, Homewood, IL 60430;
Rink: 708/957-0100

ILLINI FSC
University of Illinois Arena, 406 E. Armory Drive, Urbana, IL 61801

ILLINOIS VALLEY FSC
Owens Recreation Center, Peoria Park District, 1019 West Lake Avenue, Peoria, IL 61614; Rink: 309/686-3369

NORTHERN ICE SC
Fox Valley Ice Arena & Fitness, 1000 S. Kirk Road, Geneva, IL 60134

NORTHERN ILLINOIS SC
Carlson Artic Ice Arena, 4150 N. Perryville Road, Loves Park, IL 61111

FSC OF ROCKFORD, INC
Riverview Ice House, 324 N. Madison St, Rockford, IL 61107; Rink: 815/963-7408

SKOKIE VALLEY SC
Wilmette Centennial Park Rink, 2300 Old Glenview Road, Wilmette, IL 60091;
Rink: 847/256-9666

SPRINGFIELD FSC
Franklin Nelson Center, 1501 N. 5th Street, Springfield, IL 62702;
Rink: 217/753-2800

WAGON WHEEL FSC
Barrington Ice Arena, Pepper & Commercial, Barrington, IL 60010; Rink: 817/381-1777

WINDY CITY FSC
McFetridge Sports Center, 3843 N. California Avenue, Chicago, IL 60618;
Rink: 312/478-0210

INDIANA
BLOOMINGTON FSC, INC.
Frank Southern Ctr/Ice Arena, 1965 S.
Henderson, Bloomington, IN 47401;
Rink: 812/349-3740

FORT WAYNE ISC, INC.
McMillen Indoor Ice Arena, McMillen Park, PO Box 9537, Fort Wayne, IN 46806; Rink: 219/427-6730

GREATER EVANSVILLE FSC
Swonder Ice Rink, 201 N. Boeke Road, Evansville, IN 47711; Rink: 812/479-0989

INDIANA/WORLD SK ACAD FSC, INC.
Indiana/World Skating Academy, Pan-Am Plaza, 201 S. Capitol Avenue #001 Indianapolis, IN 46225; Rink: 317/237-5565

ISC OF INDIANAPOLIS, INC.
Carmel Ice Skadium, 1040 3rd Avenue SW, Carmel, IN 46032;
Rink: 317/844-8889

WINTER CLUB OF INDIANAPOLIS, INC.
Indiana State Fair Coliseum, 1202 E. 38th Street, Indianapolis, IN 46205;
Rink: 317/927-7622

LINCOLN CENTER FSC
Hamilton Center Ice Arena, 2501 Lincoln Park Drive, Columbus, IN 47201; Rink: 812/376-2686

SYCAMORE ISC
Perry Park Ice Rink, 541 East Stop 11 Road, Indianapolis, IN 46227;
Rink: 317/888-0070

IOWA
AMES FSC
Ames/ISU Ice Arena, 1505 Gateway Hills Park Drive, Ames, IA 50010;
Rink: 515/292-6835

DES MOINES FSC
Metro Ice Sports Arena, 5100 72nd Street, Urbandale, IA 50322;
Rink: 515/278-9757

NORTH IOWA FSC
North Iowa Ice Arena, Highway 18 W. Mason City, IA 50616; Rink: 515/424-3547

NORTHEAST IOWA FSC
Young Arena, 125 Commercial Street, Waterloo, IA 50701

FSC OF THE QUAD-CITIES
Quad City Sports Center, 700 W. River Drive, Davenport, IA 52802;
Rink: 319/355-4558

SIOUX CITY SILVER BLADES
Sioux City Auditorium, 801 4th Street, PO Box 3183, Sioux City, IA 51102-3183

KANSAS
KANSAS CITY FSC
The Rinks, 19900 Johnson Drive, Shawnee, KS 66218; Rink: 913/441-3033

SILVER BLADES FSC OF KC
King Louie Ice Chateau, 8788 Metcalf, Overland Park, KS 66212;
Rink: 913/648-0130

WICHITA FSC, INC.
Ice Sports Center of Wichita, 505 W Maple, Wichita, KS 67213;
Rink: 316/337-9150

KENTUCKY
FSC OF KENTUCKY
Broadbent, 4710 Robards Lane, Louisville, KY 40218; Rink: 502/451-0112

LOUISVILLE FSC
Iceland, 1701 UPS Drive, Louisville, KY 40223

NORTHERN KENTUCKY SC
Northern Kentucky ISC, 2638 Anderson Road, Crescent Springs, KY 41017

THOROUGHBRED FSC
Lexington Ice Center, 560 Eureka Springs Drive, Lexington, KY 40517; Rink: 606/269-5686

LOUISIANA
FSC OF NEW ORLEANS, INC.
Municipal Auditorium, 1201 St. Peter Street, New Orleans, LA 70116

MAINE
SC OF BRUNSWICK
Dayton Arena, Bowdoin College, College Street, Brunswick, ME 04011
Rink: 207/725-3000

SC OF MAINE
Kennebec Ice Arena, Whitten Road, Box 216, Hallowell, ME 04347; Rink: 207/622-6354

MARYLAND
THE BALTIMORE FSC, INC.
Mt. Pleasant Ice Arena, 6101 Hillen Road, Baltimore, MD 21239; Rink: 410/444-1888

ICE CLUB OF BALTIMORE, INC.
Northwest Ice Rink, 5600 Cottonworth Avenue, Baltimore, MD 21209; Rink: 410/433-4970

BAY COUNTRY FSC
Talbot County Community Center, 10028 Ocean Gateway, Easton, MD 21601; Rink: 410/758-2788

BOWIE FSC
Bowie Ice Rink, 3330 Northview Drive, Bowie, MD 20716; Rink: 301/249-2244

CHESAPEAKE FSC AT ICE WORLD, INC.
Ice World, 1300 Governor Court, Abingdon, MD 21009; Rink: 410/612-1000

COLUMBIA FSC (MD)
Columbia Ice Rink, 5876 Thunder Hill Road, Columbia, MD 21045; Rink: 410/730-0322

FREDERICK FSC
Frederick Sports & Ice Arena, 1288 Riverbend Way, Frederick, MD 21701; Rink: 301/662-7362

THE GARDENS FSC OF MARYLAND
The Gardens Ice House, 13800 Old Gunpowder Road, Laurel, MD 20707; Rink: 301/953-0100

MASSACHUSETTS
ACADEMY SC
Theodore Iorio Arena, Cushing Academy School Street, Ashburnham, MA 01430; Rink: 508/827-7800

SC OF AMHERST, INC.
Mullins Center, University of Massachusetts, Amherst, MA 01003; Rink: 413/545-3990

ARLINGTON CATHOLIC HIGH SCHOOL (SA)
Stoneham Arena, 101 Montvale Avenue, Stoneham, MA 02180

BABSON SC, INC.
Babson Recreation Center, 150 Great Plains Avenue, Wellesley, MA 02181; Rink: 617/239-6000

BANCROFT SCHOOL FIGURE SKATING CLUB (SA)
Worcester SC, 284 Lake Avenue, Worcester, MA 01605

BAY PATH FSC
Loring Arena, Fountain Street, Framingham, MA 01701; Rink: 508/620-4852

BISHOP FENWICK HIGH SCHOOL (SA)
Carl Sacco, 99 Margin Street, Peabody, MA 01960

THE SC OF BOSTON
SC of Boston, 1240 Soldiers Field Road, Boston, MA 02135; Rink: 617/782-5900

BOSTON COLLEGE (CC)
Boston College Campus, McHugh Forum, Chestnut Hill, MA 02167

BOSTON UNIVERSITY (CC)
Walter Brown Arena, 275 Babcock Street, Boston, MA 02215; Rink: 617/353-2748

THE BOURNE SC, INC.
The John Gallo Ice Arena, 231 Sandwich Road, Bourne, MA 02532; Rink: 508/759-8904

BRAINTREE HIGH SCHOOL TEAM (SA)
William Wasser, 128 Town St. Braintree, MA 02184

BURLINGTON HIGH SCHOOL (SA)
Linda Jennings, 123 Cambridge Street, Burlington, MA 01803

CAMBRIDGE SC
Cambridge Skating Club, 40 Willard Street, Cambridge, MA 02138; Rink: 617/354-9743

CAPE COD SC, INC.
Joseph P. Kennedy, Jr., Memorial Skating Rink, Bearses Way, Hyannis, MA 02601; Rink: 508/790-6346

CHRISTMAS BROOK FSC
Lansing Chapman, Williams College, Latham Street, Williamstown, MA 01267; Rink: 413/597-2433

SC OF CLARK MEMORIAL
Clark Memorial Rink, 155 Central Street, Winchendon, MA 01475; Rink: 508/297-0869

COLONIAL FSC
Nashoba Valley Olympia, Massachusetts Avenue, Route 111, Boxborough, MA 01719; Rink: 508/263-3450

COMMONWEALTH FSC
Randolph Ice Arena, 240 North Street, Randolph, MA 02368; Rink: 617/963-4053

CUSHING ACADEMY (SA)
Theodore Iorio Arena, Cushing Academy, Ashburnham, MA 01430; Rink: 978/827-7800

DANVERS HIGH SCHOOL FIGURE SKATING CLUB (SA)
Burbank Ice Arena, 51 Symonds Way, Reading, MA 01867

EVERETT HIGH SCHOOL FIGURE SKATING (SA)
Everett Veterans Memorial Rink, 49 Elm Street, Everett, MA 02149

FALMOUTH FSC
Falmouth Ice Arena, Off Palmer Avenue, Falmouth, MA 02540; Rink: 508/548-7080

FLAGG POND SC
ASIAF Skating Rink, Larch Street, Brockton, MA 02401; Rink: 508/583-6804

FONTBONNE ACADEMY (SA)
Ellen Sullivan, 930 Brook Road, Milton, MA 02186

FRANKLIN HIGH SCHOOL SC (SA)
Veteran's Memorial Rink, Franklin, MA 02038

GARDNER HIGH SCHOOL (SA)
Theodore Iorio Arena, 39 School Street, Ashburnham, MA 01430

GREENFIELD AREA FSC
Collins-Moylan Arena, Barr Ave, Greenfield, MA 01301; Rink: 413/772-6891

HAVERHILL FSC
Veterans Memorial Skating Arena, Brook Street, Haverhill, MA 01831

HAYDEN RECREATION CENTRE FSC, INC.
John P. Chase Skating Facility, 24 Lincoln Street, Lexington, MA 02173; Rink: 617/862-5575

SC OF HINGHAM, INC.
Pilgrim Arena, 75 Recreation Park Dr., Hingham, MA 02043; Rink: 617/749-6660

HOPKINTON HIGH SCHOOL-MIDDLE SCHOOL (SA)
Claire Wright, Hayden Rowe Street, Hopkinton, MA 01748

IORIO ICE CLUB
Iorio Arena at Walpole, 2130 Providence Highway, PO Box 227, Walpole, MA 02081; Rink: 508/660-2005

KING PHILIP R.H.S. FIGURE SKATING CLUB (SA)
Nashoba Valley Olympia, Acton, MA 02093

LITTLE SUN VALLEY SC, INC.
Ray Smead Ice Arena, 1780 Roosevelt Avenue, Springfield, MA 01109; Rink: 413/781-2599

LYNNFIELD HIGH SCHOOL FSC (SA)
Bill Adams, 275 Essex Street, Lynnfield, MA 01940

MANSFIELD HIGH SCHOOL (SA)
Iorio Arena at Walpole, 2130 Providence Hwy, Walpole, MA 02081

MARTHA'S VINEYARD REGIONAL HIGH SCHOOL (SA)
Martha's Vineyard Arena, Edgartown-V.H. Road, Oak Bluffs, MA 02557

MARTHA'S VINEYARD FSC
Martha's Vineyard Arena, Edgartown-Vineyard Haven Road, Oak Bluffs, MA 02557; Rink: 508/693-4438

MASCONOMET HIGH SCHOOL FSC (SA)
Joseph Casey, 20 Endicott Road, Topsfield, MA 01983

MIDDLEBOROUGH HIGH SCHOOL (SA)
Asiaf Rink Brockton High School, Brockton, MA 02401

MIT FSC (CC)
Massachusetts Institute of Technology Johnson Athletic Center, 77 Mass. Avenue, Cambridge, MA 02139; Rink: 617/253-4497

MONADNOCK FSC
Gardner Veterans Skating Rink, Veterans Drive, Gardner, MA 01440

MONTROSE SCHOOL FSC (SA)
West Suburban Arena, PO Box 403, Natick, MA 01760

MURDOCK MIDDLE HIGH SCHOOL (SA)
Wendee Jacob, 2 Memorial Drive, Winchendon, MA 01475

SC OF NATICK
West Suburban Arena, PO Box 403, Windsor Avenue, Natick, MA 01760; Rink: 508/655-1013

NAUSET REGIONAL HIGH SCHOOL (SA)
Cindy Edwards, Cable Road, PO Box R, North Eastham, MA 02651

NEW ENGLAND FSC
New England Sports Center, 121 Donald Lynch Blvd., Marlboro, MA 01752; Rink: 508/229-2700

NEWBURYPORT FSC
Henry Graf Jr. Skating Rink, 27 Low Street, Newburyport, MA 01950; Rink: 978/462-8112

NORTH READING HIGH SCHOOL (SA)
Burbank Ice Arena, 51 Symonds Way, Reading, MA 01867; Rink: 781/942-2271

NORTH SHORE SC
Burbank Ice Arena, 51 Symonds Way, Reading, MA 01867

NORTH STAR FSC
North Star Youth Forum, Bridle Lane, Westboro, MA 01581; Rink: 508/366-9373

NORTHEASTERN UNIVERSITY (CC)
Matthews Arena, Northeastern University, 238 St. Boltolph Street, Boston, MA 02115; Rink: 617/373-2705

NORTHERN MIDDLESEX SPINNERS
Janas Rink, Douglas Road, Lowell, MA 01852

NORWELL HIGH SCHOOL (SA)
Theodore Iorio Arena, 39 School St, Cushing Academy, Ashburnham, MA 01430

PATRIOT FSC
Merrimach Valley Arena, 654 S Union Street, Lawrence, MA 01842; Rink: 508/649-6391

PILGRIM SC
Hobomock Ice Arena, Hobomock Street, Pembroke, MA 02359; Rink: 781/294-0260

PINGREE SCHOOL (SA)
Johnson Rink, 537 Highland Street, S Hamilton, MA 01982

PITTSFIELD FSC
Pittsfield Boys & Girls Club, 16 Melville St., Pittsfield, MA 01201; Rink: 413/448-2725

RANDOLPH JR.-SR. HIGH (SA)
Randolph Ice Arena, 240 North Street, Randolph, MA 02368

RIVERS SCHOOL (SA)
Jim McNally, 333 Winter Street, Weston, MA 02193

SANDWICH HIGH SCHOOL (SA)
Gallo Ice Arena, 231 Sandwich Road, Bourne, MA 02532

SILVER BLADES SC
Bridgewater Ice Arena, 20 Bedford Park, Bridgewater, MA 02324; Rink: 508/279-0600

SILVER STREAKS SC
McVann-O'Keefe Memorial Rink, 511 Lowell Street, Peabody, MA 01960; Rink: 978/535-2110

SOUTH SHORE SC
Rockland Rink, 599 Summer Street, Rockland, MA 02370, Rink: 617/871-5135

SC OF SOUTHERN NEW ENGLAND
Southeastern Mass. Arenas, 310 Hathaway Blvd., New Bedford, MA 02740; Rink: 508/997-1416

THE SC OF SPRINGFIELD
Skate Inc., 125 Capital Drive W. Springfield, MA 01089; Rink: 413/781-6215

ST. BERNARD'S HIGH SCHOOL (SA)
Wallace Civic Center, John Fitch Highway, Fitchburg, MA 01420

STONEHAM FSC
Unicorn Arena, 101 Montvale Avenue, Stoneham, MA 02180; Rink: 617/279-2628

SYMMETRIC FSC
Veteran's Memorial Rink, Panther Way, Franklin, MA 02038; Rink: 508/528-2333

TABOR ACADEMY (SA)
Howard Johnson Arena, Tabor Academy, Marion, MA 02738; Rink: 508/748-2000

TRITON REGIONAL HIGH SCHOOL (SA)
Henry Graf Jr. Skating Rink, 27 Low Street, Newburyport, MA 01950; Rink: 978/462-8112

WAKEFIELD HIGH SCHOOL (SA)
Burbank Ice Arena, 51 Symonds Way, Reading, MA 01867

WALLACE FSC, INC.
Wallace Civic Center, 1000 John Fitch Highway, Fitchburg, MA 01420; Rink: 508/345-7593

WESTBORO HIGH SCHOOL FSC (SA)
Nashoba Valley Olympia, Box 793, Acton, MA 01720

WESTON HIGH SCHOOL (SA)
Mrs. Lee Marsh, 444 Wellesley Street, Weston, MA 02193

WILMINGTON FSC
Wilmington Arena Authority Inc., Ristuccia Expo Center, 190 Main Street, Wilmington, MA 01887; Rink: 508/657-3976

WINCHESTER FSC
Burlington Ice Palace, 36 Ray Avenue, Burlington, MA 01803; Rink: 617/229-6442

WINTHROP SKATING ASSOC, INC.
Larson Rink, 45 Pauline Street, Winthrop, MA 02152; Rink: 617/846-5770

SC OF WORCESTER, INC.
Worcester Skating Rink, 284 Lake Avenue, Worcester, MA 01604; Rink: 508/755-0582

YARMOUTH ICE CLUB, INC.
Tony Kent Arena, Gages Way, S. Dennis, MA 02660; Rink: 508/760-2400

MICHIGAN

ALPENA FSC
Mich-E-Kewis Park, U.S. 23 South, Alpena, MI 49707; Rink: 517/354-8191

ANN ARBOR FSC
The Ann Arbor Ice Cube, 2121 Oak Valley, Ann Arbor, MI 48103; Rink: 313/213-1600

BERKLEY ROYAL BLADES FSC
Berkley Ice Arena, 2300 Robina, Berkley, MI 48072; Rink: 248/546-2460

FSC OF BIRMINGHAM, MI
Birmingham Ice Arena, 2300 E. Lincoln, Birmingham, MI 48009; Rink: 248/647-7926

CALUMET FSC
Calumet Armory, Red Jacket Road, Calumet, MI 49913; Rink: 906/337-2205

COPPER COUNTRY SKATING ACADEMY
John J. MacInnes Arena, 1400 Townsend Dr. Houghton, MI 49931; Rink: 906/487-2578

DEARBORN FSC
Michael Adray Arena, 14900 Ford Road, Dearborn, MI 48126; Rink: 313/943-4098

DETROIT SC, INC.
Detroit Skating Club, Inc., 888 Denison Court, Bloomfield Hills, MI 48302; Rink: 248/332-3000

ESCANABA AREA FSC
Wells Sports Complex, 1647 174 Road, Escanaba, MI 49894; Rink: 906/786-3995

FARMINGTON HILLS FSC
Farmington Hills Ice Arena, 35500 Eight Mile Road, Farmington Hills, MI 48335

FLINT SC
Ima Ice Arena, 3501 Lapeer Road, Flint, MI 48503

FLINT 4 SEASONS FSC
Flint Iceland Arenas, 1160 S Elms Road, Flint, MI 48532; Rink: 810/635-8487

FRASER FSC
Fraser Ice Arena, 34400 Utica Road, Fraser, MI 48026; Rink: 810/294-4136

GARDEN CITY FSC
Garden City Ice Arena, 200 Log Cabin Road, Garden City, MI 48135

GREATER GRAND RAPIDS FSC
Michigan National Ice Center, 2550 Patterson Avenue SE, Grand Rapids, MI 49546; Rink: 616/940-1423

GROSSE POINTE SC
Grosse Pointe Community Rink, 4831 Canyon, Detroit, MI 48224; Rink: 810/885-4100

HIAWATHA SC
Pullar Stadium, 435 E. Portage Avenue,

Sault Ste. Marie, MI 49783; Rink: 906/632-6853

ICE BOX FSC
Ice Box Sports Arena, 21902 Telegraph Road, Brownstown Twp., MI 48183; Rink: 313/676-6429

ICE CRYSTALS FSC
Pat O'Donnell Civic Center, E. 4972 Jackson Road, Ironwood, MI 49938; Rink: 906/932-0602

ICE REFLECTIONS-MOUNTAIN VIEW FSC, INC.
Mountain View Ice Arena, 400 E. Hughitt Street, Iron Mountain, MI 49801; Rink: 906/774-1480

KALAMAZOO FSC
Lawson Ice Arena, Western Michigan University, 2009 Howard Street, Kalamazoo, MI 49007; Rink: 616/387-3050

LAKE EFFECT FSC
Belknap Arena, 30 Coldbrook NE, Grand Rapids, MI 49503

LAKELAND SC
Lakeland Arena, 7330 Highland Road, Waterford, MI 48327; Rink: 810/666-1910

LANSING SC
Lansing Ice Arena, 1475 Lake Lansing Rd., Lansing, MI 48912; Rink: 517/482-1597

MARQUETTE FSC
Lakeview Arena, 401 E. Fair Avenue, Marquette, MI 49855; Rink: 906/228-0490

MELVINDALE FSC
Melvindale Kessey Arena, 4300 S. Dearborn Street, Melvindale, MI 48122

MICHIGAN STATE UNIVERSITY (CC)
Munn Ice Arena, 1 Chestnut Road, 213 Jenison Fieldhouse, E. Lansing, MI 48824; Rink: 517/353-4698

MIDLAND FSC
Midland Civic Arena, 515 E. Collins, Midland, MI 48640; Rink: 517/832-8438

MT. PLEASANT FSC
Comm. Rec. Center of Isabella, 5165 E. Remus, Mt. Pleasant, MI 48858; Rink: 517/772-9623

NORTH STAR FSA
Cheboygan Ice Rink/Pavilion, 480 Cleveland Avenue, Cheboygan, MI 49721

NORTH SUBURBAN FSC
John Lindell Arena, 1403 Lexington Boulevard, Royal Oak, MI 48073-2408; Rink: 810/544-6690

PLYMOUTH FSC
Compuware Sports Arena, 14900 Beck Rd., Plymouth, MI 48170; Rink: 313/459-6686

PORT HURON FSC
McMorran Place Auditorium, 701 McMorran Blvd., Port Huron, MI 48060; Rink: 810/985-6166

PORT HURON NORTHERN HIGH SCHOOL (SA)
McMorran Auditorium, 701 McMorran Blvd., Port Huron, MI 48060; Rink: 810/985-6166

PORTAGE LAKE FSC
John J. MacInnes Arena, Michigan Tech

University, 1400 Townsend Drive, Houghton, MI 49931; Rink: 906/487-2578

PRECISION SC OF WESTERN MICHIGAN UNIV. (CC)
Lawson Arena, Western Michigan University, Kalamazoo, MI 49008

SKATE COMPANY SC
Lincoln Park Community Center, 3525 Dix, Lincoln Park, MI 48146; Rink: 810/386-4075

SOUTHWEST MICHIGAN SC
Wings Stadium/the Annex, 3600 Vanrick Drive, Kalamazoo, MI 49002; Rink: 616/345-1125

ST. CLAIR SHORES FSC
St. Clair Shores Civic Arena, 20000 Stephens Drive, St. Clair Shores, MI 48080; Rink: 810/445-5350

THE TROY ACADEMY OF FIGURE SKATING
Troy Sports Complex, John R Complex, 1819 E Big Beaver, Troy, MI 48083

TWIN BAYS SC
Howe Arena, 1125 W. Civic Center Drive, Traverse City, MI 49684; Rink: 616/922-4818

UNIVERSITY OF MICHIGAN SC (CC)
Yost Ice Arena, 1000 S. State Street, Ann Arbor, MI 48109; Rink: 313/764-4600

WESTLAND FSC
Westland Sports Arena, 6210 N. Wildwood, Westland, MI 48185; Rink: 313/729-4560

WYANDOTTE FSC
Benjamin F. Yack Arena, 3131 Second Street, Wyandotte, MI 48192; Rink: 810/246-4515

MINNESOTA

ALBERT LEA FSC
Albert Lea City Arena, 701 Lake Chapeau Drive, Albert Lea, MN 56007; Rink: 507/377-4374

ALEXANDRIA FSC
Runestone Community Center, 802 3rd Avenue W. Alexandria, MN 56308; Rink: 612/763-4466

BABBITT FSC
Babbitt Arena, South Drive, Babbitt, MN 55706

BEMIDJI FSC, INC.
Neilson-Reise City Arena, 23rd & Ash Avenue, Bemidji, MN 56601; Rink: 218/751-9536

FSC OF BLOOMINGTON
Bloomington Ice Garden, 3600 W. 98th Street, Bloomington, MN 55420; Rink: 612/948-8842

BRAEMAR-CITY OF LAKES FSC
Braemar Arena, 7501 Ikola Way, Edina, MN 55439; Rink: 612/941-1322

BROOKLYN PARK FSC
Brooklyn Park Community Center, 5600 85th Avenue N. Brooklyn Park, MN 55443

BURNSVILLE-MN VALLEY FSC
Burnsville Ice Center, 251 Civic Center Parkway, Burnsville, MN 55337; Rink: 612/895-4650

CHASKA FSC
Chaska Community Center, 1661 Park Ridge Drive, Chaska, MN 55318

CHISHOLM SC
Chisholm Sports Arena, 1st St. NW, Chisholm, MN 55719-1649; Rink: 218/254-2635

CROOKSTON FSC
Crookston Civic Arena, 220 E. Robert, Crookston, MN 56716

DULUTH FSC
Duluth Entertainment & Convention Ctr, 350 Harbor Drive, Duluth, MN 55802; Rink: 218/722-5573

EDEN PRAIRIE FSC
Eden Prairie Community Center, 16700 Valley View Road, Eden Prairie, MN 55344; Rink: 612/949-8470

FERGUS FALLS SC, INC.
Fairgrounds Ice Arena, Highway 59 S. Fergus Falls, MN 56537;
Rink: 218/736-6941

GREENWAY EMERALD ICE
Hodgins Berardo Arena, 200 Curley Avenue, Coleraine, MN 55722

HIBBING FSC
Hibbing Memorial Ice Arena, 400 23rd Street E. Hibbing, MN 55746;
Rink: 218/263-4379

INTERNATIONAL FALLS FSC
Bronco Arena, Independent School District #3, 11th Street, Int'l Falls, MN 56649; Rink: 218/283-2424

LAKE MINNETONKA FSC
Minnetonka Ice Arena, 3401 Williston Road, Minnetonka, MN 55345;
Rink: 612/939-8310

LAKES FSC
Lakes Sports Arena, Rossman Avenue, Fairgrounds, Detroit Lakes, MN 56501;
Rink: 218/847-7738

MANKATO FSC
All Seasons Arena, 301 Monks Avenue, Mankato, MN 56001; Rink: 507/387-6552

MAPLEWOOD FSC
Aldrich Arena, 1850 White Bear Avenue, Maplewood, MN 55109

FSC OF MINNEAPOLIS
Breck Ice Center, 5800 Wayzata Boulevard, Minneapolis, MN 55416;
Rink: 612/545-1614

NEW ULM FSC
Vogel Arena, 122 S. Garden, New Ulm, MN 56073; Rink: 507/354-8321

NORTHERN BLADES FSC
White Bear Lake Sports Center, 1328 Hwy 96, White Bear Lake, MN, 55110;
Rink: 612/429-8571

NORTHERN LIGHTS FSC
O'Leary Park VFW Arena, 711 3 Street SE, East Grand Forks, MN 56721;
Rink: 218/773-1851

OWATONNA FSC
Four Seasons Arena, Steele City Fairgrounds, Owatonna, MN 55060;
Rink: 507/451-1093

PARK RAPIDS FSC
Park Rapids Community Center, 200

Huntsinger Avenue, Park Rapids, MN 56470

RIVERSIDE FSC
Riverside Arena, 501 NE 2nd Avenue, Austin, MN 55912; Rink: 507/437-7676

ROCHESTER FSC
Rochester Olmsted Rec Center, 21 Elton Hills Drive NW, Rochester, MN 55901; Rink: 507/288-7536

ROSEVILLE FSC
Roseville Ice Arena, 1200 Woodhill Drive, Roseville, MN 55113;
Rink: 612/415-2160

ST. CLOUD FSC
Municipal Athletic Complex, 5001 8th Street N. St Cloud, MN 56303;
Rink: 320/255-7223

ST. PAUL FSC, INC.
Augsburg Ice Arena, 2323 Riverside Avenue, Minneapolis, MN 55454;
Rink: 612/330-1251

STAR OF THE NORTH SC
Ira Civic Center Arena, 3rd Avenue & 14th Street NW, Grand Rapids, MN 55744; Rink: 218/326-2591

STARLIGHT ICE DANCE CLUB
Parade Ice Garden, 600 Kenwood Parkway, Minneapolis, MN 55403;
Rink: 612/370-4904

THIEF RIVER FALLS SC
Huck Olson Memorial Civic Center, Brooks Ave. N., Thief River Falls, MN 56701

TRI-COUNTY FSC
Farmington Ice Arena, 114 W. Spruce Street, Farmington, MN 55024;
Rink: 612/463-2510

VACATIONLAND FSC, INC.
Brainerd Area Civic Center, 502 Jackson Street, Brainerd, MN 56401;
Rink: 218/825-3005

WINONA FSC
Bud King Ice Arena, 670 E. Front Street, Winona, MN 55987

MISSISSIPPI
MISSISSIPPI FSC
The Ice Park, 2280 Lakeland Drive, Flowood, MS 39208; Rink: 601/939-8333

MISSOURI
CARRIAGE FSC, INC.
The Carriage Club, 5301 State Line, Kansas City, MO 64112; Rink: 816/363-1310

CHESTERFIELD VALLEY FS ACADEMY
Ice Sports Complex, 168 N. Outer Forty, Chesterfield, MO 63005;
Rink: 314/537-4200

CREVE COEUR FSC
Creve Coeur Ice Arena, 11400 Old Cabin Road, Creve Coeur, MO 63141;
Rink: 314/432-3960

JEFFERSON CITY FSC
Washington Park Ice Arena, 700 Kansas Street, Jefferson City, MO 65109

MISSISSIPPI VALLEY FSC
North County Ice Arena, 2577 Redman Road, St. Louis, MO 63136;
Rink: 314/355-7374

THE SHOW ME BLADES SC
The Ice Plaza Galleria, 2001 Independence, Cape Girardeau, MO 63701; Rink: 314/335-4405

ST. JOSEPH FSC, INC.
Bode Ice Arena, 2500 SW Parkway, St. Joseph, MO 64503; Rink: 816/271-5506

ST. LOUIS SC
Brentwood Ice Arena, 2505 S. Brentwood Blvd, St Louis, MO 63144;
Rink: 314/962-4806

ST. PETERS FSA
St. Peters Rec Plex, 5200 Mexico Road, St. Peters, MO 63376

MONTANA
FSC OF BILLINGS, INC.
Centennial Arena, 427 Bench Blvd, Billings, MT 59105

BUTTE FSC
Butte Civic Center, 1370 Harrison Avenue, Butte, MT 59701; Rink: 406/782-5971

GREAT FALLS FSC
Four Seasons Arena, State Fairgrounds, Great Falls, MT 49404;
Rink: 406/453-1311

HELENA FSC
Queen City Ice Palace, 400 Lola Street, Helena, MT 59601; Rink: 406/443-1442

WHITEFISH FSC
Mountain Trails Ice Rink, 725 1/2 Wisconsin Avenue, Whitefish, MT 59937;
Rink: 406/862-8244

YELLOWSTONE VALLEY FSC
MetraPark Arena, 308 Sixthe Avenue N. Billings, MT 59101

NEBRASKA
BLADE & EDGE FSC OF OMAHA
Hitchcock Ice Arena, 45th & Q Streets, Omaha, NE 68117; Rink: 402/444-4955

LINCOLN ICE SKATING ASSOC.
The Ice Box, State Fair Park, 1800 State Fair Drive, Lincoln, NE 68501; Rink: 402/437-1636

FSC OF OMAHA
Hitchcock Ice Arena, 45th & Q Streets, Omaha, NE 68117; Rink: 402/444-4955

NEVADA
LAS VEGAS FSC
Santa Fe Ice Arena, 4949 N. Rancho Drive, Las Vegas, NV 89130;
Rink: 702/658-4992

NEW HAMPSHIRE
BISHOP BRADY HIGH SCHOOL (SA)
Suzanne Walsh, 25 Columbus Avenue, Concord, NH 03301

CHESHIRE FSC
Cheshire Fair Ice Arena, Monadnock Highway, PO Box 76, E. Swanzey, NH 03446; Rink: 603/357-4740

CONCORD FSC
Douglas N. Everett Arena, 15 Loudon Road, Concord, NH 03301;
Rink: 603/225-5633

SC AT DARTMOUTH, INC.
Thompson Arena, Hanover, NH 03755

GRANITE STATE FSC
Lee Clement Arena, New England

College, 12 Bridge Street, Henniker, NH 03242; Rink: 603/428-6321

GREAT BAY FSC, INC.
Dover Ice Arena, 110 Portland Avenue, Dover, NH 03820; Rink: 603/743-6060

HAVERHILL FSC, INC.
Veterans Memorial Ice Skating Rink, Brooks Street, Haverhill, MA 01831

MONADNOCK REGIONAL JR-SR HIGH SCHOOL FST (SA)
Cheshire FSC, Rt. 12, N. Swanzey, NH 03431

SOUTHERN NEW HAMPSHIRE SC
John F. Kennedy Coliseum, 303 Beech Street, Manchester, NH 03104;
Rink: 603/624-6567

TRINITY HIGH SCHOOL (SA)
Deborah Hanson, 581 Bridge Street, Manchester, NH 03104

NEW JERSEY
ATLANTIC CITY FSC, INC.
Ventnor City Ice Rink, New Haven & Atlantic Avenues, Ventnor, NJ 08406;
Rink: 609/823-8982

BEAR MOUNTAIN FSC, INC.
Fritz Dietl Ice Rink, 639 Broadway, Westwood, NJ 07675; Rink: 201/666-9883

SC OF BRIDGEWATER
Bridgewater Sports Arena, 1425 Frontier Road, Bridgewater, NJ 08807;
Rink: 908/627-0006

ENGLEWOOD FIELD CLUB
Englewood Field Club, 341 Engle Street, Englewood, NJ 07631;
Rink: 201/568-0094

ESSEX SC OF NJ, INC.
South Mountain Arena, 560 Northfield Avenue, West Orange, NJ 07052
Rink: 201/731-3828

ESSEX HUNT CLUB
Essex Hunt Club, Holland Road, Peapack, NJ 07977; Rink: 908/234-0062

THE FOUR SEASONS FSC
The Coliseum, 333 Preston Avenue, Voorhees, NJ 08043

GARDEN STATE SC
American Hockey & Ice Skating Center, 1215 Wyckoff Road, Farmingdale, NJ 07727; Rink: 908/919-7070

HOLLYDELL FSC
Hollydell Ice Arena, 601 Hollydell Drive, Sewell, NJ 08080-0472;
Rink: 609/589-5599

MONTCLAIR INSIDE EDGE SC
Montclair Arena, 41 Chestnut Street, Montclair, NJ 07042; Rink: 201/744-6088

SC OF MORRISTOWN NJ, INC.
William G. Mennen Sports Arena, 161 E. Hanover Avenue, Morristown, NJ 07960;
Rink: 201/326-7651

NORTH JERSEY FSC, INC.
Fritz Dietl Ice Rink, 639 Broadway, Westwood, NJ 07675; Rink: 201/664-9812

PRINCETON SC, INC.
Baker Rink, Princeton University, PO Box 26, Princeton, NJ 08542

PRINCETON DAY SCHOOL (SA)
Lois Rowe, PO Box 75, The Great Road, Princeton, NJ 08542

PRINCETON UNIVERSITY FSC (CC)
(Collegiate Club) University, Princeton, NJ 08544

RARITAN VALLEY FSC, INC.
Old Bridge Arena, 1 Old Bridge Plaza, Old Bridge, NJ 08857; Rink: 908/679-3100

RIVER'S EDGE FSC
Twin Rinks of Pennsauken, 6725 River Road, Pennsauken, NJ 08110; Rink: 609/488-9300

SOUTH MOUNTAIN FSC, INC.
South Mountain Arena, 560 Northfield Avenue, West Orange, NJ 07052; Rink: 201/731-3828

NEW MEXICO
ALBUQUERQUE FSC
Outpost Ice Arena, 9530 Tramway Blvd. NE, Albuquerque, NM 87122; Rink: 505/856-7594

NEW YORK
ACHILLES FSC, INC.
Achilles Rink, Union College, Schenectady, NY 12301; Rink: 518/370-6134

SC OF THE ADIRONDACKS, INC.
Ronald B. Stafford Arena, Plattsburgh State Field House, Rugar Street, Plattsburgh, NY 12901; Rink: 518/564-3060

THE ALEXANDRIA BAY FSC
Alexandria Bay Municipal Arena, Bolton Avenue, Alexandria Bay, NY 13607; Rink: 315/482-9360

AMHERST SC, INC.
Audubon Recreation Center, 1615 Amherst Manor Drive, Amherst, NY 14221; Rink: 716/684-3887

BEAVER DAM WINTER SPORTS CLUB
Beaver Dam Winter Sports Club, 99 Kaintuck Lane, Locust Valley, NY 11560; Rink: 516/671-1923

BINGHAMTON FSC
Grippen Park Ice Rink, Grippen Avenue, Endicott, NY 13760; Rink: 607/748-9461

BRONXVILLE SC
E.J. Murray Memorial Skating Center, 348 Tuckahoe Road, Yonkers, NY 10710; Rink: 914/377-6469

BROOME-CHENANGO WINTER CLUB
Polar Cap Ice Arena, PO Box 319, Katelville & River Road, Chenango Bridge, NY 13745; Rink: 607/648-9888

BUFFALO SC, INC.
State University College at Buffalo Ice Arena, 1300 Elmwood Avenue, Buffalo, NY 14222

CAMILLUS FSC
Shove Park Rec Facility, Slawson Drive. Camillus, NY 13031; Rink: 315/487-5085

CANTIAGUE FSC, INC.
Cantiague Park Rink, W. John Street, Hicksville, NY 11801; Rink: 516/935-3501

CLAYTON FSC
Clayton Recreation Park Arena, E. Line Rd. Clayton, NY 13624; Rink: 315/686-4310

CLIFTON FINE FSA
Clifton Fine Arena, Main Street, Star Lake, NY 13690; Rink: 315/848-2578

CLINTON FSC
Clinton Arena, 36 Kirkland Avenue, Clinton, NY 13323; Rink: 315/853-5541

CORNELL FSC OF ITHACA
Lynah Rink, Cornell University, Ithaca, NY 14850; Rink: 607/255-3793

CORTLAND FSC, INC.
Alumni Ice Arena, SUCC PO Box 2000, Cortland, NY 13045

DUTCHESS FSC
McCann Ice Arena, Mid-Hudson Civic Center Plaza, Poughkeepsie, NY 12601

SC OF FINGER LAKES, INC.
Wilson Ice Arena, SUNY Campus, Geneseo, NY 14454

FULTON FSC, INC.
Fulton Recreation Center, W. Broadway, Fulton, NY 13069; Rink: 315/598-5379

GENESEE FSC
Frank Ritter Memorial Arena, 51 Lomb Memorial Drive, Rochester, NY 14623; Rink: 716/475-6165

GLENS FALLS FSC
Glens Falls Civic Center, 1 Civic Center Plaza, Glens Falls, NY 12801; Rink: 518/798-0366

GREAT NECK FSC, INC.
Parkwood Ice Rink, Wood Road, Great Neck, NY 11023; Rink: 516/487-2976

THE HARVEY SCHOOL (SA)
The Harvey School Rink, 260 Jay Street, Katonah, NY 10536

HESSIAN LAKE FSC
Bear Mountain Ice Rink, Bear Mountain State Park, Bear Mountain, NY 10911-0427; Rink: 914/786-2701

HICKORY HILL FSC
Westchester Skating Academy, 91 Fairview Park Drive, Elmsford, NY 10523

HUDSON-MOHAWK FSC
RPI'S Houston Field House, Peoples Avenue, Troy, NY 12180; Rink: 518/276-6262

HUDSON VALLEY FSC
Ice Time Sports Complex, Lakeside Road, Newburgh, NY, 12550; Rink: 914/567-0005

JAMESTOWN SC
Allen Park Ice Rink, Elizabeth Avenue, Jamestown, NY 14701; Rink: 716/483-0614

KEN-TON FSC
Lincoln Arena, Decatur & Parker Blvds, Kenmore, NY 14223; Rink: 716/833-7757

THE SC OF LAKE PLACID
Olympic Center Arena, Main Street, Lake Placid, NY 12946; Rink: 518/523-3325

LONG ISLAND FSC
Long Beach Arena, 150 W. Bay Drive, Long Beach, NY 11561; Rink: 516/431-6501

MALONE FSC
Malone Ice Arena, State Street, Malone, NY 12953

MASSENA FSC, INC.
Massena Arena, Harte Haven Plaza, Massena, NY 13662; Rink: 315/769-3161

METROPOLITAN FSC, INC.
Iceland Skating Rink, 3345 Hillside Avenue, New Hyde Park, NY 11040; Rink: 516/746-1100

THE SC OF NEW HARTFORD
New Hartford Recreation Center, Mill Street, New Hartford, NY 13413; Rink: 315/724-0600

NEW HARTFORD HIGH SCHOOL FSC (SA)
New Hartford Recreation Center, Mill Street, New Hartford, NY 13413

THE SC OF NEW YORK, INC.
Sky Rink at Chelsea Piers, 23rd Street & Hudson River, Pier 61, New York, NY 10011; Rink: 212/336-6100

NIAGARA UNIVERSITY SC
Niagara University Ice Complex, Lewiston Road, Niagara Univ., NY 14109; Rink: 716/286-8782

NORFOLK NORWOOD FSC
Norfolk Community Center, Clinton Street, Norfolk, NY 13667

NORTH COUNTRY SC
Rouses Point Recreation Center, 39 Lake Street, Rouses Point, NY 12979; Rink: 518/297-6852

OGDENSBURG FSC
Edgar Allen Newell, 2nd Golden Dome, 1101 State Street, Ogdensburg, NY 13669; Rink: 315/393-5320

OLEAN AREA SC
Olean Rec Center Ice Complex, Front & State Streets, Olean, NY 14760; Rink: 716/373-7465

OSWEGO FSC, INC.
A. J. Crisafulli Skating Rink, Fort Ontario, Oswego, NY 13126; Rink: 315/343-4054

PARK FSC, INC.
Flushing Rink, Worlds Fair Grounds, Flushing Corona Park, Corona, NY 11326, 908/842-6160

THE POTSDAM FSC
Pine Street Arena, Sandstoner Park, Potsdam, NY 13676; Rink: 315/265-4030

PROSPECT PARK FSC
Kate Wollman Rink Alliance '95 Prospect Park West, Brooklyn, NY 11215

RIT FSC (CC)
Frank Ritter Memorial Arena, 51 Lomb Memorial Drive, Rochester, NY 14623

SC OF ROCKLAND NEW YORK
Sport-O-Rama, 20 College Road, Monsey, NY 10952; Rink: 914/356-3919

RYE FSC, INC.
Playland Ice Casino & Manager, Playland Parkway, Rye, NY 10580

SALT CITY FIGURE SKATERS, INC.
Meachem Rink, Seneca Turnpike, Syracuse, NY 13203; Rink: 315/492-0179

SHAMROCK FSC, INC.
Salmon River Central Sch Arena, Ft. Covington Bombay Road, Ft. Covington, NY 12937; Rink: 518/358-9510

SKANEATELES FSC
W.G. Allyn Arena, Jordan Street, Skaneateles, NY 13152; Rink: 315/685-7757

ST LAWRENCE FSC, INC.
Appleton Arena, St. Lawrence University, Leigh Street, Canton, NY 13617; Rink: 315/229-5011

STATE UNIVERSITY COLLEGE FSC (CC)
Ira S. Wilson Ice Arena, State University College, Geneseo, NY 14654

STATUE OF LIBERTY SKATING INST.
The War Memorial Ice Rink, Victory Blvd, Staten Island, NY 10301

SYRACUSE FSC, INC.
Lysander-Radisson Ice Arena, 2725 W. Entry Road, Baldwinsville, NY 13027; Rink: 315/635-1555

THOMAS CREEK FSC
Thomas Creek Ice Arena, 80 Lyndon Road, Fairport, NY 14450; Rink: 716/223-2160

SC OF TUPPER LAKE, INC.
Tupper Lake Civic Center, McLaughlin Avenue, Tupper Lake, NY 12986; Rink: 518/359-3881

UNCLE SAM SKATING CLUB
Knickerbacker Rec Skating Rink, 103rd Street & 8th Avenue, Troy, NY 12182; Rink: 518/235-0215

SC OF UTICA
Utica Memorial Auditorium, Oriskany Street W. Utica, NY 13057; Rink: 315/738-0164

FSC OF WATERTOWN, INC.
Fairgrounds Ice Arena, William T. Field Drive, PO Box 101, Watertown, NY 13601; Rink: 315/785-7836

SC OF WESTCHESTER
Alan H. Young, 126 Penn Road, Scarsdale, NY 10583

SC OF WESTERN NEW YORK
Leisure Rinks Southtowns, 75 Weiss Road, West Seneca, NY 14224; Rink: 716/822-4713

WHITE PLAINS FSC
Ebersole Ice Rink, 53 Lake Street, White Plains, NY 10605; Rink: 914/682-4390

THE WINTER CLUB
The Winter Club, Route 25A, Huntington, NY 11743

YONKERS FSC
E.J. Murray Memorial Skating Center, 348 Tuckahoe Road, Yonkers, NY 10710

NORTH CAROLINA
CAPE FEAR FSC
Cleland Sports Complex, Fort Bragg, NC 28307; Rink: 910/396-5127

CAROLINAS FSC
IceHouse, 400 Towne Centre Blvd. Pineville, NC 28134; Rink: 704/889-9000

CENTRAL CAROLINA SC
Triangle Sportsplex, One Dan Kidd Drive, Hillsborough, NC 27278; Rink: 919/644-0339

CHARLOTTE FSC
Ice Chalet, Eastland Mall, 5595 Central

Avenue, Charlotte, NC 28212;
Rink: 704/568-0772

SC OF NORTH CAROLINA
Ice Works; 2601 Raleigh Blvd. Raleigh,
NC 27604

TWIN CITY ISC
Lawrence Joel Mem Colis. Annex, 300
Deacon Blvd. Winston-Salem, NC 27105;
Rink: 910/727-2978

NORTH DAKOTA
BISMARCK FSC, INC.
VFW All Seasons Arena, 1200 N.
Washington Street, Bismarck, ND
58501; Rink: 701/222-6588

BORDER BLADES FSC
Fido Purpur Arena (City Arena), 1210
7th Avenue S. Grand Forks, ND 58201;
Rink: 701/746-2764

BOTTINEAU FSC
Bottineau Community Arena, Railroad
Avenue & 7th Street, Bottineau, ND
58318

HAZEN FSC
Hazen All Seasons Arena, Corner of 3rd
Avenue & Hwy 200, Hazen, ND 58545

JAMES RIVER FSC
Wilson Arena, 7th Street & 12th Avenue
NE, Jamestown, ND 58401;
Rink: 701/252-3939

LAKE REGION SC
Burdick Arena, Highway 20 N. Devils
Lake, ND 58301; Rink: 701/662-8418

MAGIC CITY FSC
All Seasons Arena, 2005 Burdick
Expressway E., Minot, ND 58701;
Rink: 701/857-7620

RED RIVER VALLEY FSC
John E. Carlson Coliseum, 807 - 17th
Avenue N., Fargo, ND 58102;
Rink: 701/241-8154

SOUTHERN VALLEY FSA
Stern's Sports Arena, 1026 N. 11th
Street, Wahpeton, ND 58075;
Rink: 218/643-5159

OHIO
AUBURN FSC
Auburn Ice Palace, 9999 Washington
Street, Auburn, OH 44023

BOWLING GREEN SC
Bowling Green University Ice Arena,
Mercer Road, Bowling Green, OH
43402-0035; Rink: 419/372-2264

BOWLING GREEN STATE
UNIVERSITY (CC)
BGSU Ice Arena, Bowling Green State
University, Mercer Road, Bowling Green,
OH 43403; Rink: 419/372-2264

BROOKLYN FSC OF OHIO
Brooklyn Recreation Center, 7600
Memphis Avenue, Brooklyn, OH 44144;
Rink: 216/398-7024

CHILLER FSC
Chiller, 7001 Dublin Park Drive, Dublin,
OH 43017; Rink: 614/764-1000

FSC OF CINCINNATI
Sports Plus Cincinnati, 10765 Reading
Road, Cincinnati, OH 45241-5499;
Rink: 513/769-1010

CLEVELAND SC
Cleveland Skating Club, 2500 Kemper
Road, Shaker Heights, OH 44120;
Rink: 216/791-2800

COLUMBUS FSC
Ohio State University Ice Rink, 390
Woody Hayes Drive, Columbus, OH
43210-1167; Rink: 614/292-4154

EUCLID BLADE & EDGE CLUB, INC.
Clifford E. Orr Arena, 22550 Milton
Avenue, Euclid, OH 44123;
Rink: 216/731-8440

FORESTWOOD FSC OF PARMA
OHIO
Ries Rink, 5000 Forestwood Drive,
Parma, OH 44134; Rink: 216/885-8870

GARFIELD HEIGHTS FSC
Dan Kostel Recreation Center, 5411
Turney Road, Garfield Heights, OH
44125; Rink: 216/475-7272

GEM CITY FSC
Sportstown Ice Center, 10561 Success
Lane, Centerville, OH 45458

GREENBRIER FSC
Greenbrier Ice Rink, 6200 Pearl Road,
Parma Heights, OH 44130;
Rink: 216/842-5005

KENT SC
Kent State Univ. Ice Arena, Loop Road,
Kent, OH 44242; Rink: 303/672-2415

MENTOR FSC
Mentor Civic Arena, 8600 Munson
Road, Mentor, OH 44060;
Rink: 216/255-1777

MIAMI UNIVERSITY
Goggin Ice Arena, Miami University,
Oxford, OH 45056; Rink: 513/529-3343

THE OHIO STATE UNIVERSITY FSC (CC)
The Ohio State Univ. Ice Rink, 390
Woody Hayes Drive, Columbus, OH
43210

OXFORD SC
Goggin Ice Arena, Miami University,
Oxford, OH 45056; Rink: 513/529-3343

PAVILION SC OF CLEVELAND HTS
Pavilion Recreation Center, 1 Monticello
Boulevard, Cleveland Hts., OH 44118;
Rink: 216/691-7373

QUEEN CITY FSC
Northland Ice Center, 10400 Reading
Road, Cincinnati, OH 45241;
Rink: 513/563-0008

SHAKER FSC
Thornton Park Ice Rink, 20701 Farnsleigh
Road, Shaker Heights, OH 44122

SILVER STREAK FSC, INC.
Hancock Recreational Center, 3430
N. Main Street, Findlay, OH 45840

SOUTH DAYTON FSC
Kettering Rec Ctr Ice Arena, 2900
Glengarry Drive, Kettering, OH 45420;
Rink: 513/296-2587

TROY SC
Hobart Arena, 255 Adams Street, Troy,
OH 45373; Rink: 937/339-2911

WEST SHORE FSC
North Olmsted Rec Complex, 26000

Lorain Road, North Olmsted, OH
44070; Rink: 216/734-8200

WINTERHURST FSC
Winterhurst Ice Rink, 14740 Lakewood
Heights Blvd., Lakewood, OH 44107;
Rink: 216/228-4030

OKLAHOMA
EDMOND FSC
Arctic Edge Ice Arena, 14613 N. Kelley,
Oklahoma City, OK 73013

OKLAHOMA CITY FSC, INC.
Iceland Sports Center, 3200 N.
Rockwell, Bethany, OK 73008;
Rink: 405/789-2090

TULSA FSC, INC
Tulsa Ice Arena, 6910 S 101st E. Avenue,
Tulsa, OK 74133; Rink: 918/254-7272

OREGON
CAROUSEL FSC
Valley Ice Arena, 9250 SW Beaverton-
Hillsdale Highway, Beaverton, OR 97005;
Rink: 503/297-2521

EUGENE FSC
Lane County Ice, 796 W. 13th Avenue,
Eugene, OR 97402; Rink: 541/687-3615

LLOYD CENTER ISC
Lloyd Ctr Mall Ice Chalet, 2201 Lloyd Ctr,
Portland, OR 97232; Rink: 503/288-4599

PORTLAND ISC
Ice Chalet-Clackamas Town Ctr, 12000
SE 82nd, Portland, OR 97266

PENNSYLVANIA
BEAVER COUNTY FSC
Beaver County Ice Arena, Brady's Run
Park, Road 1, Box 526, Beaver Falls, PA
15010; Rink: 412/728-4330

SC OF BUCKS COUNTY
Face Off Circle, 1185 York Road, Warmin-
ster, PA 18974; Rink: 215/674-1345

COLONIAL SC
Grundy Recreation Center, 474 Beaver
Street, PO Box 117, Bristol, PA 19007;
Rink: 215/788-3311

FSC OF ERIE
Erie Civic Center, 809 French Street, PO
Box 3412, Erie, PA 16508;
Rink: 814/898-3755

HAVERFORD SC
Skatium, Darby & Manoa Roads, Haver-
town, PA 19083; Rink: 610/853-2225

HERSHEY FSC
Hershey Park Arena, 100 W. Hershey
Park Drive, Hershey, PA 17033;
Rink: 717/534-3891

JOHNSTOWN FSC
Cambria County War Mem. Arena, 326-
350 Napoleon Street, Johnstown, PA
15901; Rink: 814/536-5156

LANCASTER FSC
Lancaster Ice Rink, 371 Carerra Drive,
Lancaster, PA 17601

ICE CLUB OF LANCASTER
Regency Sports Rink, 2155 Ambassador
Circle, Lancaster, PA 17603

LEHIGH VALLEY SC
Lehigh Valley Ice Arena, 3323 7th St.,
Whitehall, PA 18052; Rink: 215/434-6899

MEADVILLE FSC
Meadville Area Rec Complex, 800
Thurston Rd., Meadville, PA 16335; Rink:
814/724-6006

SC OF MT. LEBANON
Mt. Lebanon Rec Ctr Rink, 900 Cedar
Blvd, Mt Lebanon, PA 15228;
Rink: 412/561-4363

OLD YORK ROAD SC
Church & Old York Rds, Elkins Park, PA
19027; Rink: 216/635-2770

PENGUIN FSC, INC.
Ice Palace, 623 Hanover Ave, Allentown,
PA 18103; Rink: 215/435-3031

PENN STATE FSC
Penn State Ice Pavilion, Pollack &
McKean Roads, University Park, PA
16802-1216; Rink: 814/865-4102

UNIVERSITY OF PENNSYLVANIA (CC)
The Class of 1923 Ice Rink, 3130 Walnut
St., Philadelphia, PA 19104-6327

PHILADELPHIA SC & HS
Philadelphia Skating Club & Humane
Society, 220 Holland Ave., Ardmore, PA
19003; Rink: 215/642-8700

PITTSBURGH FSC, INC.
Blade Runners Icecomplex, 66 Alpha Dr,
Pittsburgh, PA 15238;
Rink: 412/826-0800

QUAKER CITY FSC
Melody Brook Ice Rink, Route 309 &
Lenhart Rd, Colmar, PA 18915;
Rink: 215/822-3613

TWIN PONDS FSC
Twin Ponds W. Family IS Complex, 101
Salem Church Rd N., Mechanicsburg, PA
17055; Rink: 717/795-7663

SC OF WARWICK
Warwick Twin Ricks Inc., 1621 Mearns
Road, Warwick, PA 18974

WESTMINSTER FSC OF ERIE
J.M. Cochran Memorial Arena, W. 38th &
Cherry Sts., Erie, PA 16509;
Rink: 814/838-6458

WHITE ROSE FSC
Memorial Park Ice Rink, Corner
Rockdale & Vander Aves, York, PA 17403;
Rink: 717/843-3959

WISSAHICKON SC
Wissahickon Skating Club, 550 W.
Willow Grove Ave, Philadelphia, PA
19118; Rink: 215/247-1759

WYOMING VALLEY ISC
Ice-A-Rama, Coal Street at N. Sherman,
Wilkes Barre, PA 18702;
Rink: 717/820-0137

RHODE ISLAND
PAWTUCKET & PROVIDENCE FS
Lynch Arena, 25 Beatty St, Pawtucket, RI
02860; Rink: 401/728-7420

SMITHFIELD FSC
Smithfield Municipal Ice Rink, 101
Pleasant View Ave, PO Box 17121,
Smithfield, RI 02917; Rink: 401/233-1051

WARWICK FIGURE SKATERS
Thayer Memorial Rink, 975 Sandy Lane,
Warwick, RI 02886; Rink: 401/739-9000

SOUTH CAROLINA
GREENVILLE FSC, INC.
The Pavilion Rec Complex, 400
Scottswood Dr., Greenville, SC 29615;
Rink: 803/322-7529

SOUTH DAKOTA
WATERTOWN SC
Watertown Ice Arena, 112 21st St. SW,
Watertown, SD 57201

TENNESSEE
FSC OF MEMPHIS
Ice Chalet of Memphis, 4451 American
Way, #1 Mall of Memphis, Memphis, TN
38118; Rink: 901/362-8877

NASHVILLE FSC
Centennial Sportsplex, 222 25th Ave N.,
Nashville, TN, 37203; Rink: 615/862-8480

TEXAS
AUSTIN FSC
Chaparral Ice, 14200 I.H. 35 North,
Austin, TX 78728; Rink: 512/252-8500

BLUEBONNET FSC
Galleria Ice Skating Center, 13350 Dallas
Parkway #50, Dallas, TX 75240;
Rink: 214/392-3363

THE CAPITAL OF TEXAS FSC
Austin Ice at Northcross Mall, 2525 W.
Anderson Lane, Austin, TX 78757

DALLAS FSC, INC.
Dr. Pepper Star Center, 211 Cowboys
Pkwy. Irving, TX 75063;
Rink: 214/831-2480

THE FSC OF TEXAS
Texas Ice Stadium, 18150 Gulf Fwy.,
Friendswood, TX 77546;
Rink: 281/486-7979

HOUSTON FSC
Galleria Ice Skating Center, 5015
Westhelmer, Houston, TX 77056;
Rink: 713/621-7609

ICELAND FSC OF HOUSTON
Aerodrome Willowbrook, 8220 Willow
Place N. Houston, TX 77070;
Rink: 281/84-SKATE

LONE STAR FSC
Int'l SC of TX at Ice Bound, 4020 W.
Plano Parkway, Plano, TX 75026-0277;
Rink: 972/758-7528

SAN ANTONIO FSC
Crystal Ice Palace, 12332 IH-10 W #12,
San Antonio, TX 78230;
Rink: 210/696-0234

TEXAS GULF COAST FSC
Aerodrome Ice Skating Complex, 16225
Lexington, Sugar Land, TX 77479;
Rink: 281/265-7465

UTAH
COTTONWOOD HEIGHTS FSC
Cottonwood Heights Rec Center, 2700
E 7500 S, Salt Lake City, UT 84121;
Rink: 801/943-1334

UTAH FSC
Bountiful Recreation Center, 150 W. 600
North, Bountiful, UT 84010;
Rink: 801/298-6220

WASATCH FSC
The Ice Sheet, 4390 S Harrison Blvd
Ogden, UT 84403; Rink: 801/479-8579

VERMONT
BARRE FSC
B.O.R. Skating Rink, Seminary Hill, Barre,
VT 05641

BRATTLEBORO FSC, INC.
Nelson Withington Ice Rink, Memorial
Park, Brattleboro, VT 05302;
Rink: 802/257-2311

CHAMPLAIN VALLEY FSC
G.H. Paquette Municipal Arena, Leddy
Park, Burlington, VT 05401;
Rink: 802/864-0123

STOWE SC, INC.
Jackson Arena, PO Box 730, Stowe, VT
05672; Rink: 802/253-6148

VERMONT SC
C. Douglas Cairns Rec Arena, Dorset
Park, PO Box 9482, S. Burlington, VT
05407; Rink: 802/658-5577

VIRGINIA
SC OF NORTHERN VIRGINIA
Fairfax Ice Arena, 3779 Pickett Road,
Fairfax, VA 22031; Rink: 703/323-1132

RICHMOND FSC, INC.
Skate Nation Richmond, 636 Johnston
Willis Dr., Richmond, VA 23236;
Rink. 804/378-7465

TIDEWATER FSC
Iceland of Virginia Beach, 4915 Broad St.,
Virginia Beach, VA 23462;
Rink: 804/490-3999

ICE CLUB OF WASHINGTON
Mt Vernon Recreation Center, 2017
Belle View Blvd., Alexandria, VA 22307

WASHINGTON FSC
Mt Vernon Recreation Center, 2017
Belle View Blvd., Alexandria, VA 22307;
Rink: 703/768-3224

WASHINGTON
BELLINGHAM FSC
Whatcom County Sports Arena, 1801
W. Bakerview Rd, Bellingham, WA 98225

HIGHLAND SC
Highland Ice Arena, 18005 Aurora
Avenue N. Seattle, WA 98133;
Rink: 206/546-2431

LAKEWOOD WINTER CLUB
Sprinker Recreation Center, 14824
South C St. Suite 108, Tacoma, WA
98444; Rink: 206/537-2600

LILAC CITY FSC
Eagles Ice Arena, N. 6321 Addison,
Spokane, WA 99207; Rink: 509/489-9303

SEATTLE SC
Olympic View Ice Arena, 22202 70th
Ave. W. Mountlake Terrace, WA 98043

SPOKANE FSC, INC.
Ice House, 12600 E. Euclid, Spokane,
WA 99216

TRI-CITIES FSC
Tri-Cities Coliseum, 7100 W. Quinault,
Kennewick, WA 99336

WALLA WALLA FSC, INC.
YWCA Ice Chalet, 213 S. First, Walla
Walla, WA 99362; Rink: 509/525-2575

WENATCHEE FSC
Wenatchee Riverfront Ice Rink, 2 Fifth
St, Wenatchee, WA 98801;
Rink: 509/664-5994

YAKIMA ISC INC
Yakima Ice Arena, 1700 E. Beech St.,
Yakima, WA 98901; Rink: 509/248-7638

WEST VIRGINIA
CHARLESTON FSC
Charleston Civic Ctr. Ice Arena, 200
Civic Center Drive, Charleston, WV
25301; Rink: 304/357-7465

HUNTINGTON FSC
Huntington Civic Arena, One Civic
Arena Plaza, Huntington, WV 25704

MASON-DIXON FSC
Morgantown Munic Rink, Mississippi St.,
White Park, Morgantown, WV 26505;
Rink: 304/292-6865

WHEELING FSC
Wheeling Park Ice Rink, 1801 National
Road, Wheeling, WV 26003;
Rink: 304/242-3770

WISCONSIN
BLACK RIVER FALLS FSC
Jackson County Arena, Highway 54
West, Black River Falls, WI 54615;
Rink: 715/284-9974

CHIPPEWA FSC
Chippewa Falls Ice Arena, PO Box 131,
Chippewa Falls, WI 54729

CRYSTAL ICE FSC
K.B. Willett Ice Arena, 1000 Minnesota
Ave., Stevens Point, WI 54481

DEPERE FSC, INC
DePere Ice Recreation Center, 1450
Fort Howard Ave, De Pere, WI 54115;
Rink: 414/339-4097

EAGLE RIVER FSC
Eagle River Sports Arena, 4149 Highway
70 E. Eagle River, WI 54521;
Rink: 715/479-4858

EAU CLAIRE FSC
Hobbs Ice Arena, 915 Menomonie St.,
Eau Claire, WI 54701;
Rink: 715/839-5040

FOND DU LAC BLUE LINE FIGURE
SKATING
Blue Line Club, 550 Fond du lac Ave.,
Fond du Lac, WI 54935;
Rink: 414/922-3233

GREATER MILWAUKEE FSC
Wilson Recreation Center, 4001 S. 20th
St, Milwaukee, WI 53221;
Rink: 414/281-6289

JANESVILLE FSC
Janesville Civic Ice Arena, 821 Beloit
Ave, Janesville, WI 53545;
Rink: 608/755-3014

LAKELAND FSC
Lakeland Hawks Ice Arena, 7661 Old
Highway 51, Minocqua, WI 54548;
Rink: 715/356-6762

M & M FSC
Civic Center Domes, 2000 Alice Ln.,
Marinette, WI 54143

FSC OF MADISON, INC.
Madison Ice Arena, 725 Forward Dr.,
Madison, WI 53711; Rink: 608/271-1022

NORTHWOODS FSC
Badgerland Civic Center, 301 Walnut St.,
Spooner, WI 54801; Rink: 715/635-6144

PORTAGE COUNTY FSC
K.B. Willett Ice Arena, 1000 Minnesota
Avenue, Stevens Point, WI 54481

RHINELANDER FSC
Rhinelander Ice Arena, 2021 E. Timber
Dr., Rhinelander, WI 54501

SOUTHPORT SC
Kenosha County Ice Arena, 7727 60th
Avenue, Kenosha, WI 53142;
Rink: 414/694-8011

SPARTA AREA FSC
Sparta Community Ice Arena, 1121 E.
Montgomery, Sparta, WI 54656

SUPERIOR FSC
Wessman Arena, 2701 Catlin Avenue,
Superior, WI 54880; Rink: 715/394-8361

SWAN CITY ICE SKATERS
Beaver Dam Family Center, 609 Gould
St., Beaver Dam, WI 53916;
Rink: 414/885-9816

TIMBERLINE SC
Marathon County Park Dept, Ice Arena,
Marathon Park, Garfield Avenue,
Wausau, WI 54401; Rink: 715/847-5367

VALLEY FSC
Tri-County Ice Arena, 700 E. Shady Lane,
Neenah, WI 54956; Rink: 414/731-9731

WAUPUN FSC
Waupun Community Center, E. Spring
St, Waupun, WI 53963;
Rink: 414/324-4514

WISCONSIN FSC, INC.
Petit National Ice Center, 500 S. 84th
Street, PO Box 144009, Delafield, WI
53018; Rink: 414/266-0100

WISCONSIN RAPIDS FSC
South Wood County Rec Center,
2711 16th St. S, Wisconsin Rapids, WI
54494

WYOMING
CASPER FSC
Casper Ice Arena, 1801 E. 4th, Casper,
WY 82601; Rink: 307/235-8484

JACKSON HOLE FSC
Snow King Center Ice Rink, 150 E. Snow
King Ave., Jackson, WY 83001;
Rink: 307/733-5200

SWEETWATER FIGURE
SKATING ASSOC.
Rock Springs Family Rec Center, 3900
Sweetwater Drive, Rock Springs, WY
82901-4506; Rink: 307/352-1445

UNITED STATES FIGURE
SKATING ASSOCIATION
20 First Street, Colorado Springs, CO
80906; 719/635-5200

CANADIAN FIGURE
SKATING ASSOCIATION
1600 James Naismith Drive, Gloucester,
Ont., KIB 5N4; 613/748-5635

INTERNATIONAL SKATING
UNION
Chemin de Primerose 2, 1007 Lausanne,
Switzerland; (+41) 21 612 66 66

GLOSSARY OF TERMS

Accountant—An official at a figure skating competition who compiles and computes marks awarded by the judges to determine the placement of competitors.

Axel jump—One of the most difficult jumps, it takes off from the forward outside edge and is landed on the back outside edge of the opposite foot. A single Axel consists of one-and-a-half revolutions, a double is two-and-a-half revolutions, and a triple is three-and-a-half revolutions. Named for its inventor, Axel Paulsen, it is easily recognizable since it is the only jump that takes off from a forward position.

Block—A formation in precision skating whereby the skaters line up one behind the other in more than two straight lines, into a block formation. The block moves on the ice, utilizing the entire surface.

Camel spin—A spin done on one leg, with the nonskating leg, or free leg, extended in the air in a position parallel to the ice. The body remains in this "spiral" position while spinning.

Check—A term coaches use when talking about stopping or controlling the rotation of a skater's body. For example, on a jump, the "check out" is when the air rotation is completed and the skater starts to land. Turns on the ice, such as three-turns, also "check" on the exit from the turn.

Circle—A maneuver in precision skating where skaters are linked and rotate with step combinations in a circular motion. Skaters move forward or backward as they try to hold the formation of a perfect circle.

Combination spin—The combining of several spins where the skater changes feet and positions while maintaining speed throughout the entire spin.

Compulsory dances—In ice dancing, the two compulsory dances are each worth 10 percent of the total score. All skaters perform the same two selected dances, which have prescribed rhythms and specific steps that must be done in an exact manner with exact placement on the ice. At some competitions, only one dance is competed, and then it is worth 20 percent of the total score.

Crossovers—A method of gaining speed and turning corners in which skaters cross one foot over the other. There are both forward and backward crossovers.

Death spiral—A pair move in which the man spins in a pivot position while holding one hand of his partner, who is spinning in a horizontal position with her body low and parallel to the ice.

Draw—The process by which the starting or skating order for each event is determined. It is conducted by either the competition referee or the chair in the presence of other judges (closed draw) or in an open setting where the athletes participate and actually draw a number from a pouch (open draw).

Edge jump—A jump where the skater takes off from the entry edge of the skating foot without bringing the free foot in contact with the ice to assist the takeoff. The Axel, loop, and Salchow are common edge jumps.

Edge quality—Characterized by a stable arc and controlled body rotation. An edge is ideally without subcurves or wobbles, and initiated by placing the body and blade on an angle to the surface of the ice and stepping on the required edge. This edge and arc will ideally commence immediately at the point where the skate takes the ice or a turn is completed, and travel uninterrupted until a required transition takes place. Depth of edge refers to the acuteness of the arc and the angle of the blade.

Edges—The two sides of the skate blade on either side of the grooved center. There is an inside edge—the edge on the inner side of the leg—and an outside edge—the edge on the outer side of the leg. There is also a forward and backward for each edge, all of which add up to a total of four different edges.

Eligible—Skaters or competitions that meet the requirements and follow the rules of the USFSA and/or the ISU. All eligible skaters, judges, and officials are members of the USFSA and have not participated in any activities, competitions, or events that are not sanctioned by the USFSA or the ISU.

Extension—Extension is the controlled stretching of the free leg complemented by an upright body posture. The extended leg is held in an unbroken line. The height of the extension is determined by the type of movement being executed. However, the final extended position should always be attained in a controlled fashion.

Flip jump—A toe pick–assisted jump, taken off from the back inside edge of one foot and landed on the back outside edge of the opposite foot.

Flow—The ability to maintain a constant speed across the ice while executing various skating elements. Flow also refers to the length of time it takes for the speed generated from a single stroke to diminish.

Footwork—A sequence of step maneuvers carrying the skater across the ice in patterns, generally straight, circular, or serpentine. Intended to show the precision and dexterity of the skater's movements.

Free dance—In ice dancing, the free dance, which comprises 50 percent of a dance team's total score, is relatively unrestricted, and skaters select the mood and tempo as long as it is danceable. Skaters are allowed four minutes to display their full range of technical skills, interpretation, and inventiveness.

Free side—Opposite to the skating side is the "unemployed" side (the free side of the body). This refers to the non-weight-bearing side (foot, leg, hip, arm, and shoulder).

Free skate—The free skate counts for 66.7 percent of a skater's or team's final score in Singles and Pairs. It does not have required elements, so skaters select their own music and theme, and choreograph the many jumps, spins, and footwork that best display their technical and artistic skills. The free skate (for the Senior level) has a length of four and a half minutes for men and pairs, and four minutes for ladies.

Free-skating posture—The skater's back is straight and the head is up. The spine and head are perpendicular to the surface of the ice. The arms are extended out from the shoulders and are level and relaxed. The free leg is extended in a straight line and slightly turned out from the free hip to the free toe.

Hand-to-hand loop lift—In pair skating, a lift in which the man raises his partner, who is in front of him and facing the same direction, above his head. The woman, in the sitting position with her hands behind her, remains facing the same direction, while her partner supports her by the hands.

Hydrant lift—In pairs, a lift in which the man throws his partner over his head while skating backwards, makes half a turn, and catches his partner facing him.

Intersection—In precision skating, a required element for the precision short program and a common precision formation, it is any type of maneuver that incorporates movement of one part of the team through the other part of the team.

Layback spin—Generally performed by women, the layback spin involves an upright spin position in which the head, shoulders and back are arched backwards.

Lifts—Pair moves in which the man lifts his partner above his head with arm(s) fully extended. Lifts consist of precise ascending, rotational, and descending movements.

Line—In precision skating, a formation in which the skaters are arranged in a single line, side by side. For the precision short program, the line must extend across the width of the ice surface and travel the full length of the ice.

Long program—Slang term for the free-skating portion of the Singles and Pairs competitions.

Loop jump—An edge jump that takes off from a back outside edge and lands on the same back outside edge.

Lutz jump—A toe pick–assisted jump, that takes off from a back outside edge and lands on the back outside edge of the opposite foot. The skater glides backwards on a wide curve, taps the toe pick into the ice, and rotates in the opposite direction of the curve. The jump is named for its inventor, Alois Lutz.

Ordinal—Each skater or team is given a score that is converted into an ordinal or "place." The skater or team that receives the highest marks from a judge is awarded the first-place mark or ordinal from that judge.

Original dance—The second competition phase in ice dancing, it counts for 30 percent of the team's total score. Skaters are given a prescribed rhythm (such as the paso doble or rhumba) with a defined tempo range and must create a completely original version of the dance. It has a time limit of two minutes.

Overhead lifts—The group of pair lifts in which one or both of the man's arms are fully extended as he holds his partner overhead. The man does not let go of his partner during the lift, except momentarily during changes in her position or during the dismount.

Platter lift—In pairs, a lift in which the man raises his partner overhead with his hands resting on her hips. She is horizontal to the ice, facing the man's back, in a platter position.

Power—Obvious and rapid acceleration, often from a standstill position, achieved by a forceful, gripping pressure exerted by the skating leg against the surface of the ice. Power includes maintaining or increasing speed while executing various skating elements. Power is relative to the size of the skater, but it can always be attained with proper stroking technique.

Presentation mark—The second of two marks awarded when judging the Singles' and Pair's short program and free skate, and the original and free dance. Judges consider the program's relationship to the music. Speed, utilization of the ice surface, carriage, and style; and originality, and unison.

Referee—The official at a competition who has full authority over all aspects of the event and is the chairperson for the panel of judges. It is the referee's responsibility to ensure that all USFSA rules are observed, that a high standard of judging is maintained, and that all technical aspects of the competition are satisfactory.

Regionals—The first of two qualifying competitions en route to the U.S. Championships. The USFSA breaks the United States into nine regional areas and holds competitions. Skaters must place in the top four at their regional event to advance to the sectionals.

Required elements mark—The first mark given by the judges in the

Singles and Pairs short program, evaluating how well each element is performed. Deductions are made based on the errors skaters make as they execute the required elements.

Salchow—An edge jump that takes off from the back inside edge of one foot and lands on the back outside edge of the opposite foot. Created by Ulrich Salchow.

Sanction—Permission or approval given by the USFSA or the ISU to member clubs, competition organizers, individuals, or national federations to conduct competitions, shows, or events featuring eligible athletes. Registered USFSA athletes can participate only in sanctioned activities.

Sectionals—The second and final qualifying competition en route to the U.S. Championships. The top four finishers from each sectional advance to the U.S. Championships. There are three sectionals—Eastern, Midwestern and Pacific Coast.

Shadow skating—Any movement in pairs skating performed by both partners simultaneously while skating in close proximity.

Short program—Official name for a two minute, forty-second program in Singles and Pairs that consists of eight required elements and is set to music of the skater's choice. No more than eight required elements can be done. Failure to complete or elimination of, any element is penalized in the scoring.

Sit spin—A spin done in a "sitting" position. The body is low to the ice with the skating (spinning) knee bent and the nonskating, or "free" leg extended.

Skating side—The side of the body bearing the skater's weight at a given moment. For example, when a skater skates on the right foot, the right side of the body is the skating side. (The right foot, leg, hip, shoulder, and arm comprise the skating side.)

Spiral—A move in which a skater demonstrates flexibility and a fluid line by extending the nonskating leg to the rear at hip level or higher.

Spiral sequence—A sequence of steps that incorporates various spirals in a pattern across the ice. When performed in a sequence, spirals may be done going forward,

backward, in a straight line, on a curve, on an inside or outside edge.

Square—Refers to the relationship of the skater's shoulders and/or hip bones to the skating foot. If the hip bones are facing the same direction as the skating foot, the hips are said to be square. The skater's shoulders can also be positioned square to the skating foot.

Star lift—In pairs, a lift in which the man raises his partner into the air by her hip, from his side. She is in the scissor position, with either one hand touching his shoulder or both in a hands-free position.

Starting order—The result of the draw that lists the order in which the athletes will compete in and the group each athlete will warm up in prior to competition.

Step sequence—A sequence of steps that immediately follow one another, executed in time to music, and choreographically related to each other.

Stroking—Fluid movement used to gain speed, in which a skater pushes off back and forth from the inside edge of one skate to the inside edge of the other skate.

Technical merit mark—The first of two marks awarded when judging the free skate (Singles and Pairs) and the free dance (Ice Dancing). It measures the difficulty, variety, and cleanness of the performance.

Technical program—Former term for the short program.

Technique mark—The first of two marks awarded when judging the compulsory dance, based on the conformity of the dance steps, accuracy, style, form, and carriage.

Throw jump—A pair move in which the male partner assists the woman into the air; she then executes one, two, or three revolutions, and lands skating backwards.

Timing/expression mark—In ice dancing, the second of two marks awarded when judging compulsory dances, based on steps corresponding to the beat of the music, with correct timing, and in a clear expression of the nature of the dance.

Toe loop—A toe pick–assisted jump that takes off and lands on the same back outside edge.

Toe overhead lift—A lift in which the man swings his partner from one side of his body around behind his head and into a raised position. She is facing the same direction as the man, in a split position.

Toe picks—The teeth at the front of the blade, used primarily for jumping and spinning.

Twist lifts—The group of pair lifts where both partners begin skating backward and the man lifts his partner over his head and tosses her in the air. While airborne, she will do anywhere from a half to two-and-a-half revolutions. The man catches his partner and places her back on the ice.

Wheel—A precision skating formation in which skaters form lines that are connected and rotate from one central point, similar to the spokes on a bicycle wheel.

Photograph and figure page references are in italics.

ACKNOWLEDGMENTS

Many people at the United States Figure Skating Association have been helpful in the creation of this book. We'd like to thank Oscar Iobst, Janet Champion, Margaret Ann Wier, Don Laws, Leann Miele, and Megan Faulkner. For vital review, we'd also like to thank Jay Miller, Blaine Fowler, Sheila Collins, Christy Krall, and Bob Crowley, and for careful attention and wisdom, Jerry Lace and Pat Hagedorn. The passion, knowledge and commitment each of these people poured into their involvement make this volume unique among skating books.

Beth Davis opened the doors of the World Figure Skating Museum and Hall of Fame. Her enthusiasm and constant good cheer in the face of foolish questions and requests for help were invaluable, as were the efforts of Karen Cover.

At ABC Sports, Bob Apter gave the project the green light, and many hours of work by Pam Miller, Mary Landergan and Pat Shimonov made it real. Lana Sherman's close review was also crucial. Ann Limongello was always there when we needed her, as was Ida Astute.

Paul Harvath and Dave Black offered quick help and beautiful photos; Dale Mitch offered years of experience and wisdom.

At Simon & Schuster, our friend Constance Herndon always believed. With a true eye, patience, a firm hand when necessary and a serious love for books, she brought in this project. Andrea Au kept the trains moving, and associate publisher Annik LaFarge is surely its godmother.

The staff of Balliett & Fitzgerald rose to the occassion as never before, thanks to Maria Fernandez, Liz Barrett, Michael Walters, Rachel Aydt, Vijay Balakrishnian, and Irene Agriodimas. Thanks as well to copy editor Jane Herman and proofreader Donna Stonecipher.

The final two people were the first. Bill O'Rourke at Hakan and Associates made this all happen, becoming a good friend in the process, and, finally, thanks to Kristin Matta, who deserves a gold medal as much as any Olympic skater. She's a tireless worker for the sport of figure skating, and this book would not be here without her.

—Balliett & Fitzgerald

In addition, the USFSA would also like to thank Balliett & Fitzgerald for undertaking such an ambitious project. Special thanks go to Tom Dyja who turned an idea into a reality and whose dedication and endless enthusiasm is evident throughout.

—USFSA

Photography Credits

World Figure Skating Museum and Hall of Fame: iv-v, 2, top and bottom, 4-25, 27, 32, 34-47, 49-52, 55-56, 60, 74 top and bottom, 76 bottom, 77-78, 80, 83, 127, 139-147, 170, 172, 177, 183-185, 186 top right and bottom right, 191-193, 201-202, 210, 216, 212, 222, 224-225, 228-229, 242 bottom, 243 top and bottom

ABC, Inc.: 26, top and bottom, 148-149, 153 bottom right, 158, 187 bottom, 205 top right, bottom right, 213 top

Dave Black: i, ii-iii, vi-1, 3, 28 top, 29 top, 66, 70, 75, 129, 138, 160, 166-167, 174, 176 198 top, 199, 221, 232-235, 239

Rob Brown/ABC, Inc.: 63, 151 upper right, 187 top

Jacqueline Duvoisin/ABC, Inc.: 126

Steve Fenn/ABC, Inc.: 62, 151 bottom left and bottom right, 162, 165, 226

Heinz Kleutmeier/ABC, Inc.: 54, 57-58, 61, 150, 151 upper left, 159, 197 bottom, 198 bottom, 206 top, 215, 245 bottom

Manny Millan/ABC, Inc.: 87, 99 left

Craig Sjodin/ABC, Inc.: 29 bottom, 30-31, 67-69, 71, 73, 79 top and bottom, 94, 95, 96, 99 right, 128, 133, 135, 152, 153 top left, 154 all photos, 157, 161, 163, 168, all photos, 171 all photos, 173, 175, 179, 182, 186 top left and bottom left, 188-190, 196, 197 top right, 204, 205 bottom left, 206 bottom, 207-209, 211, 218-219, 231, 236-237, 242 top, 244, 245 top

Tony Triolo/ABC, Inc.: 59, 65, 169

Jerry Cooke/Sports Illustrated: 194

Neil Leifer/Sports Illustrated: 53

Manny Millan/Sports Illustrated: 28 bottom

John G. Zimmerman/Sports Illustrated: 48, 195

Michelle Harvath: 132, 134 top and bottom, 153 bottom left and top right, 156, 213 bottom, 240

Paul Harvath: 64, 72, 81, 89, 97, 136-137, 155, 181, 197 top left, 200

Dan Helms: 130 top and bottom, 131 top and bottom

Mary Tiegreen: 176, 227

THE AUTHORS

The United States Figure Skating Association is the nation's leading sanctioning organization for the sport of figure skating. Its coaches and executives have been deeply involved in every stage of this book's creation, establishing its content, selecting its photos from an extraordinary archive, and vetting every detail for accuracy and precision. The USFSA is located in Colorado Springs, Colorado.

America's most beloved figure skater, **Peggy Fleming** won three consecutive World Championships along with the gold medal at the 1968 Olympic Winter Games. She lives in California.

Thomas Dyja is a novelist and sports historian. He lives in New York City.

A former associate editor of *Newsweek* and senior editor of *Parade*, **Mary Alice Kellogg** has covered figure skating for the last six Winter Olympic Games. She lives in New York City.

Formerly an attorney, **Suzanna Miller** is now a freelance writer specializing in figure skating. She also works behind the scenes for televised figure skating events. She lives in Brooklyn, New York.

Dale Mitch is the former director of the World Figure Skating Museum & Hall of Fame, as well as the former editor of *Skating* magazine. He lives in Colorado Springs, Colorado.

Carl Poe is a member of the Sports Medicine Committee of the USFSA and is an off-ice strength and conditioning coach for many skaters. He lives in Woodridge, Illinois.

Ralph Routon, who has extensively covered figure skating and the Olympics, is currently the executive sports editor and a columnist for the Colorado Springs *Gazette*. He lives in Manitou Springs, Colorado.

Along with partner Ken Shelley, **JoJo Starbuck** won three U.S. pairs titles, earned two bronze medals in the World Championships, and participated in two Olympic Winter Games. She lives in New Jersey.